D0281057

Cambridge Opera Handbooks

Giacomo Puccini
La bohème

CAMBRIDGE OPERA HANDBOOKS

Published titles

Giacomo Puccini
La bohème

ARTHUR GROOS AND ROGER PARKER

CAMBRIDGE
UNIVERSITY PRESS

Published by the Press Syndicate of the University of Cambridge
The Pitt Building, Trumpington Street, Cambridge CB2 1RP
40 West 20th Street, New York, NY 10011–4211, USA
10 Stamford Road, Oakleigh, Melbourne 3166, Australia

First published 1986
Reprinted 1991, 1995

Printed in Great Britain at the University Press, Cambridge

British Library cataloguing in publication data

Groos, Arthur
Giacomo Puccini: La bohème – (Cambridge
opera handbooks)
1. Puccini, Giacomo. bohème, La
I. Title II. Parker, Roger
782.1′092′4   ML410.P89

Library of Congress cataloguing in publication data

Groos, Arthur
Giacomo Puccini, La bohème.
(Cambridge opera handbooks.)
Bibliography: p.
"Discography by Malcolm Walker": p.
Includes index.
1. Puccini, Giacomo, 1858–1924. Bohème.
I. Parker, Roger. II. Title. III. Title: Bohème.
IV. Series.
ML410.P89G76   1986   782.1′092′4   85–28076

ISBN 0 521 26489 8 hard covers
ISBN 0 521 31913 7 paperback

WD

CAMBRIDGE OPERA HANDBOOKS

General preface

This is a series of studies of individual operas, written for the serious opera-goer or record-collector as well as the student or scholar. Each volume has three main concerns. The first is historical: to describe the genesis of the work, its sources or its relation to literary prototypes, the collaboration between librettist and composer, and the first performance and subsequent stage history. This history is itself a record of changing attitudes towards the work, and an index of general changes of taste. The second is analytical and it is grounded in a very full synopsis which considers the opera as a structure of musical and dramatic effects. In most volumes there is also a musical analysis of a section of the score, showing how the music serves or makes the drama. The analysis, like the history, naturally raises questions of interpretation, and the third concern of each volume is to show how critical writing about an opera, like production and performance, can direct or distort appreciation of its structural elements. Some conflict of interpretation is an inevitable part of this account; editors of the handbooks reflect this – by citing classic statements, by commissioning new essays, by taking up their own critical position. A final section gives a select bibliography, a discography and guides to other sources.

v

To Bonnie and Lynden

La più divina delle poesie
è quella, amico, che c'insegna amare!

Contents

Illustrations

The illustrations appear by permission of the following: Fig. 1: Musée Carnavalet; figs. 4, 7, 8 and 9: G. Ricordi and Co.: Archivio Storico Ricordi; figs. 2 and 3: Peter Ross Collection; fig. 5: the Trustees of the Pierpont Morgan Library.

Preface

Our aim, quite simply, was to produce a book of hard facts and new critical opinions about *La bohème*. In the event, this proved surprisingly difficult. One might assume that what is without doubt one of the three or four most popular operas in the repertory would have primary materials in abundance, and have generated a formidable scholarly and critical literature, with the essential documents easily available in annotated modern editions. This is, after all, rapidly becoming the case with Verdi's mature operas, and has long been so with many of Wagner's. But in fact the relative lack of scholarship, or even of less-than-casual criticism, in Puccini studies very soon became apparent. In biographical matters, much of the story remains untold: Mosco Carner's critical biography is of course a most important milestone (one to which we make reference more than once), but his is necessarily a synoptic view; in spite of the magnificent *Carteggi pucciniani* and several more recent collections, much of Puccini's voluminous correspondence remains unpublished, some of it unavailable; the contemporary periodical literature, at least so far as *La bohème* is concerned, has hardly been considered by modern commentators and biographers – even Ricordi's house journal, the *Gazzetta musicale di Milano*, has received scant attention (and, as we shall see, it in fact constitutes an important source of information on the opera's genesis and the composer's activities during the period of composition); much of what is written in the memoirs of Puccini's friends and colleagues turns out to be unreliable, the *vero* and the *ben trovato* mingling freely in the syrup of hagiography.

The position vis-à-vis sources for the genesis of the opera is, if anything, even worse. Publication of the drafts and sketches for the libretto, promised long ago, has not occurred; only fragments of the musical sketches have appeared; and although the autograph score is available for study, and stands as awesome testimony to Puccini's mania for revision, we cannot even arrive at a 'definitive edition' of the musical text, as the proof stages between the autograph and the first published score have not surfaced.

And what of criticism and analysis? The latter, at least as the term is understood these days, hardly exists, and although current work on Verdi's music may perhaps change this quite soon, William Drabkin's essay on the music is something of a pioneering effort, as is our attempt to offer a close reading of the opera's extremely sophisticated libretto. Criticism there is in plenty, but the best of it (at least from a literary point of view) is almost entirely negative. Being supercilious about Puccini began very early in the century, and continues as a vigorous practice among the musical élite. However, *La bohème* is now nearly 100 years old; its cultural context should be perceptible, and this context undoubtedly illuminates and enriches our experience of the work. To offer one example, such considerations tend to draw attention to the sheer difficulty of *fin de siècle* (post-Wagnerian and post-Verdian) operatic composition, the extent to which each work had to create its own artistic cohesion, even its own aesthetic standards, in the face of an imposing but increasingly fragmented tradition.

In this sense, our book has a limited scope. In practical terms, we were restricted to sources available in the United States (though good friends in Germany and Italy did help out with important missing items), and to what could be seen in a brief research trip to Italy. We cannot pretend to anything like completeness. In critical terms, we sorely missed the extensive and varied body of scholarship that exists for other great opera composers. It did increasingly seem, though, as if our work had one important advantage: from quite an early stage it was the product of close collaboration, not just of two authors, but of two disciplines. The exchange between a literary critic and a musicologist constantly served both as a stimulus and as a corrective, helping to modify the necessarily limited perspective that each of us brought to the opera. The result, we hope, offers an insight into the complexities and richness of one of Puccini's great works.

Cornell University
Ithaca, New York
Easter 1985

Acknowledgements

It is a great pleasure to thank some of the people who have helped us during the writing of this book. Our contributors Jerrold Seigel, William Drabkin, and Malcolm Walker were all prompt and courteous, and William Ashbrook deserves special mention for his advice and friendship at every stage, and his critical reading of the entire typescript. Many others, both in Europe and the U.S., were generous with their advice and assistance: Peter Ross furnished us with photographs from his private collection; Francesco Degrada gave us the benefit of his unique knowledge of the Puccini sources; Pierluigi Petrobelli and Julian Budden offered many interesting musical insights at an early stage; Alfred Karnein and Steven Scher helped us to obtain copies of rare documents; Lenore Coral, Nelly Furman, Sander Gilman, Peter Uwe Hohendahl, and Steven Kaplan aided us with bibliographical information; Gina Psaki was unfailingly helpful in clearing up numerous problems of transcription and translation, and her appearance as co-author of the Appendix is only partial recognition of her assistance with many parts of the book. We are also indebted to the staff of various libraries and archives. In particular to M.° Giampiero Tintori and his staff at the Museo teatrale alla Scala; J. Rigbie Turner of the Pierpont Morgan Library in New York; Martin Chusid, Director of the American Institute for Verdi Studies, also in New York; and the Staff of the various Cornell libraries. Excellent editorial advice came from Rosemary Dooley and Penny Souster of Cambridge University Press; long-suffering secretarial assistance from Carol Cook, Tanis Furst, and Jennifer Hymoff. Finally, we would like to thank Bonnie Buettner, for her editorial and translating skills, and for her occasionally uncalled-for good humour.

Jerrold Seigel's contribution 'The rise of Bohemia' is reprinted by permission of *The New Republic*, © 1983, *The New Republic*, Inc. Extracts from Heinrich Mann's *Ein Zeitalter wird besichtigt* in Ch. 8 appear by permission of Aufbau-Verlag.

Source materials

In quoting from the libretto, we have been forced, as all Puccini scholars are, to make frequent compromises between the vocal score and early printed versions of the libretto. The latter supply us with often vital information about prosody and, wherever possible, their lineation has been preserved; but on many occasions the vocal score offers a different reading, one that is clearly 'definitive', and must be followed. References to rehearsal numbers hold good for all modern vocal and orchestral scores of the opera.

In the genesis and libretto chapters, the following frequently cited standard sources have been abbreviated as follows:

CP = *Carteggi pucciniani*, ed. Eugenio Gara (by letter number)
M = George Marek, *Puccini: A Biography* (by page number)
P = Giuseppe Pintorno, *Puccini: 276 lettere inedite* (by letter number)

All translations (from French, German, and Italian) are our own, unless otherwise stated. A major exception is the letters quoted from Marek, for which original texts are not available. Close dots (…) reproduce a common Italian punctuation; open dots [. . .] mark ellipses in quoted sources. Our operatic heroine sports a diacritical mark (Mimì), while her literary forebear's nationality makes such accentual prompting unnecessary.

1 *The rise of Bohemia*

BY JERROLD SEIGEL

Its borders were youth and hope, gaiety and despair, love, poverty, courage, cold, and the hospital. To nineteenth-century explorers, Bohemia was a real country with real inhabitants but not marked on any map. They traced its frontiers with a mixture of reality and fantasy. We inherit their problem of just where to locate Bohemia, and whom to count among its citizens. To be able to say how many Rodolfos and Mimìs were shivering and starving in their garrets in year X and how many half a century later, how long youth lasted and what level of middle-class comfort awaited those who gave up or escaped: if nothing else, charts and graphs might make *La bohème* a respectable subject. But in this way as in others Bohemia resists respectability. It cannot be mapped and graphed and counted because it was never wholly an objective condition. Bohemia had outward signs of membership: clothing, occupation, gait, rhythm of life. But it had to be entered through the mind, through some consciousness of belonging. Whether a certain form of dress or rhythm of life was bohemian or not depended – and still does – on how it was meant or taken. Bohemian gestures were symbolic actions.

Our map must place Bohemia at the intersection of life and cultural symbol. To enter it might have real and unforeseen consequences, sometimes even tragic ones; but to go in was always to make a gesture and a statement – about oneself, about society. Because Bohemia was half life and half symbol, to invent the name was not far from discovering the thing. That invention can be traced to a period, the 1830s and 1840s, and to a place, Paris. By 1850 the word was shedding its literal association with gypsies and its first extended ties with a shady underworld of beggars and con men to take on the meaning best enshrined for most of us in Puccini's opera. One man contributed more than anyone else to this transformation: the author of the stories that gave Puccini his characters, Henry Murger.

1

Murger was not the first to write about Bohemia in this sense, and many who have done so since have sought to belittle him. Understandably: Murger was a mediocre writer and in some ways not a very admirable person. Those who associate Bohemia with the forward thrust of the artistic avant-garde or the high ground of moral heroism have treated him with disdain, wishing he would go away. But in the history of Bohemia, Murger will not go away. He is there whenever the phenomenon is to be defined or described. The enormous success of his play *La Vie de bohème*, written with Théodore Barrière in 1849, first gave the image of Bohemia wide currency, and provoked the earliest sustained discussion of what it was and what it meant. The play's half-dozen revivals through the century kept that dialogue alive. Murger's death in 1861 was marked by a large public funeral, a widely supported subscription for a memorial monument, and a further round of debate about Bohemia: newspaper and magazine articles to begin with, then no less than three biographies, all seeking to capture the true meaning of Murger's life.[1]

What made this second-rate writer so pervasive a symbol? The simplest answer is not the least important, though it is often overlooked: chronology. When Murger first offered his tales and sketches in a small newspaper, mostly during 1846, they were hardly noticed. Three years later the play based on those stories was the talk of Paris. Daily papers could not restrain their astonishment at the size of the crowds – and of box-office sales. The broad enthusiasm was only partly brought on by the explosions of wit several critics hailed in the dialogue. Behind it lay the experience of revolutionary upheaval. The toppling of the government in February of 1848, followed by the bloody civil war in June and the agitations that continued under the Second Republic, all gave a new edge to the contemplation of undisciplined young people living out their hostility to respectable society in the shadowy reaches of Paris. Murger's characters were seldom inspired by political conviction or passion. His work gave heart to those who wanted to see the French put aside public confrontations for the other great national enthusiasm, the poetry of private life. But other observers found very different hopes in Murger. To the radical young reviewer for *La Réforme*, the theatrical presentation of bohemian life was a reminder of all the inner contradictions in bourgeois society that drove its heirs to flee toward its margins. Their commitment to a life of freedom, work, and pleasure was a warning that the society which corrupted those values was rotten and weak, and would have to pay.[2]

Murger's impact was strong partly because it was first felt at a moment of revolutionary crisis. As that crisis receded it left a residue of issues that would recur to challenge every generation of the modern European bourgeoisie. That Bohemia had to be a temporary phase if its inhabitants were to avoid disaster was one of Murger's strongest convictions. In the play of 1849 this conviction inspired Rodolphe's self-centred vision of Mimi's death as the end of his own youth; two years later, in the preface to his book of bohemian tales, Murger rejected longer residency in Bohemia as a cul de sac.[3] Murger himself was always seeking the way out of Bohemia, and it is more than ironic that the success of his bohemian tales offered him the first real chance to find it. He yearned for nothing more than a regular, comfortable, and established bourgeois existence. But he never succeeded in achieving one. His habits were too irregular, his output too small, and he never learned to write successfully about any other subject. Hence his original link to Bohemia remained, undiluted by any other public identity. His explicit advocacy of conversion from Bohemian to bourgeois made him appeal to many who had found the path or sought it. At the same time, his own inability to escape altogether from Bohemia made him also the symbol of the deeper and more persisting alienation felt by others. The contrast between those two views structured the debate about Murger that followed his death in 1861. These issues are perennial in modern life, but they were especially intense for the members of Murger's own generation. Young in the 1840s, they felt the full impact of the failed revolutionary expectations of 1848. They were the first generation who had to make some kind of peace with the refusal of bourgeois society to transform itself into something else. Murger met their need, spinning a thread of continuity between revolt and reconciliation, youth and age.

Murger's Bohemians did their dance of closeness and distance to bourgeois life to a rhythm of constant ambivalence. Their lives revolved around the opposite poles of commitment to artistic poverty and fascination with bourgeois wealth. It was this, rather than any genuine artistic vocation, that occupied centre stage in Murger's *mise-en-scène*. In the preface to his book of 1851, Murger claimed that the real subjects of his tales were the 'true' Bohemians, poor young men with genuine artistic callings for whom the passage through Bohemia was a necessary apprenticeship. Murger distinguished these true Bohemians from the crowd of those he called 'amateurs' who surrounded them: young bourgeois seeking excitement or living out their youthful rebellions in the protective anonymity of Paris.[4] Yet the distance between the two groups was smaller than he wanted to believe. Indeed, if we accept Murger's definition of the professionals as those with a real artistic calling, then he was never far from being an amateur Bohemian himself, an artist who could write successfully about nothing but Bohemia. He represented those for whom being an artist seldom found fulfilment through doing the work; instead it meant living the life.

Murger's sketches and stories became the classic image of Bohemia because they depicted a life that was both less and more than the artistic apprenticeship he claimed. The form of that life was modelled on the experiences of poor young artists trying to enter the world of culture in an age of market relationships. But their style of life was here appropriated for a different purpose: dramatizing the ambivalence felt by young – and not so young – bourgeois toward their own social destinies. Bohemia enacted the polarities of wealth and poverty, work and indulgence, duty and liberation, and thus acquired its theatrical quality of being half life and half symbol. The identity of the artist was the mirror in which Bohemians explored their wider ambivalence toward bourgeois life.

Mirrors are of different sorts, however. They can magnify or diminish, sharpen or blur. Once the mirror of Bohemia existed, it was available to others. Whether it diffused or intensified the tensions of modern life depended on who was holding it up. There is space to mention – briefly – two such standard-bearers here. Both had Murger's work very much in mind when they described their own Bohemias; each deliberately departed from him. The first is nearly forgotten today, although he was famous as an arch-Bohemian in the 1850s. He was Alexandre Privat d'Anglemont, journalist, night-walker, café-fixture, friend of Murger and Courbet and Baudelaire, the man to whom Murger declared and everyone repeated: 'You are not a Bohemian, you are Bohemia.'[5] Privat was the great master of *blague*, of leg-pulling, tall-tale-telling, and self-obfuscation, the ultimate *Luftmensch* of body and spirit. We know practically nothing certain about his life because, as one of his friends recounted, he would tell his story to anyone on the slightest provocation, but he never told it twice the same way. Privat once considered writing about the artists, writers, and women who made Murger famous, but never did. Instead he wrote about another underside of Paris, a region also named Bohemia but which Murger determinedly excluded when he sought to draw its boundaries. This was the shadowy gaslight world of slum-dwellers and down-and-outers, ragpickers and peddlers, acrobats and organ grinders, the lower depths of society.

Privat's reports were especially famous for their accounts of the surprising and inventive forms of surviving and making do that grew up in the empty corners of nineteenth-century society, the activities and employments called *métiers inconnus*. Parisians had long been fascinated by these murky figures, present in the pages of Eugène Sue. Privat's characters were as colourful as any. One called himself the *boulanger en vieux*, collector of stale bread from which he provided pet food and even soup croutons; another filled attics with dog and cat dung in order to make breeding grounds for worms to be sold as fish bait. There was the widow Vanard who scavenged lemon peels, making perfumes and flavourings of them; and Matagatos, the scourge of stray cats, supporting himself by selling them to cheap bistros where they could pass for rabbit stew.

Court records show that judges of the time often believed that the *métiers inconnus* were merely invented by vagabonds and con men as trumped-up defences against criminal charges. Privat's reports gave a very different picture. Not only were the unknown activities real, they were inspired by virtues and a vision that was altogether respectable. Privat's people did not live from hand to mouth. They rose above their condition. Each was animated by an inspiration, an idea. Each worked steadily and responsibly to turn that idea into an enterprise that benefited both himself and others. Some did very well, thank you, and Privat was happy when his publicity helped them to do better. His message was that the outer edges of Parisian life were not swamps waiting to sink the forward motion of modern civilization, but potential sources of innovation and progress.

Murger and Privat represented Bohemia in ways that were conservative, integrative; in their mirrors the tensions of bourgeois life were diffused, relaxed. Both stood at the opposite pole from another noted and self-conscious Bohemian, Jules Vallès. Vallès provides the model mid-nineteenth-century example of the Bohemian as rebel and revolutionary. His prominence in the

Commune of 1871 was a strong reason why some people at the time saw that uprising as an outburst of bohemianism. His autobiographical trilogy, *Jacques Vintras*, described his life trajectory as a progress from bohemianism to revolutionary radicalism, and his collection of 1865, *Les Réfractaires* (a good modern rendering would be *The Refuseniks*), evoked a Bohemia that was consciously desperate and menacing where Murger's had been hopeful and light-hearted.[6]

Most writers about Bohemia have followed Vallès's own lead in stressing the contrasts between his version of *La bohème* and Murger's. Yet the two shared more than Vallès wanted to believe, especially from the perspective of his wholehearted identification with revolution after 1871. Before that date, Vallès's attitude toward bourgeois society was less one of clear and determined opposition than of deep and pained ambivalence. As a journalist and writer during the Second Empire, Vallès was always a republican, a socialist, and an outsider. But that did not keep him from seeking accommodations with society or yearning to be accepted by it. His primary commitment was to individuality, and this made him as suspicious of regimentation when it was demanded from the left as when it was sponsored by the right. Although he chafed at Bonapartist restraints on political activity, his ferocious individualism probably got freer rein within them that it could have in a situation in which political loyalties would have been more constantly and publicly tested. Vallès suggested as much when he said he had felt freest when writing for the conservative but independent-minded *Le Figaro*.[7]

One hears the authentic accents of his speech in an article he published in the autumn of 1861:

Sirs! there is a misunderstanding between us! In every man who takes up a pen, a palette, a chisel, a pencil, whatever, the bourgeois sees a useless person; in every bourgeois, the man of letters sees an enemy. Sad prejudice, foolish opinion, unhappy antagonism. Our cause is the same, the valiant cause of the parvenus.[8]

The Bohemians he called *réfractaires* were themselves parvenus, individuals who sought to arrive at their personal goals by the sheer force of their pride and imagination, rejecting the paths traced out in advance by others. Unlike Privat d'Anglemont's people, they were not born on the margins of respectability. But their identification with the qualities of inventiveness and independence supposed to animate bourgeois society was so intense that it demolished the conventional limitations within which ordinary people found security. Their lives were heroic and sometimes led to the edges of revolt. But their hopes and visions were seldom fulfilled. Pouring out their hearts in a cloud of heroic but useless fantasy, they imagined things never done and books never written. They lived in the stale, winy atmosphere of defeat.

That Vallès painted their fate in darker colours than either Murger or Privat reflects the disappointments of his own and his family's history. Vallès's father was an Auvergnat peasant who sought to rise into the bourgeois world through education, passing his *baccalauréat* and becoming a secondary school teacher. But like many similar people in the nineteenth century, Vallès learned early that when people like his family claimed bourgeois status, they might have to pay for their pretension in the coin of failure and rejection. That experience cast the mould for the ambivalence toward bourgeois society that drove Vallès in contradictory directions until the outbreak of revolution and repression in 1871 resolved it for him. His identification with the defeated, the *vaincus*, there found its apotheosis.

In different ways Murger, Privat, and Vallès all occupy exemplary space in the landscape of nineteenth-century Bohemia. That they do helps us to see beyond the most common approach to Bohemia in cultural history, the one that frames the subject primarily in terms of the social position of art and artists. The figure of the artist was central to bohemianism not because Bohemia was made up of artists, but because the nineteenth century made the artist's intense preoccupation with self-examination and self-development symbolic of wider issues in individual and social life. The French Revolution did away with the corporate basis of society dominant in the old regime. For the first time society was constructed on principles that claimed to place each individual in it not through some intermediate adherence to a corporation, an order, or a guild, but on the basis of pure individuality. To develop one's individuality, through education, independence, inventiveness – what Hegel called free subjectivity – was the expectation placed on all members of civil society. Access to these possibilities for self-development was the distinguishing mark of membership in the modern bourgeoisie. There was a point beyond which this cultivation of self ceased to be socially useful, becoming egocentric, anarchic. Bohemia grew up where the boundaries and limits of bourgeois existence were murky and uncertain. It was a space within which the potentialities set free in bourgeois life were continually thrown up against the barriers erected to contain them.

Only when we have recognised this basic independence of the history of Bohemia from the history of art and artists can we grasp the nature of their interdependence. A good place to approach it is through the greatest of the nineteenth-century poets associated with Bohemia, Charles Baudelaire.

More often than not Baudelaire detested Bohemia, sharing a hostility felt by other modernist figures, including the Goncourt brothers and Flaubert. His anti-bohemianism was double-pronged. Baudelaire's preferred personal style was elegant, refined. He aspired to be a Dandy, to embody the aristocratic impassiveness and hard polish of a Beau Brummel, living the whole of his life in front of a mirror. To him, the Bohemian's spontaneity, his social and sexual promiscuity, his life under the stars, were all anathema. Baudelaire found bohemianism suspect from an aesthetic point of view, too. Bohemia was one important locus of the modern artistic heresy that identified art with natural feeling. Baudelaire, as we know, rejected this identification. Beauty was the product not of sentiment but of imagination; it belonged not to nature but to artifice. The followers of Murger, Baudelaire wrote the year Murger died, rejected the hard work and discipline that real artistic creation required.[9]

Baudelaire also aspired to the union of art and life, but on the Dandy's terms, not the Bohemian's. The Dandy sought to make life an art by imposing his image of self-contained perfection on it, cancelling out his natural self through the power of artifice. It was a heroic undertaking, one always on the edge of failure. The Dandy was a creature from another age, glowing like the sun in the twilight zone between the eras of aristocracy and democracy. Historically doomed, the Dandy's impassiveness was also personally impossible. It was shattered by the passion that drove the genuine artist – what Baudelaire called 'the passion for seeing and feeling'.

Out of the dissolution of Baudelaire's Dandyism there emerges the other Baudelaire: the penniless inhabitant of dingy hotels, the poet fascinated by prostitution, the celebrant of inebriation, the explorer of drugs. These experiences and postures were expressions of that artistic passion for seeing and feeling that marked the limits of aesthetic Dandyism. The modern artist had to enter the realm of imagination and beauty on the only ground available: the ground of pure personal experience. Baudelaire recognised this meant abandoning Dandyism for the Bohemian regions from which his other side was always in flight. In this mood, Baudelaire wrote of the need to glorify the vagabond bohemian life, celebrating it 'as the cult of multiplied sensation'.

Baudelaire is the paradigm case of tension between the authentic, committed artist – as distinct from Murger's amateurs – and Bohemia. Writers and painters intent on fulfilling some inner vision by realising it in finished work have seldom failed to grasp the distinction between their lives and those who appropriate their surface and gestures for the different purpose of dramatising ambivalence toward bourgeois life. To confuse art with the life of art is to devalue the products by dissolving them in conditions that may be necessary but are certainly not sufficient to produce them. Yet, however real the distinction between art and life may be, it is also very fragile. Baudelaire lived in Bohemia despite himself. Much of the history of modern art since his day has followed his example. Deprived of transcendence, modern art has had to nurture itself on real, subjective experience. Increasingly it has turned from a search for beauty to a confrontation with the conditions of that experience. The ideal of beauty, to which Baudelaire still held, has receded in much of the modern avant-garde he inspired, replaced by the dramatisation of the conflict between art and life.

The dimensions of that conflict emerged clearly at the end of the nineteenth century. As the social and political structures of the Third Republic revealed an ability to enthrone philistinism and absorb conflict and dissent despite the moral decadence of public life, artists and political militants experienced a common attraction for extreme postures. In 1892 the symbolist poet Pierre Quillard equated art with opposition to contemporary life: 'Whoever communicates to his brothers in suffering the secret splendour of his dreams acts upon the surrounding society in the manner of a solvent and makes all those who understand him, often without their realisation, outlaws and rebels.'[10]

Such a vision gave credence and support to the position Baudelaire fought off even as he recognised its powerful appeal in Murger's example: that the artist could be identified as clearly by the lived dramatisation of his antibourgeois self-consciousness as by the work he did. This image would become a central preoccupation of modernism, from Alfred Jarry through Cubism and Dada to Surrealism. The features of Bohemia that were most suspect to Baudelaire were precisely the ones that made it a breeding ground for avant-garde consciousness: once fused with life, art was free to embody the pure subjectivity that constantly corroded the objective limits of ordinary existence. This vision reached its most complete embodiment in the Surrealist insistence that the proper medium of art was life, not literature.

Almost from the start Bohemia has expanded outward from its French homeland to colonise other countries. It found its classic American expression (not its first) in Greenwich Village during the years before and after World War I, later reappearing as the Beat Generation and Hippiedom. These Bohemias, like their original archetypes, have nurtured themselves on the merger of art and life, mixing rebellion with ambition, simultaneously sponsoring real artistic vocations and appropriating the artist's image to dramatise ambivalence toward the beckoning destinies of ordinary social life. Privat's *blague* and Murger's identification of art with the liberated spontaneity of those who live in the name of it have reappeared in more recent modernist forms: action painting, pop art, minimalism. The locus of bohemian experience may have shifted, from inside Murger's garret to Kerouac's *On the Road*, but its explorers have continued to be those whose literary vocations often find expression in writing about nothing else. In the twentieth century as in the nineteenth, Bohemians move in and out of political engagement, sometimes ranging themselves like Vallès behind the banner of revolt, but impelled by a commitment to individual liberation that can also send them back into political indifference or isolation.

Bohemia has also changed its relationship to society in our century. Its forms of life and signs of membership – hair, dress, irregular work patterns, drugs, unconventional sexual behaviour – have broken free of the marginal spaces that once confined them. Increasingly they are becoming accepted features of ordinary life. That development may be taking place most rapidly in the United States, where the weight of convention and tradition is lighter than in Europe. But its effects are visible even in France, the original home of everything packed into the notion 'bourgeois'. This diffusion of Bohemia into everyday life is a sign that its theatre of marginality has always been a revelation of potentialities taking shape at the hidden centre of modern society. In every generation the cultivation of self opens up new terrain, pushing back or circumventing the boundaries society erects to contain and limit it. Yet the demand to set limits to what individuals do in the pursuit of subjective satisfactions continually reasserts itself. Perhaps the need for Bohemia is receding now, even as the free spaces within which it originally developed grow rarer and less accessible. We may have to imagine a future without Bohemians. If so we will miss their vitality and inventiveness. And we will need some new mirror in which to explore the conditions – and the limitations – of our liberation.

2 Synopsis

Act I: In the garret

Large window from which one sees an expanse of snow-covered roofs. To the right a stove. A table, a bed, a wardrobe, four chairs, an artist's easel with a sketched canvas and a stool: a few books, many bundles of paper, two candlesticks. A door in the centre, another to the left.

The curtain rises to reveal Rodolfo and Marcello in what we will later find to be characteristic actions. Marcello, working discontentedly on his Biblical canvas 'The Crossing of the Red Sea' and suffering badly from the cold, keeps moving around and blowing on his hands. Rodolfo, the young poet, stares meditatively out over the grey skies of Paris. The orchestra, at first plainly in tune with Marcello, establishes an atmosphere of restless energy. A heavily accented, dotted-rhythm figure, destined to dominate this opening section, is thrown from instrument to instrument, exploring a wide orchestral space. The origin of this theme in a composition from Puccini's student days entitled *Capriccio sinfonico* has often been noted: the composer may even have found it an apt musical reminiscence of his own days of artistic struggle.[1] Whatever the cause, its blend of lively adventure and playful scholasticism is perfectly suited to the situation.

Marcello's first words immediately set the verbal tone:

> Questo Mar Rosso – mi ammollisce e assidera
> come se addosso – mi piovesse in stille.
> Per vendicarmi, affogo un Faraon!

> This Red Sea dampens and freezes me
> As if it were raining on me in drops.
> As revenge, I'll drown a Pharaoh!

Conversational, gently mocking the inflated language of

nineteenth-century melodrama ('Per vendicarmi . . .'), this opening nevertheless represents a moment of great significance in Italian opera. There is no formal prolegomenon, no scene-setting chorus or conversation of secondary characters. We are emphatically *in medias res*; a slice of life has opened before us. Rodolfo's counter-statement belatedly gestures toward the more conventional descriptive mode, but again there is an ironic twist, the poet's potentially romantic vista being marred by grey skies and belching smoke:

> Nei cieli bigi
> guardo fumar dai mille
> comignoli Parigi,
>
> In the grey skies
> I watch Paris smoke
> from a thousand chimneys,

The melody of 'Nei cieli bigi' is another self-borrowing (this time from *La lupa*, an abortive project of 1894), but again is skilfully adapted to the present situation, its relaxed rhythm and broad contours, as well as a number of harmonic details, making it an ideal complement to the opening, 'symphonic' theme – a kind of 'second subject' that offers a lyrical counterpart.

After 'Nei cieli bigi' the 'symphonic' theme returns, to be repeated with ever-increasing urgency as Marcello's disgust at the cold takes on even greater colloquial force ('Ho un freddo cane' – 'I'm damned cold'). He proposes sacrificing the chair, but Rodolfo hits on a piece of 'poetic' justice: with a renewed version of 'Nei cieli bigi', he announces that they will burn his own five-act drama. The orchestral texture shimmers with harp arpeggios and a solo flute as Act I is crammed into the stove and they huddle round to enjoy its fleeting warmth.

The philosopher Colline enters, throwing down a pile of books, and soon Act II goes into the flames. The orchestra depicts the reviving fire with a brilliant texture of pizzicato strings and detached woodwind and brass chords; but even though the rest of the play soon follows, the flame quickly dies. Colline and Marcello prepare to exact justice from the author of this 'fragile drama'. They are interrupted by a robust unison theme that heralds two boys carrying food, wine, cigars and wood. The boys are followed by the composer Schaunard who, to variants of the unison theme, proceeds to tell the bizarre story of his newfound wealth: engaged by an Englishman to speed a neighbour's parrot to an early grave by means of incessant musical performance, he eventually took matters into his own hands, charmed the owner's maid, and had the creature poisoned with parsley. At the grandiose climax of this tale, Schaunard realises that his set-piece description is coming a poor second to the pleasures he has brought with him. But he manages to deny the others a taste of the food. It is Christmas Eve and they must eat in the Latin Quarter, whose evocative odours Schaunard sings of in a gently oscillating theme of parallel triads. The mood of boisterous fun is re-established and everyone prepares to leave. Suddenly, a knock on the door freezes the action.

It is Benoît, the landlord, come to claim the long overdue rent. Marcello takes charge; drinks are proffered; and Benoît is encouraged to discuss his amorous conquests. As the wine takes its effect, the old man makes no secret of his preferences:

> Le donne magre sono grattacapi
> e spesso ... sopracapi ...
> e son piene di doglie –
> per esempio mia moglie ...
>
> Thin women are headaches
> and often ... horns ...
> and they are full of complaints –
> for example my wife ...

And this mention of his wife gives the Bohemians their chance. In a magnificent verbal and musical parody of serious opera, they denounce Benoît's 'obscene desires' and peremptorily push him from the room, only to collapse in laughter the moment he has gone.[2] The oscillating triads of the Latin Quarter theme return, and again the friends prepare to leave; but, to a further reprise of 'Nei cieli bigi', this time on solo violin, Rodolfo announces that he must stay at least briefly to finish an article. The others, somewhat tipsy by now, descend the stairs, the Bohemians' theme turning from purposeful descent to uncontrollable slither. Rodolfo sets to work.

For a second time in the act, there is a knock at the door. A quiet string chord, followed by an intense version of the theme which will begin her monologue, introduces Mimì. Timidly she begs a light for her candle, but is suddenly overcome by a fit of coughing and faints into Rodolfo's arms. He sprinkles water on her face – a gesture uncannily imitated by pizzicato violins – and she revives. Composure regained, she sips a glass of wine, takes up her candlestick (now lighted by Rodolfo), and leaves with a demurely exchanged

'Buona sera'. But she is gone for no more than a moment before reappearing in some agitation, saying that she has lost the key to her room. The pace of the encounter now quickens and a new melodic idea, in part characterised by clarinets in thirds, takes over. A draught blows out Mimì's candle; Rodolfo, hurrying to her aid, extinguishes his own; they are left in darkness. Both grope for the key, which Rodolfo soon finds and, with a stifled exclamation, surreptitiously pockets. The brisk music that has accompanied this episode slows down to begin a steep modulatory progression as Rodolfo inches his way toward Mimì. As the modulation finally reaches its goal, their hands 'accidentally' touch, and this time it is Mimì who cries out in surprise. The stage is set for one of the most famous monologues in all opera.

Rodolfo's 'Che gelida manina', difficult to classify formally, is perhaps best described as in two unequal parts, with a brief transitional passage. The first part invokes the central poetic image associated with Mimì, the 'tiny frozen hand', then sets the scene:

> Ma per fortuna – è una notte di luna,
> e qui la luna l'abbiamo vicina.

> But luckily – it is a moonlit night,
> and here we have the moon close to us.

and poses the central question ('Chi son?' – 'Who am I?'), again making use of a solo flute and harp to give luminosity to the string texture. This ends with a question – 'Vuole?' – which Mimì demurely declines to answer. Then comes the transition: a clear, succinct statement of the bohemian ideal:

> Chi son? – Sono un poeta.
> Che cosa faccio? – Scrivo.
> E come vivo? – Vivo.

> Who am I? – I'm a poet.
> What do I do? – I write.
> And how do I live? – I live.

At the end of this description, almost unobtrusively, the music slips into the main key of the larger, final section. This is itself in two parts, the first a broader, common-time version of 'Nei cieli bigi'. Then, at 'Talor dal mio forziere', the voice expands as the poet expatiates; the melody moves into characteristic triplet divisions that give an improvisatory air; and finally, on the word 'speranza', a 'hope' which by now is clearly pinned on Mimì, an optional line takes the tenor up to high *c*. From there the melody falls to a questioning close, but as if in response to the vocal outburst, the orchestra continues to explore new registers in its final cadence. The initial impression of Mimì's answering autobiographical monologue is of maximum contrast. The widely spaced final chord of 'Che gelida manina' is followed by a single note and, in place of Rodolfo's assertive bohemianism, we have a simple, prosaic answer to the question of identity:

> Sì.
> Mi chiamano Mimì,
> ma il mio nome è Lucia.

> Yes.
> They call me Mimì,
> but my name is Lucia.

The musical theme which accompanies this declaration, already heard at Mimì's first entrance, assumes the status of a leitmotif by virtue of its repetition and prominence, and will be used to telling effect later in the score. The dominant impression of the monologue is of restraint (stage directors should note that Mimì is instructed in the score to remain seated throughout). In broad contour, Mimì's 'sketch' is similar to Rodolfo's, in that it has two parts, divided by a direct question (in her case, 'Lei m'intende?'). But although in the second half thoughts of the coming spring impel a climax of Rodolfo-like intensity, the final moments return to understatement, and are concluded in a musical and verbal idiom as near to actual speech as possible:

> Altro di me non le saprei narrare.
> Sono la sua vicina
> che la vien fuori d'ora a importunare.

> I wouldn't know what else to tell you about myself.
> I am your neighbour
> who comes at an odd hour to beg a favour.

From the courtyard below we hear the Bohemians, anxious for Rodolfo to join them. He sends his friends away and turns to find Mimì bathed in moonlight. The visual image fuses with Marcello's parting words 'Trovò la poesia!' ('He found poetry!'), to create the final duet 'O soave fanciulla!' ('O sweet young girl!'), which at its climax returns triumphantly to the 'Talor dal mio forziere' theme from Rodolfo's aria. From there some moments of tonal flux underpin a playful exchange between the newfound lovers: Should they go out? Wouldn't it be cosier to remain here? But Mimì side-steps the issue and, to a reprise of the opening of 'Che gelida manina', they again link hands – though this time with a mock excess of formality. And so they disappear from sight, Mimì floating up to a high *c* (marked *perdendosi* in the score) as they dreamily repeat 'Amor! Amor! Amor!' Harp harmonics slowly descend through the final chord. The curtain falls.

Act II. In the Latin Quarter

Christmas Eve. A crossroads which at its centre forms a kind of square; shops, hawkers of all kinds; to one side the Café Momus. Rodolfo and Mimì wander in the crowd, Colline is by a rag shop, Schaunard is buying a pipe and a horn at a second-hand shop, Marcello is pushed here and there with the tide of people. A great, motley crowd: bourgeois, soldiers, serving girls, boys, children, students, seamstresses, gendarmes, etc. It is evening. The shops are decorated with lanterns and glowing lamps; a large lamp lights the entrance to the Café Momus. The café is so crowded that several bourgeois are obliged to sit at a table outside in the open.

In considering the second act, a mere twenty minutes or so of hectic activity, we should bear in mind its original position as the concluding scene of Act I. We can then see it in a traditional context, as an example of that most imposing of nineteenth-century Italian operatic forms, the *concertato finale*, the grand sonic and scenic climax at the mid-point of a drama, often dominated musically by a central, static moment of reflection (in this case Musetta's 'Quando me'n vo' ').[3] However, once this traditional paradigm is accepted, one can only marvel at the skill with which Puccini also maintains and integrates the musical strands set out in Act I: the Bohemians' boisterous fun and, of course, the sentimental passion of Rodolfo and Mimì.

The act begins with an emphatic brass rendition of the parallel triads associated in Act I with Schaunard's quiet evocation of the Latin Quarter. Soon the orchestra is overlaid with a myriad of vocal interventions: tradespeople calling their wares, café patrons shouting orders, bystanders flustered at all the moving to and fro, and Schaunard haggling over a horn which obstinately sounds $e\flat$ when he wants a *d*. This bustle of energy is interrupted by a musical and dramatic 'close focus' onto Mimì, Rodolfo and the other

1   The Café Momus, sketch by Thomas Boys (1819)

Bohemians, and a shift to the waltz time so characteristic of this act. The two lovers emerge from the crowd to enter a bonnet shop while Colline collects a coat he is having mended and Marcello flirts with the girls. A further waltz theme takes over as more saleswomen appear and Rodolfo and Mimì (the latter with a new pink bonnet) reappear. With a return to the Latin Quarter theme, the crowd engulfs the scene briefly, but soon Colline, Schaunard and Marcello carry a table out from the Café Momus and, by their noisy joviality, drive away the more sober clients. There is a brief, light-hearted but nevertheless ominous exchange between Rodolfo and Mimì on the subject of jealousy. Parpignol, the toy-seller, is heard in the distance. Then Rodolfo introduces Mimì to his friends. Both the words and the music recall the autobiographical monologues which closed Act I, but now, significantly, they are fused: Rodolfo's 'perchè son io il poeta' is a clear verbal reference to *his* aria, while the music repeats a phrase of Mimì's ('mi piaccion quelle cose'):

> Questa è Mimì,
> gaia – fioraia.
> Il suo venir completa
> la bella compagnia,
> perchè son io il poeta,
> essa la poesia.

> This is Mimì,
> a happy flower maker.
> Her arrival completes
> this fine company,
> because I am the poet,
> she, poetry.

and are capped by a formal lyric stanza from Rodolfo ('Dal mio cervel' – 'From my brain'). The Bohemians respond to all this extrovert passion with a dry exchange of Latin tags.

As everyone takes a seat, the stage undergoes yet another invasion. Enter Parpignol, the toy-seller, surrounded by a crowd of pestering children. Their breathless demands are quickly countered by a bevy of mothers who attempt to scold them home. Soon the mothers relent (it is, after all, Christmas Eve), and Parpignol goes on his way with an army of satisfied youngsters. Again, we close in on the main characters and, with a skilful thematic link, Marcello questions Mimì about *her* present, the bonnet. This gives a pretext for what is in effect a miniature, shared aria, 'Una cuffietta a pizzi, tutta rosa, ricamata' ('A lace bonnet, all pink, embroidered'). The first 'stanza', sung by Mimì, is characterised by a rhythmic ambiguity (bars of 3/4 injected into 2/4) that lends a conversational air to the melody. The second is taken by the Bohemians in turn: Colline (with the aid of judicious transposition), Schaunard, Marcello and finally, in a climax of intensity, Rodolfo. Mimì then interjects her rhythmically ambiguous line, and the whole delightful episode ends with a vigorous toast:

> E via i pensier!
> Alti i bicchier!
> Beviam! ... beviam! ...
>
> Away with thoughts!
> Raise high the glasses!
> Let's drink! ... let's drink! ...

'Ch'io beva del tossico!' ('Let me drink poison!') shouts Marcello, the suddenness of the change of mood reflected in an extreme harmonic *non sequitur*. His former mistress Musetta has appeared, and her tripping 9/8 theme (with syncopated bass for added rhythmic bite) immediately establishes the presence of an important new personality. She is followed, puppy-like, by Alcindoro, 'a pompous and affected old man' (according to the stage direction) and plainly one who, matched up against Musetta, is fighting well outside his weight. *His* primary purpose, it would seem, is to avoid undue fuss and ostentation, something which makes Musetta a singularly inappropriate choice of partner. Mimì is evidently intrigued and, as Musetta continues to chatter incessantly, Marcello supplies an acid portrait:

> Il suo nome è Musetta;
> cognome: Tentazione!
> Per sua vocazione
> fa la rosa dei venti;
>
> Her name is Musetta;
> surname: Temptation!
> And her vocation
> is to act the compass card . . .

Musetta, seemingly oblivious to the insults being thrown at her, becomes increasingly agitated by the lack of recognition the Bohemians (and especially Marcello) are offering her. Finally the strain becomes too much and, to Alcindoro's horror, she hurls a plate to the ground. The tension continues to mount, interrupted only by a brief passionate exchange between Rodolfo and Mimì, who are quite unaffected by the quarrel surrounding them. Now Musetta plays her trump card: seduction. The action freezes and, in a dreamy waltz time, she celebrates her own magnetism:

> Quando me'n vo' soletta per la via
> la gente sosta e mira,
> e la bellezza mia tutta ricerca in me
> da capo a piè.
>
> When I walk alone through the street
> people stop and stare,
> and all seek in me my beauty
> from head to foot.

'Quando me'n vo' ', the 'largo' of our *concertato finale*, is certainly the longest set piece of the opera, and has a suitably complex articulated structure. The first part, its 'exposition', is a clear ABA form, Musetta's two statements of the main theme being interrupted by a contrasting section in which the prevailing descending melodic motion is reversed. The theme itself is remarkable in several respects. One (to touch on a point which will be discussed in greater detail in chapter 5) is that, for such a famous *melody*, its initial means of characterisation is primarily harmonic (the first three chords); another that it is suffused with counterpoint. The orchestral countersubjects of the opening are soon given greater focus as Mimì joins Musetta in answering phrases to conclude the first section. The middle portion of the ensemble introduces themes from earlier in the act; Marcello and Musetta move closer together; but there is still the troublesome Alcindoro. In an inspired moment, Musetta shrieks of pain in her foot, her elderly lover stoops to investigate, and so allows Marcello to pour forth his declaration in an unrestrained reprise of the main melody of the ensemble ('Gioventù mia'). A final thrilling cadence (with both Mimì and Musetta on high *b*) is capped by the orchestra, *fff tutta forza*, as Alcindoro rushes off to mend Musetta's offending shoe; but this noisy climax is suddenly replaced by a passage of the utmost restraint. 'Siamo all'ultima scena!' ('We have reached the final scene!') says Schaunard and, sure enough, the bill unobtrusively appears. Needless to say, the Bohemians rummage fruitlessly through their pockets. A military tattoo heard in the distance gives an added sense of urgency. Eventually, Musetta saves the day: she instructs the waiter to add their bill to hers, and places it on Alcindoro's table with a neat couplet:

E dove s'è seduto
ritrovi il mio saluto!

And where he was seated
he will find my farewell!

The Bohemians repeat the couplet in pious four-part harmony, just as the tattoo arrives onstage, headed by a magnificent drum major. Marcello and Colline hoist Musetta onto their shoulders as everyone follows the parade to suitably martial music.[4] And so we are left with poor Alcindoro, hurriedly returning with a new pair of shoes. He is ceremoniously presented with the bills; he sees the deserted stage and, to a final, triumphant statement of the Latin Quarter theme, sinks dumbfounded into a chair.

Act III: The Barrière d'Enfer

Beyond the barrière (tollgate) the outer boulevard and, in the far background, the Orleans road that disappears long past the tall houses and the February fog; on this side, to the left, a tavern and the small square at the tollgate, to the right the Boulevard d'Enfer; to the left the Boulevard St Jacques. Also to the right the beginning of the Rue d'Enfer which leads straight to the Latin Quarter. The tavern has as its sign Marcello's picture 'The Crossing of the Red Sea', but below it, in large letters, is painted instead 'At the Port of Marseilles'. To the sides of the door are also painted frescoes of a Turk and a zouave with an enormous laurel crown around his fez. In the wall of the tavern, which faces toward the tollgate, a window on the ground floor from which comes a pink glimmer of light. The plane trees that border the tollgate square, grey, tall and in long rows, extend from the square diagonally toward the two boulevards. Between the plane trees are marble benches. It is February: snow is everywhere. As the curtain rises there is in the sky and on the houses the uncertain whiteness of early dawn. Seated in front of a brazier, customs officers are dozing. From the tavern, at intervals, shouts, the clink of glasses, laughter. A customs officer comes out of the tavern with wine. The tollgate is closed. Behind the closed tollgate, stamping their feet from the cold and blowing on their frozen fingers, are some road sweepers.

As became something of a tradition in Puccini's operas, the third act opens with an evocation of atmosphere, a celebration of ambience. The bleak, snow-covered scene is matched by a sparse orchestral texture (flute and harp, yet again), and a theme of descending open fifths which at first sounds like an etiolated version of the Latin Quarter theme. Road sweepers impatiently shout to be let in; a customs officer eventually complies. From the tavern come richer harmonies, after which we hear Musetta sing a fragment of 'Quando me'n vo''. Milkmaids and peasant women enter through the tollgate, the latter breaking into a lively melody.

As Mimì enters from the direction of the Latin Quarter, the strings sound a brief, fragmented version of her leitmotif, 'Mi chiamano Mimì'; she seems disorientated, and soon breaks into a fit of violent coughing. After checking with an officer that this is the correct tavern, she asks a serving girl to fetch Marcello. There is a brief return to the atmospheric music of the opening, but soon the Bohemians' theme announces Marcello, who explains that he and his friends have been living at the tavern for some time, Musetta teaching singing while he paints decorative figures.

As Marcello invites Mimì to come in from the cold, there begins a passage of sustained lyricism which lasts virtually without interruption to the end of the act. Though it has no obvious parallel in traditional nineteenth-century operatic forms, this act's basic structure is as clear as it is age-old. We move according to the principle of *crescit eundo* (progressive growth), a gradual increase of characters, of dramatic intensity, and of musical complexity; from the relatively static, monochrome opening duet, to the changing emotions of the trio, and finally to the richly developed juxtaposition of contrasting couples in the closing quartet. 'Oh, buon Marcello, aiuto!' ('Oh, good Marcello, help me!') cries Mimì, and pours forth her heart. To a theme based both harmonically and melodically on descending triads (in fact an impassioned version of the idea that opened the act), she explains how Rodolfo's jealousy is destroying their relationship, and how last night they parted after yet another bitter quarrel. Her lament flowers into an intense soprano–baritone duet, with Marcello assuming the role of father confessor, as is so often the case with Verdian set pieces for these voice types. But soon, violent coughing again overtakes Mimì. Distant strains of 'Nei cieli bigi' announce that Rodolfo is about to appear. Mimì will not see him, and Marcello ushers her away; she remains close at hand to overhear the conversation.

Rodolfo at first seems to be of boundless bohemian energy and good spirits. 'Nei cieli bigi' still sounds as he hurriedly announces:

2 Photograph, with musical illustration, of a moment from Act III, possibly from the first production

> Marcello. Finalmente!
> Qui niun ci sente.
> Io voglio separarmi da Mimì.

> Marcello. At last!
> Here no one can hear us.
> I want to separate from Mimì.

Marcello will have none of this. With a sinister chromatic scale – the inevitable *topos* of jealousy, at least since Verdi's *Otello* – he chides Rodolfo with a verbosity fully worthy of Boito:[5]

MARCELLO   Tu sei geloso.
RODOLFO   Un poco.
MARCELLO   Collerico, lunatico, imbevuto
           di pregiudizi, noioso, cocciuto!

MARCELLO   You are jealous.
RODOLFO   A little.
MARCELLO   Choleric, lunatic, soaked
           in prejudice, boring, pig-headed!

Rodolfo counters with 'Mimì è una civetta' ('Mimì is a coquette'), which describes her supposed infidelities to a theme whose unusual harmonic simplicity and uncharacteristically low tessitura should alert us to its insincerity. But the strain of maintaining this false insouciance is too great. Rodolfo breaks down and, as he admits his undiminished love for Mimì, the music expands both vocally and harmonically. The slow death-knell of 'Mimì è tanto malata!' ('Mimì is so ill!') moves into a distinctive rhythm in parallel triads that graphically evokes the spasms of Mimì's cough ('Una terribil tosse' – 'A terrible cough') before the death-knell returns with interpolations from Marcello and the still-hidden Mimì.[6]

'Mimì's coughing and violent sobs reveal her presence', says the stage direction and, as Rodolfo hurries to her aid, a reprise of the 'cough' theme merges into an altered version of her leitmotif. Hardly have the two lovers touched before we hear Musetta's shameless laughter from the tavern, and Marcello's exasperated reaction. The stage is set for the final quartet, which Mimì leads off in a highly unconventional manner. Her opening statement comprises disjointed versions of previous material, which flower into lyricism only with the defining phrase 'Addio, senza rancor!' ('Farewell, without bitterness!'). She will leave Rodolfo and return to her 'solitary nest'; he can collect together her few possessions and pass them on, but he may (if he wishes) keep her pink bonnet. The melody is still punctuated with repetitions of past music (from her Act I monologue), and there is an insistence on the 'defining' word of the act, 'Addio'; but after Rodolfo's first distraught response the set piece proper begins.

The quartet is one of extreme emotional and thematic juxtaposition, a type made famous by Verdi, most recently in *Otello* and *Falstaff*. As the lovers say a passionate farewell, Marcello and Musetta argue violently over a trivial incident – though, with perhaps too evident irony, one that revolves around Marcello's jealousy at Musetta's 'coquettish' behaviour. The contrast in mood, looked at from the libretto alone, is at times jarringly abrupt:

MUSETTA	Pittore da bottega!
MARCELLO	Vipera!
MUSETTA	Rospo!
MARCELLO	Strega!
MIMÌ	Sempre tua per la vita!

3 Photograph, with musical illustration, of a moment from Act III, possibly from the first production

MUSETTA	Fifth-rate painter!
MARCELLO	Viper!
MUSETTA	Toad!
MARCELLO	Witch!
MIMÌ	Always yours for the rest of my life!

but in the musical setting it acquires a logic and persuasiveness through Puccini's skilful placing of the argument in the interstices of the lovers' lyrical phrases. Musetta and Marcello violently stride off in opposite directions; Mimì and Rodolfo slowly exit together, as they did at the end of Act I. They dreamily resolve to postpone their separation until the coming of spring. 'Ci lascierem alla stagion dei fior!' ('We will part at the season of flowers!'); and, again as in Act I, their final notes are sung off-stage, distance softening resignation, just as it had earlier cast a sentimental veil over their first declaration of love.

Act IV: In the garret

As in Act I. Marcello again stands in front of his easel, while Rodolfo is seated at his table: they wish to persuade each other that they are working indefatigably, though in fact they do nothing but gossip.

A vigorous, abbreviated version of the Bohemians' theme, and of course the same set and characters, immediately announces that Act IV is to be a kind of recapitulation of Act I. Again we enter *in medias res*:

MARCELLO (*continuando il discorso*)
          In un coupé?
RODOLFO   Con pariglia e livree.
          Mi salutò ridendo.

MARCELLO (*continuing the conversation*)
          In a coupé?
RODOLFO   With a pair and livery.
          She greeted me, laughing.

The lady is Musetta. Marcello unsuccessfully pretends to be unaffected by the recollection, and both return to work with highly visible assiduity. Now it is Marcello's turn to unleash the wolves of memory: he has seen Mimì in a carriage 'dressed like a queen'. Rodolfo is equally poor at hiding his agitation, and their renewed attempt to return to work is even more half-hearted. Marcello surreptitiously pulls a bunch of ribbons from his pocket and kisses it; an altered fragment of Rodolfo's Act I aria speaks eloquently for *his* thoughts. Both settle down to the true purpose at hand: a leisurely and nostalgic recollection of times past.

'O Mimì tu più non torni' ('Oh Mimì you return no more') is a duet of great simplicity, as befits an indulgence of nostalgia, the gently oscillating tonic–dominant bass quite unlike earlier lyrical sections; but its plainly articulated ABA form allows for a powerful coincidence of musical and dramatic action when Rodolfo takes Mimì's bonnet from a drawer at the climactic reprise of the first section. The solo violin coda (with a characteristically Puccinian turn to the subdominant region) completes the sentimental picture.

The essential action of Act I again repeats itself as Schaunard and Colline enter with food and boisterous high spirits. But, to suit the more sombre, abbreviated context, this time there are only loaves of bread and a solitary herring. The music that accompanied Schaunard's Act I entrance is again heard, and as Colline takes the stage – an apt metaphor, as this entire scene is one of overt play-acting, each character trying to outdo the others – 'his' brief Act I entrance theme takes over. A mock ballroom scene, with appropriate musical gestures, is quickly followed by a mock duel, in which words and music take another affectionate side-swipe at the melodramatic clichés of earlier nineteenth-century Italian opera.

The climax of this pell-mell of activity has Colline and Schaunard capering around the room in pretended combat, Marcello and Rodolfo dancing together, and the orchestra playing in wild abandon. Then, quite suddenly, both music and action come to a brutal halt. The door swings open on Musetta: she has brought Mimì, who is gravely ill, and who can be seen on the topmost stair, recovering from the exertion of the climb. To a painfully intense, chromatically inflected version of her leitmotif, Mimì is carried in by Rodolfo and laid down on the bed. A restrained reprise of part of Mimì's Act I aria accompanies Musetta's narration: how she met Mimì in the street, and how Mimì, sensing the approach of death, begged to be taken to Rodolfo. But Mimì herself feels better: 'Ah, come si sta bene qui!' ('Ah, how comfortable one feels here!') she sings and, raising herself up a little, embraces Rodolfo. The music here is a skilful blend of their Act I arias, a conflation made possible by the relative narrowness of Puccini's melodic idiom.

As this section draws to a lyrical close, anxious comments are passed between Musetta and the other Bohemians: there is no food or medicine; Mimì looks desperately ill. And, as if to confirm their fears, Mimì's closing words strike an ominous tone (though they are, as is almost everything in this act, also redolent of past events):

> Ho tanto freddo …
> Se avessi un manicotto! Queste mie mani
> riscaldare non si potranno mai? (*tosse*)

> I'm so cold …
> If only I had a muff! Can these hands of mine
> never be warmed? (*coughs*)

Mimì continues briefly to control the action, greeting Schaunard and Colline, and attempting to reconcile Musetta and Marcello. Musetta then draws Marcello away and instructs him to sell her earrings in order to bring a doctor and some cordial. To a fragile reminiscence of the waltz tune which in Act II accompanied Mimì's longing gaze into the shops of the Latin Quarter, she decides to go with Marcello and buy Mimì a muff: perhaps it will be her final request. They leave hurriedly.

During this last conversation, Colline has taken off his overcoat; now he sings the famous aria of farewell to this beloved garment. 'Vecchia zimarra' ('Old coat') is in one sense a vocal settling of the score for the second 'minor' Bohemian, a balance for Schaunard's Act I narration. The words retain some bohemian playfulness and irony, particularly the solemn academic references to Italy's state pawn shops, called Monte di Pietà:

> Vecchia zimarra, senti,
> io resto al pian, tu ascendere
> il sacro monte or devi.
> Le mie grazie ricevi.
>
> Old coat, listen,
> I will stay on the plain, you must now
> ascend the sacred mountain.
> Receive my thanks.

The music, set in the clearest of ABA forms, is disarmingly simple and, as with so many of Puccini's finest moments, gains its effect primarily from the context. Its key, subdued orchestral texture, freshness of musical invention (as one of few substantial passages in the act not repeated from elsewhere), low vocal sonority, and dramatic situation all break new ground. The extreme musical simplicity is thus necessary, emphasising its contextual position in a way more complex numbers could never do.

Colline puts his coat under his arm and slowly leaves, taking Schaunard with him. An orchestral interlude transforms a restrained version of Schaunard's theme, full of 'academic' suspensions, into the climactic theme of Rodolfo's Act I aria as Mimì awakens and stretches her hand out to Rodolfo. Then with a sudden turn to the minor comes Mimì's 'Sono andati?' ('Have they gone?'). In poetic terms, this short aria is something of an anomaly – a shift into hyperbole that is uncharacteristic of Mimì's usual discourse. Perhaps some of this rubs off onto the music, which is certainly Mimì's most nakedly expressive; but again, the dominant impression is of an effect gained through great simplicity of musical means.

The aria drifts into further repetitions from Act I, with Mimì dreamily recalling her leitmotif in a series of chromatic transformations. Rodolfo takes out the bonnet and places it on her head, and the most extended musical and verbal reprise from Act I begins as they recall their first meeting: the unlit candle; the search for the key; the chance meeting of hands. It culminates, inevitably, in the opening of 'Che gelida manina', sung by Mimì with the evocative orchestral countersubject played on muted violins, harp and flute. But, quite suddenly, all is action again. A sudden spasm cuts short Mimì's reprise; Schaunard returns, soon followed by Musetta and Marcello bearing the muff and a cordial. As a spirit lamp is prepared for the medicine, Musetta gives Mimì the muff, which she eagerly seizes. With evident irony, the opening of 'Che gelida manina' returns as Mimì slips her hands into the muff and again lapses into memories and sleep. Her final words reveal the continuing poetic and dramatic images that have surrounded her from the beginning:

> Qui ... amor ... sempre con te! ...
> Le mani ... al caldo ... e ... dormire.
>
> Here ... love ... always with you! ...
> My hands ... in the warmth ... and ... to sleep.

An ominous key shift to the minor, the intrusive sound of brass instruments, a sinister motif in the bass, and yet more vague reminiscences from Act I underpin the Bohemians busily making things as comfortable as possible for Mimì. Everyone sings in the simplest recitative style. Musetta utters a brief prayer. But Schaunard, tiptoeing to the bed, discovers that Mimì's sleep is permanent, and hoarsely whispers the truth to Marcello. A ray of sunshine falls through the window onto Mimì's face. Musetta points to her shawl and Rodolfo tries to arrange it on the window to block out the light. Turning back, he becomes aware of Marcello and Schaunard. In a husky speaking voice he asks them: 'Che vuol dire quell'andare e venire ... quel guardarmi così ...' ('What does that coming and going mean ... those looks you are giving me ...'). Marcello runs to comfort him as the truth dawns. The orchestra, after three brutal bass chords, launches into an impassioned reprise of 'Sono andati?' as Rodolfo flings himself onto Mimì's bed, lifts her up and calls her name. The others all adopt attitudes of despair; the curtain falls, and the orchestra borrows the final bars of 'Vecchia zimarra' to effect a solemn close.

3 The genesis of the opera

I

We owe our earliest information about Puccini's *La bohème* to a famous and still puzzling controversy that burst upon the Milan opera world in March 1893. According to reports published by friends after his death, Puccini revealed during a casual conversation with Ruggero Leoncavallo (already celebrated as the composer of *I Pagliacci*) that he was working on *La bohème*. The admission infuriated Leoncavallo, who reminded his colleague that he had offered Puccini his own *Bohème* libretto the previous winter and thus had a prior claim on the subject.[1] Leoncavallo's claim is enhanced by the fact that he wrote libretti for other composers, and had already researched bohemian themes for his *Chatterton*; it is complicated by the fact that he had been tactfully removed from work on Puccini's previous opera, *Manon Lescaut*, and was obliged as a result of tangled earlier contractual problems to provide Puccini's publisher, Giulio Ricordi, with a new opera.[2] Since Leoncavallo has not attracted the interest of biographers, we must rely on those of Puccini, whose accounts of the meeting favour their subject. Fraccaroli, mistakenly dating the episode in the ensuing autumn, nonetheless manages to recall how Puccini and Leoncavallo met at the gallery De Cristoforis, went to the nearby Trenk alehouse, discovered to their mutual horror that they were working on the same subject, and rushed off to claim *La bohème* publicly; Adami, glossing over the meeting entirely, explains the 'strange coincidence' by having Puccini read about Leoncavallo's project in the newspaper and respond to this 'thunderbolt' with his own announcement.[3] Such is the unanimity of Puccini's early biographers.

Regardless of precisely how the argument occurred, the controversy became public knowledge during the next few days. In

31

accordance with a common means of staking a claim on operatic subjects, Leoncavallo and then Puccini announced in Milan newspapers, the *Secolo* and *Corriere della sera* respectively, that each had been working on an opera based on Henry Murger's famous novel *Scènes de la vie de bohème* (1851). Leoncavallo's statement in the *Secolo* of 20 March 1893 establishes his prior claim to the subject:

Maestro Leoncavallo wants to make it known that he contracted for the new opera last December, and has since that time been working on the music for that subject. He had not announced the opera previously, only because he wanted to retain an element of surprise. As proof of this, the distinguished artist Maurel can testify that at the time of his arrival in Milan for the rehearsals of *Falstaff*, Maestro Leoncavallo told him he was writing for him the part of Schaunard, just as Signora Frandin is able to testify that four months ago the Maestro spoke to her of the role of Musette, which was destined for her. Maestro Puccini, to whom Maestro Leoncavallo declared two days ago that he was writing *Bohème*, confessed that only upon his return from Turin a few days ago did he have the idea of putting *La bohème* to music and that he spoke of it to Illica and Giacosa who, according to him, have not yet finished the libretto. Maestro Leoncavallo's priority as regards this opera is thus indisputable.[4]

Puccini's response in the *Corriere* of 21 March diplomatically tries to defuse the issue by establishing both his ignorance of Leoncavallo's project and the advanced state of his own:

Maestro Leoncavallo's declaration in the *Secolo* yesterday must have made the public understand my complete good faith; for it is clear that if Maestro Leoncavallo, to whom I have long been tied by lively feelings of friendship, had confided to me earlier what he unexpectedly told me the other evening, I would not have thought of Murger's *Bohème*.

Now – for reasons easy to understand – I am no longer inclined to be as courteous to him as a friend and musician as I would like.

For the rest, what does it matter to Maestro Leoncavallo?

Let him compose and I will compose, and the public will judge. Precedence in art does not imply that one must interpret the same subject with the same artistic ideas. I desire only to make it known that for about two months, i.e. since the first production of *Manon Lescaut* in Turin [1 February], I have been working intently on my idea and have made no secret of it to anybody.   (CP 81)

Puccini's disclaimer actually raises as many questions as it answers. To be sure, his team of librettists, Luigi Illica and Giuseppe Giacosa (who had rescued *Manon Lescaut* and would later collaborate on *Tosca* and *Madama Butterfly*), were indeed slaving away on *La bohème*. By the time the Leoncavallo–Puccini controversy became public, Illica had already completed a detailed prose scenario, to which Giacosa responded generously on 22 March: 'I have read it, and I admire you. You have been able to extract a dramatic action from a novel which has always seemed to me to be exquisite, but little suited for the stage. The first acts are marvellously sketched, but I cannot yet visualise the last one, which seems too similar to many others' (CP 82). But Puccini's assertion that *he* had been working on the opera and that this was no secret remains unsubstantiated. The composer's later account of how Murger's novel riveted his attention just after the first performance of *Manon Lescaut*, evoking irresistible memories of his own impoverished student days, has not found favour with discerning biographers, but a brief reference by Giulio Ricordi implies that the composer originally proposed the subject.[5] Nonetheless, there is no evidence that Puccini himself was seriously involved in *La bohème* – as we shall see, other matters preoccupied him.

There are indications, however, that Puccini was conspiring with the very secrecy he took such pains to deny in the *Corriere*. An undated letter to Illica reveals that while the composer was flogging his librettist to reread Murger's novel so that discussions could be conclusive ('time is pressing'), other stratagems had been attempted:

The telegram came from Paris about *la Bohème*. But to my displeasure, the novel is free, since Murger died without heirs. The play [co-authored by Murger and Théodore Barrière] is still under the copyright *of the authors*. [. . .]
Have you reread the novel? Have the French edition sent to you. I remind you: now the gauntlet has been thrown down and the job undertaken. Leoncavallo writes to me from Venice that *he* will have to wrestle with *two* colossi: you and Giacosa, and that now he's going off to study the ambience of the 'Quartier Latin'. (CP 83)

The *Carteggi pucciniani* suggests a date of February 1893 for this letter, but places it between the letters of late March and early April, thus tacitly avoiding two options, neither of which flatters the composer. If the letter was written in February, then Puccini's disclaimer to the editor of the *Secolo* that he knew nothing of Leoncavallo's *Bohème* until their meeting in Milan in late March is an outright lie. If it was written after that meeting, the situation is more complicated. Apparently mollified by the possibility of other commitments from Ricordi, Leoncavallo seems to have accepted Puccini's proposal of a gentlemanly competition, jocularly advising his rival of current 'research' while pointedly reminding him of the unequal odds. In the meantime, Puccini & Co. were attempting to obtain exclusive rights for *La bohème* behind Leoncavallo's back, having cabled Paris to inquire about copyrights for Murger's novel as well as the play written with Barrière. This explains the 'displeasure' at discovering that Murger's *Scènes* was in the public domain, and thus available to both composers.

One would think that the publicly announced competition between Puccini and Leoncavallo over the setting of the same material, compounded by constant rumours of 'industrial espionage' between their respective publishers, Ricordi and Sonzogno, would have provided a goad for the rapid completion of *La bohème*.[6] That this was not the case can be attributed to a variety of factors, not the least of which was Puccini's deep-seated insecurity about the viability of his operatic subjects: throughout his career, he toyed with projects made attractive by success on stage or by the interest of other composers, sometimes 'stealing' their material.[7] Insecurity also manifests itself in another form of behaviour that contributed to his tardy involvement in *La bohème*. Hedging his bets, he frequently considered several subjects simultaneously, in this instance toying with *La lupa* (*The She-Wolf*), based on a short story by Giovanni Verga, whose tales about Sicilian peasant life had provided his former room-mate Mascagni with the source for *Cavalleria rusticana* (1889). Puccini remained so interested in Verga's subject that he travelled to Catania in late June and early July 1894 to discuss plans for a libretto with the author, immerse himself in the local atmosphere (a crucial element in the genesis of his music), and collect photographs and other materials for staging. In announcing to Ricordi his decision to abandon this project, on 13 July 1894, Puccini cites a characteristic reason for holding back: wanting to see how *La lupa* would fare on stage.

Two other elements of Puccini's life help us to understand his belated commitment to *La bohème*. His penchant for shooting, which appears in the correspondence with unfailing regularity each autumn, elicited equally regular admonitions from Ricordi that he should 'also hunt the notes' (M 133). When the composer was arrested for hunting without a licence, the publisher exulted in the possibility of a prison term: 'Have them send you a piano, and instead of annoying wild beasts you can blast forth gunshots of melody' (M 135). But Puccini's avid pursuit of game, like his pursuit of multiple subjects, ultimately benefited *La bohème*: Musetta's waltz ('Quando me'n vo' ') originated on a boat while hunting; and Rodolfo's melody as he watches the grey sky out of the garret window ('Nei cieli bigi') derives from *La lupa*.[8]

What most impeded Puccini's involvement in *La bohème* was his growing fame as the composer of *Manon Lescaut*. Thanks to the correspondence, and to Ricordi's *Gazzetta musicale di Milano*, which carried reviews and a gossip column regularly featuring the activities of the composer, we can reconstruct something of Puccini's hectic schedule in the year or so following the premiere of *Manon* (1 February 1893). It is perhaps worth doing this in some detail. Not only was the period vital to the establishment of Puccini's international reputation, and thus a most important milestone in his career; it also offers a fascinating glimpse into the mechanics of that career, and the extent to which an efficient and widespread railway system allowed Puccini and Ricordi to take advantage of their success in a manner unimaginable to a composer such as the young Verdi fifty years earlier.[9]

The record of our hero's peregrinations begins with the *Gazzetta*'s announcement of his departure for the second production in Trent on 4 June and his return on the 30th. The duration of this stay should not surprise us: as well as attending early performances and receiving applause, Puccini often supervised the final rehearsal period of a new production, offering help and advice to singers, conductors and producers, and sometimes even revising his music. He was then present at a performance in Brescia on 25 August, and at the premiere on 3 September in his home town of Lucca, where he stayed for several weeks. On 29 October the composer was in Hamburg for preparations for the first German *Manon*, but the premiere had to be postponed, and he returned to Italy for a performance in Bologna on 4 November. By the 5th he was in Rome, supervising that city's local premiere on the 8th. Although he missed the opening night in Hamburg on 7 November, Puccini dashed back for later performances and reported their success by telegram on the 14th. In his haste to juggle appearances and make last-minute adjustments for the unexpected postponement of the Hamburg premiere, Puccini completely forgot about a carefully arranged plan to meet his sister and brother-in-law at the train station in Pisa on his return on the 6th.

Not surprisingly, Puccini was indisposed by a brief illness in December – was it simply travel fatigue, or the thought of choosing between carnival performances of *Manon* in Novara, Verona,

Ferrara, Messina, and Genoa? By 12 January 1894, Puccini had arrived in Naples to assist preparations at the Teatro San Carlo, where he attended the premiere on the 21st and remained for several days. After a rest-stop in Torre del Lago for hunting, it was back to Milan for the first La Scala production on 7 February. Recurrent health problems temporarily limited his public appearances to a performance in Pisa on 17 March, but left the hunting fever undiminished. On 12 April, Puccini left for Budapest, where the premiere on the 16th under the baton of Nikisch was a resounding success, and the composer was called out thirty times for ovations. Temporarily adopting a more leisurely pace, he left Budapest by steamer for Vienna to negotiate a contract for performances of *Manon*, returning via Munich. Back in Milan on 22 April, Puccini conveyed greetings to Illica from a colleague in Vienna and anticipated a junket to London for eight or ten days. After squeezing in a performance in Florence on 5 May, he attended the premiere at Covent Garden on the 14th, returning to work a few days later, only to be interrupted again by illness. Clearly, *La bohème* almost became the victim of Puccini's first operatic success. And even though the incessant promotional tours were undoubtedly arranged and funded by Ricordi, it is not surprising that the publisher felt it necessary to warn Puccini about the distractions of 'running the Grand Derby' (M 143) and the necessity of pacing his career: '*Bohème* must surpass *Manon* and arrive at the right time' (M 133).

The hectic promotion of his latest opera and indecision about his next project, in conjunction with frequent and insistent demands for 'speed' from his librettists, cannot have helped the impending crisis with Illica and Giacosa, both of whom had other and often more pressing commitments. Illica had delivered a detailed prose scenario by 22 March 1893. Giacosa's doggerel missive to Ricordi, dated 31 May, optimistically announces his completion of the 'thankless task' of versification and looks forward to a meeting at his office the following day:

Or mi vedo arrivato	Now I see that I have arrived
ad un buon risultato.	at a good result.
Puccini ha ormai sicura	By now Puccini has the plot
trama alle note sue.	ready for his notes.
Faremo la lettura	We will hold the reading
domani all'ore due	tomorrow at two o'clock
in via degli Omenoni.[10]	in Via degli Omenoni.

The meeting seems to have gone well. Ricordi reports on 5 June to Puccini (in Trent to oversee the second production of *Manon*), confirming some suggested revisions of the first scene, noting Illica's delivery of the Barrière act and the promise of the Latin Quarter material by Puccini's return (30 June), and suggesting that the team read it together immediately thereafter. This meeting also seems to have gone well, since on 2 July 1893 the *Gazzetta musicale* announced – also optimistically – that Giacosa and Illica 'have completed the libretto for the new opera being written by Giacomo Puccini'.

After this premature note of accord, work proceeded with revisions of the Latin Quarter and Cortile (Courtyard) scenes. But Giacosa, who expressed reservations about the last act from the very beginning, soon became dissatisfied. By early October 1893 the Barrière and Cortile acts were nearly completed, but the poet was distraught:

The trouble is that what I am doing with that libretto is not a work of art, but of indispensable, minute, and extremely wearisome pedantry. It is work that absolutely must be done; it is work that requires an artist; but it is work without stimulus and without internal warmth. [. . .] Many times I measured the completed work and that still to be completed, and congratulated myself in the certainty of freeing myself of it in a few hours. All of a sudden, I would stumble on a scene, on a strophe, which would make me curse for days [. . .]   (CP 91)

A few days later (6 October), Giacosa confesses to Ricordi his inability to shift from his own works 'of reasoning and thought' to the 'brilliant and frivolous gaiety' required by the scene at the Café Momus. It is an 'insuperable obstacle':

I don't feel it; I can't get inside it; it doesn't succeed in convincing me or in creating for me that fictitious reality without which one can accomplish nothing. I have messed up more paper on this scene and I have racked my brains more than for any of my dramatic works. For a week now, I have been stopped dead on the scene with the slap [later deleted]. I must have done it, redone it, and then gone back to do it again a hundred times. I haven't extracted one single line that I like. I have worked this evening from 11 to 3 in the morning; I started work again at 7:30; it's 5 p.m. now, and the scene has not moved ahead one step.

[. . .] I take the heroic resolution of retiring from the undertaking, certain that Illica will be able to bring it happily to a conclusion by himself. I don't want just to dash off anything. Putting line after line with the sole purpose of coming to the end and receiving the promised sum would seem to me an ungrateful and dishonest action. To my misfortune, I am not, and never have been, a quick worker.   (CP 92)

By the end of October 1893, Puccini was also having second thoughts about *La bohème*. Annoyed by the lack of information from Ricordi (who was in Paris) and by the lack of 'something from Giacosa' ('un Gia...cosa'), he suggests to Illica from Hamburg that they will work in Milan 'if not on *Bohème*, then on some other thing that we will come up with together, eh?' (CP 93). Upset by this 'eloquent postcard', Illica anxiously notified Ricordi of the impending dishonour of abandoning the 'pitched battle, desired, engaged with such publicity' (CP 94). Ricordi, 'very displeased, but not surprised', answers Illica on 2 November from the wise perspective of experience:

My personal conscience is easy. The subject was chosen by Puccini, and I did not fail to point out to him the very great dramatic and musical difficulties which one would be up against. You know very well how Puccini was carried away, how he absolutely wanted that subject and the mutual letters–polemics with Leoncavallo. And now – pardon the expression – he messes in his pants at the first difficulties.

And Illica–Giacosa first of all, and I – modestly – last of all, will we all have to come off looking like fools? Add, moreover, that I have very important interests to take care of: subject no. 1, subject no. 2, accept, reject, put aside, undertake jobs and pay Pantalone! Not hundreds, but thousands of lire are uselessly wasted by misgivings and hesitations.

In the end we are up against a question of art and interests, and a rather serious one. I, however, hope that it's only one of the usual hesitations common to composers – and very common in Puccini! – and that it will soon pass.   (CP 95)

As so often was the case, Ricordi judged the situation correctly.

II

If the first year of *La bohème*'s genesis constantly seems to verge on its exodus as well, the ensuing years are punctuated by a continual series of crises: decisive meetings in Ricordi's office; disagreement between Puccini and Illica over the basic treatment of the subject; difficulties with Giacosa over uncongenial sections of the libretto and material altered without his consent; and a series of impasses over the scenes at the Café Momus, the Barrière, and the garret in Act IV. The complexity of the issues, and the energy with which they were debated, tells us much about the status of the libretto as a kind of creative blueprint for the opera. To be sure, Puccini sometimes began with complete musical ideas around which the libretto had to be fashioned; such instances understandably provide the best-known anecdotes for biographers. But in matters of structure and duration the text was all-important; and Puccini also depended on the libretto for musical ideas far more often than is usually admitted (see pp. 110–14). His intense involvement in its development, not to mention his insistence on revision after revision, thus represents what is arguably the work's essential creative stage. And because this activity generates evidence in the form of correspondence with librettists and publishers, whereas in composition the composer is engaged with himself, the genesis of *La bohème* becomes, for the historian, in large measure the genesis of the libretto.

The initial libretto of Puccini's 1893 *La bohème* must be reconstructed from the correspondence, since Giacosa's and Illica's surviving drafts remain for the most part unpublished.[11] But the preliminary scenario appears to have resembled Leoncavallo's in several ways. The action was divided along a traditional four-act structure:

Act I, scene 1	the garret: the Bohemians
scene 2	the Latin Quarter: in the Café Momus
Act II	at the Barrière d'Enfer
Act III	the courtyard of Musetta's house
Act IV	the death of Mimì

This version also originally contained two garret scenes, an episode set *inside* the Café Momus (according to a later letter, CP 147), and a dance in the courtyard of Musetta's house – a particularly striking coincidence in the light of Leoncavallo's claims to priority, since the latter episode occupies less than a page in the novel (see p. 148). In addition, this scenario also implied a chronological progression through the year: Act I occurs on Christmas Eve, Act II in February. The Courtyard dance in Act III is in the spring or summer, and Illica wanted at one point to stage Act IV in the autumn rather than winter (CP 101).

Of even greater interest, however, is what the opera does *not* yet contain: the bohemian scene at the beginning of Act IV and – more significantly – the meeting between Rodolfo and Mimì at the end of Act I. Both gaps reflect Puccini's early 'interest' in the subject. The composer's attention seems to have been attracted first to the death of Mimì – a preoccupation with suffering that has led scholars to comment on the psychological archetype underlying the fate of so many Puccini heroines.[12] Puccini's only detailed letter from 1893 concerning the libretto fussily reminds Illica about beginning the action *in medias res*:

Remember the beginning. It's unnecessary to remind you, I know, because you will undoubtedly do it, but it is a scruple of mine. As the curtain rises the three – Colline, Schaunard, Rodolfo – are facing the window and thinking of the smoking chimneys; they are torn away from that desire for warmth by the abrupt motion of one of them who grabs a chair and throws it on the fire – but is there paper? Rodolfo sacrifices his play – their comments act by act – and then after the feeble flame, the fire dies down. Seated around the table in attitudes of discomfort, they gripe about their poverty. It is Christmas Eve; everybody else is celebrating and they don't have a penny. Marcello enters, they don't even turn their heads [. . .]   (CP 85)

The initial emphasis falls on the Bohemians as a group, possibly specifying details for which Puccini already had musical ideas ('smoking chimneys' ['cieli bigi'], 'the feeble flame'). Later developments introduce the two major male characters, Rodolfo and Marcello, the poet and painter, with only Rodolfo – the male lead, still unattached romantically – gazing out of the window, and thus establishing a poetic link with Mimì, who in her first aria characterises herself as looking out of her window in anticipation of spring.

These developments began with a decisive session in Ricordi's office (see pp. 147–8), the famous 'Cortile' [Courtyard] meeting, which took place sometime that winter between December 1893 and February 1894, and led – at Puccini's insistence (according to a later letter, CP 297) – to the deletion of the Courtyard act. The lengthy and extremely informative protest from Illica to Ricordi, which has tentatively been dated February 1894, deals with two consequences of that meeting: (1) the fact that 'Puccini doesn't like at all the resolution [about Mimì] decided on Sunday night' and (2) ways to complete the libretto and 'heal it of the enormous wound inflicted on it by the cutting of the Cortile'. The librettists had defended the act, which portrays Mimì's introduction to Viscount Paolo and Rodolfo's jealousy (see below, pp. 152–81), because it explained and motivated a brief separation of Mimì from Rodolfo; and they continued to defend that separation even after the deletion of the episode. Puccini, on the other hand, still wanted to begin the final act with the dying Mimì in bed, ignoring the separation of the lovers, an ending not consonant with the librettists' understanding of the novel:

The situation is pathetic, but it isn't *La bohème*! The love affair is lachrymose (and Romantic), but Murger's Mimì is more complex! You also must have a little compassion for the librettists!

In the first place, it's already a mistake if the separation between Rodolfo and Mimì does not take place on stage; imagine, then, if it doesn't take place at all! Because the essence of Murger's book lies precisely in that great freedom in love (supreme characteristic of *Bohème*!) with which all the characters behave. Think how much greater and more moving that Mimì can be who, being able to live with a lover who can give her silks and velvet and feeling herself dying of tuberculosis, goes to the cold and desolate garret to die in the arms of Rodolfo. It seems to me impossible that Puccini won't understand the greatness of it!

And yet this really is the Mimì of Murger!   (CP 101)

Puccini would insist again in July that 'I want the death to be as I have envisaged it' (CP 109), but Ricordi seems to have had 'a little compassion' for his librettists and sided with them on this issue. The separation between Mimì and Rodolfo, although clumsily motivated by brief allusions to the Viscount, remained in the final version.

Illica's second concern allows us to observe him in the process of rapid improvisation for which he was renowned. His 'phosphorescent brain cells' rapidly proceed through alternative ways of beginning the last act and alluding to the separation:

(1) And notice (and it seems to me almost an inspiration) how new it would be to begin the last act just the way the first begins. Only it is not winter but autumn. [. . .] Rodolfo gathers a leaf carried there by the wind, and the thought of Mimì returns to him.

(2) One could begin with Rodolfo alone – in the meantime let the audience know about the separation – this damned separation which is so necessary!! (There is as yet no tenor solo!)

(3) Throughout the piece our *bohèmes* do nothing but eat well and drink better: here we could show them to the audience dining on a herring divided in four [. . .]   (CP 101)

The ultimate solution would combine the first and third ideas, beginning the last act in the same way as the first, again with the cold and hungry Bohemians in their garret.

Illica's suggestions also require our more immediate attention, since they provide several clues to the development of the libretto immediately after February 1894. The allusion to the falling autumn leaf reveals his familiarity with Murger's seminal chapter, 'Francine's Muff', which supplied the model for the meeting of Rodolfo and Mimì as well as for a description of Mimì's final illness (though, in the novel, she eventually dies alone in a hospital). Indeed, Puccini's heroine, as the librettists announced in their published preface, is a composite of Francine and Mimì. At the same time, the lack of a 'tenor solo' and a reference in the same letter to the 'meeting in a garret between a poet–journalist and a seamstress' reveal that this famous scene of Act I was now being developed. It is no coincidence that Puccini's increasing commitment to *La bohème* and the progress of the Mimì–Rodolfo episode overlap during the spring and summer of 1894. Ricordi's *Gazzetta* did not officially announce that Puccini had been commissioned to compose the opera until 25 March, also taking care to announce simultaneously that Leoncavallo had been signed to write a libretto, thus resolving publicly – for the moment – the contretemps between the two composers that had erupted one year before. By 23 April 1894, Illica had produced a revision of the entire first scene that Giacosa found 'wonderful', especially 'the two self-descriptions of Rodolfo and Mimì' (CP 104). The addition seems to have provided Puccini with the 'luminous, sympathetic figure' he found lacking in *La lupa* when he informed Ricordi on 13 July that he was dropping Verga's subject (CP 106). By the end of August Ricordi writes, 'Illica told me that you finished the first part. How anxious I am to hear the duet!' (M 145). In September, his curiosity is even greater: 'And the Rodolfo–Mimì duet? Finished?' (CP 119).

III

A rough outline of *La bohème* as we know it today had thus emerged by the summer of 1894. The enlarged disposition of scenes now suggests a circular *scenic* progression and an increasing symmetry between the first and last acts:

Act I, scene 1	the garret: the Bohemians	
scene 2		meeting of Rodolfo and Mimì
scene 3	Latin Quarter: at the Café Momus	
Act II	at the Barrière d'Enfer	
Act III, scene 1	the garret: the Bohemians	
scene 2		the death of Mimì

The only significant difference between this outline and the final one of 1895 is that the scene in the Latin Quarter at the Café Momus has not yet become a separate act. Ricordi refers explicitly to a three-act structure on 2 August 1894 (M 145); Puccini's letter of 7 September confirms this (CP 118). It is difficult to determine when the Latin Quarter became an independent act, but we can trace the stages of its genesis. As we shall see, the evolution of this scene and its problems are inseparable from the development of certain other acts.

The 'brilliant and frivolous gaiety' required by the Latin Quarter had already driven the serious Giacosa to offer his resignation in 1893. The main difficulty in the ensuing drafts was that the scene evolved musically into a *concertato finale*, the traditional set piece that often concludes the middle act of a nineteenth-century Italian opera, reaching a climax of tension and/or confusion that ensuing acts resolve. The conventional *concertato finale* hinged on a complex set of articulated structures, and required a formal relationship with words and music that had become unfamiliar to late nineteenth-century librettists. A major portion of Verdi's correspondence on *Otello*, for example, is devoted to resolving problems presented by its *concertato finale*, and it is not surprising to find the same type of difficulty in *La bohème*.

Illica's letter to Ricordi of 5 January 1894 begins the new year by anticipating the worst: 'Do you really think that when we have put together the "Latin Quarter" Puccini will be happy with it? [. . . he] finds it pleasant to make work for others, in order to avoid working himself' (CP 98). Nonetheless, Illica decides to try a new canvas based on the old one, 'keeping in mind what Puccini had wanted (the little episodes)' – the building blocks of the *concertato finale*. In order to clarify the new spatial arrangement caused by the shift from inside to outside the Café Momus, Illica also enclosed a sketch, ostensibly inspired by the illustrations in Édouard Drumont's *Mon vieux Paris*. There is also agreement with Puccini's suggestions for a favourite character: 'The presentation of Musetta suits me very well'.

The famous 'Cortile' meeting that winter, as we have seen, shifted attention to the first and last acts, postponing further developments in the Latin Quarter until the summer of 1894. After Puccini decided to abandon *La lupa*, another intense meeting occurred in Ricordi's office, involving Puccini and Illica in interrelated difficulties over the Barrière act and the Latin Quarter. The crisis develops in a barrage of six letters in the twelve-day period from 13 to 24 July. Puccini remained dissatisfied with the Barrière act (an invention of Illica's) and suggested its deletion, thereby infuriating Illica, who saw himself 'used, cast aside, taken up again, and once more shoved away like a dog' (M 143). In response, Illica apparently suggested the excision of the Latin Quarter instead, provoking a petulant outburst from Puccini with counter-demands to

Ricordi: 'Must I blindly accept the Gospel according to Illica? [. . .] I have my vision of *La bohème*, but with the "Quartiere Latino" the way I described it the last time I conferred with Illica, with Musetta's scene which *I* invented: and I want the death to be as I have envisaged it, and then I am sure of producing an original and vital piece of work' (CP 109).

The session in Ricordi's office finally scheduled for 10 a.m. on Tuesday, 24 July 1894, proved anticlimactic – Illica did not appear. Ricordi rescheduled the meeting for later that day, and delivered a pointed message to his truant librettist: 'I had written to you to make an appointment with me, today at 10. Perhaps the letter didn't reach you? Anyway: whether it is a Roman brawl or an English boxing match, we must finish it once and for all!!! ...' (CP 110). Ricordi's powers of persuasion and reconciliation appear to have prevailed, and the immediately ensuing Puccini–Illica correspondence becomes a love-feast of co-operation.

An undated letter from Illica to Ricordi, clearly written soon after the meeting, announces that he has finished 'all that regards the characters' in the Latin Quarter, and will complete the 'scene with the part that concerns the setting' as soon as galley proofs arrive. Anticipating radical changes, he provides an outline of the new order of scenes, one that closely resembles the final version (CP 115). Later revision would eliminate the third scene, a *duettino* between Rodolfo and Mimì. (Puccini must have felt uncertain about the status of this scene, since a new *duettino* involving the purchase of Mimì's bonnet was added for the premiere of *La bohème* in Palermo in 1896.)[13] Puccini's response of 3 August 1894 expresses satisfaction with Illica's characterisation of Alcindoro, a *brindisi* (drinking song) for Schaunard, and especially with the *Musettata*: 'thus I have a main character complete also musically' (CP 113); while the equally short note of 18 August looks forward to collaboration in Lucca and the organisation of 'all the subscenes tied to and independent of the action at Momus' (CP 114).

During the same period, the Barrière act underwent a similar development. While Puccini's letter to Ricordi of 13 July implies an understanding with Illica about the Latin Quarter, the composer cavalierly dismisses the librettist's Barrière act (invented independently of Murger's work) as 'junk', suggesting instead that he get new ideas from the novel he was supposed to adapt: 'We should find an entirely different act, more effective both dramatically and comically. Illica can find valuable material for this by reading

Murger's works' (CP 106). As with the Cortile decision, Illica appealed to Ricordi, who seconded his favourable opinion of this act. But Puccini remained adamant: 'As for the "Barrière", I am still of the same opinion: I do not like it. There is very little that is musical in it. Only the drama has movement, and that's not enough. [. . .] I wanted a canvas that would allow me to expand a little more lyrically' (CP 109). During the decisive meeting of 24 July in Ricordi's office, a compromise appears to have been reached regarding this act as well, since Illica's letter outlining the Latin Quarter (mentioned above) promises to look for possible cuts when the galley proofs arrive.

The exchanges between Illica, Ricordi, and Puccini (Giacosa was on an Alpine walking tour) in late August and early September finally share a mutual agreement that the libretto, though still requiring further cuts, is basically complete. Illica, his eyes finally dry after finishing the death of Mimì, announces that 'Bohème is all there [. . .] the last act seems to me perhaps the best – as to effect – and is certainly a great novelty' (CP 116). Ricordi reports to Puccini on 22 August that Illica has read him the 'whole Bohème' and 'now we have really succeeded', although the lengthy libretto must still be shortened according to the 'dictates of musical necessity, as they will appear in the course of composition' (M 145). Puccini agrees that there is 'no doubt about its being an original work! And such a one!', also waxing ecstatic over the last act. But he warns that further cuts are necessary in the Latin Quarter – certain 'extravagances which Illica loves like his own sons (as if he had any)' – and that the Barrière act remains, even with changes, 'the weak act' (CP 118).

IV

Musical composition finally dominates the agenda for the late summer and autumn of 1894. The already 'finished' state of some of the musical material borrowed from earlier works, such as the *Capriccio sinfonico* for the bohemian theme and a melody from *La lupa* for 'Nei cieli bigi', as well as Puccini's interest in the meeting between Mimì and Rodolfo account for the rapid progress on Act I. Ricordi's letters of 22 August and 29 September 1894, mentioning the 'completion' of the first scene and inquiring whether the duet is 'finished', imply that Puccini had reached the stage of composition sketches. Since the composer also began with firm ideas for the

Latin Quarter and considered 'his' Musetta 'musically complete' in early August, it is understandable that he pressed for Giacosa's revised version at the beginning of September: 'I await the "Latin Quarter" revised, abridged, and corrected by the intervention of the Giacosan Buddha' (CP 118).

The momentum of the opera was halted again by two separate crises: Puccini's arrest in September for hunting without a licence, which culminated in a farcical trial,[14] and renewed difficulties in October with both librettists over the Latin Quarter. Puccini balked at setting some French stanzas by Murger and a 'Marseillaise' of medical students which Illica had proudly unearthed from a trial of the period. Then Giacosa's sluggish progress was brought to a dead halt by his discovery that Puccini had silently made changes in setting the first act. The composer was forced to write to Tito Ricordi, informing him that he was now trying to 'fix' the situation with Giacosa and 'still have him as a collaborator' (P 17). Giulio Ricordi, returning from the triumph of Verdi's *Falstaff* in Paris, epitomised the entire affair: 'It seems to me with your Bohème that I am at a ball game, in which the libretto is substituted for the ball' (M 148).

Extensive gaps in the correspondence after November 1894 make it possible to trace the further development of Acts I and II only in outline: Puccini is composing, not corresponding. The autograph score of *La bohème* records that he began the 'definitive' version of Act I on 21 January 1895 at his home in Torre del Lago and finished it on 6 June in Milan. The relatively long period required for the composition confirms that the composer's attention had again been diverted to supervising new productions of *Manon Lescaut* in Bari, Leghorn, and Fiume, the latter part of a larger junket that included Budapest and Vienna.[15] The Latin Quarter progressed more rapidly. Puccini's letters to his brother-in-law from late May through June are preoccupied with finding the right summer retreat in order to work intensively on the opera. The *Gazzetta* announced on 30 June 1895 that 'Maestro Puccini has delivered to Ricordi & Co. the orchestral score of the first two acts of his new opera *La bohème*'; the autograph does not record the completion of Act II until 19 July in Val di Nievole near Pescia, where he was the guest of Count Bertolini from late June to late November, and where a graffito on the wall of his study gives 23 July as the date of completion.[16] The discrepancy may be due to the fact that Puccini recalled the manuscript for further polishing after he had sent it in, something he definitely did on 9 August with Musetta's waltz – an action characteristic of his tendency to continue reworking already 'finished' compositions. Revisions of the Barrière scene (now Act III) commenced somewhat earlier. Ricordi's letter of 20 June 1895, in addition to confirming the new numeration of acts, reveals the publisher's artistic instinct and influence on the final shape of the opera:

Abolish many of the details. There are already too many details [. . .] and the opera would end by being a little comedy of episodes. The atmosphere is at once created by the customs officers and by the others who appear. This is sufficient. More would not interest the public.

Musetta ought to sing part of her waltz behind stage. The melody characterises her perfectly and could be reheard with pleasure. (M 150)

In spite of complaints about academic obligations and domestic turmoil, Giacosa finished the Barrière in late June, and Puccini could begin composition by mid-July (CP 125). He instructed Illica to carry out cuts and revisions, and then, following Ricordi's advice, requested a chorus to answer Musetta's repetition of her waltz melody from within the tavern. Since the musical idea had already been conceived, he asked for a particular poetic form, even providing an example in nonsense verse:

Noi non dormiam	We don't sleep
sempre beviam	we always drink
facciam l'amor	we make love
sgonfiam trattor.	we annoy innkeepers.
	(CP 126)

After a brief plea on 9 August to Ricordi, 'my best of poets, *mender of others' faults*' (CP 128), to patch up the passage where Mimì overhears that her illness is fatal, the worst was over. Puccini's versified response of 17 August includes some pointed references to his librettists and notes how Illica's 'rounded and pompous/ Giacosan rhymes/ make the simple verses/ of Mimì and Musetta/ seem strange to me'. Nonetheless, there is praise for the concluding quartet:

Adesso viene il buono	Now there comes the good,
la pagina perfetta	the perfect page,
scritta in un solo tono	written in a single tone
con battibecchi e baci	with squabbles and kisses
che alternansi fra loro!	alternating with each other!
	(P 20)

Puccini orchestrated the Barrière act rapidly. The *Gazzetta* proclaims its completion on 8 September; the autograph – lagging behind Riccordi's optimism – is dated the 18th. The publisher's suggestions had created the right atmosphere, and Puccini now seems to have found precisely what he found lacking the previous summer, a 'canvas that would allow me to expand a little more lyrically' (CP 109). Saving the beginning until last, Puccini created one of his famous third-act orchestral preludes.

Very happy with the act as a whole, he announces that he is 'exceedingly pleased' with the first scene, but warns of unusual orchestral requirements: 'I warn you that we shall need four bells. Matins are rung from the Hospice of Marie-Thérèse and the nuns are coming down to pray. *Ensemble*: xylophone, bells, carillon, trumpets, drums, cart-bells, cracking of whips, carts, donkeys, tinkling of glasses – a veritable arsenal' (CP 138). Ricordi's apparent objections to unusual dynamic extremes had to be justified with reference to the highest authority: 'As for the *pp*'s and *ff*'s of the score, if I have overdone them it is because, *as Verdi says*, when one wants *piano* one puts *pppp*' (CP 141).

Our knowledge of the final stages of Act IV is more complete than for any other act, since complications and deliberations from August to November 1895 produced the largest portion – most of it unfortunately undated – of correspondence on *La bohème*. Puccini, aware of Giacosa's inability to warm to Act IV and then to versify it, began prodding the poet for a final revision in mid-March, well before he had even completed the composition of Act I. The brusque request to 'send me the last act as soon as possible – revised' (CP 121) failed to achieve the desired result; as did a plea in doggerel in early April:

Ti rammento l'atto quarto,	I remind you of the fourth act,
perch'io presto me ne parto.	because I have to leave soon.
Cerca, trova, taglia, inverti,	Look, find, cut, invert,
ché tu re sei, tra gli esperti.	as you are the king among experts.
Ti ricordi di ridurre	Have you remembered to reduce
le scenette in cima all'atto?	the little scenes beginning the act?
Quando tutto sarà fatto,	When everything is done,
qual sospiro emetterem![17]	what a sigh we will heave!

By June, continued pressure from Puccini, eager to finish the Barrière act and move on, precipitated an eruption reminiscent of the one that almost terminated the collaboration in 1893. The prisoner of an academic committee for examinations in Italian literature, something apparently even worse than the 'Puccini torture', Giacosa complained to Ricordi, 'I swear to you that I can't go on' revising everything 'twenty times' (CP 122). On 25 June, with his household in the middle of a move, he protested:

I confess to you that I'm tired to death of this constant remaking, retouching, adding, correcting, cutting, piecing together, extending on the one hand and reducing on the other. [. . .] I've written this damned libretto from beginning to end three times and certain sections four and five times. How am I supposed to finish at that rate? [. . .] I swear to you they'll never trap me into doing libretti again! [. . .] Tomorrow I'm [. . .] installing myself all alone in some quiet hotel. And there, not having a family (which is always a source of distraction), I will have finished in a few days. But will it be finished then? Or will we have to start all over from the beginning?
(CP 123)

With this outburst, Giacosa seems to have left the polishing of remaining portions of the libretto largely in the hands of Illica.

Puccini originally intended to take a brief hunting vacation after orchestrating Act III, hoping to 'terrorise my beloved *palmipeds*, which have long been panting for my murderous and infallible lead. Boom!' (CP 138). But the outing had to be postponed, and he began work on the last act almost immediately. Faced with a mass of material that seemed too long and needed to move more rapidly, he suddenly felt fatigued. And with good reason: the beginning of Act IV was to have included a mock *credo* against women by Schaunard – in imitation of Iago's famous *credo* in Verdi's *Otello* – and a *brindisi* (drinking song) in praise of water – inspired by Murger's 'Water Drinkers'. While the initial *credo* produced by Illica seemed out of character, Giacosa's *brindisi* seemed uncomposable, since verses for the quartet employed different metres for parts to be sung simultaneously. Puccini insisted nonetheless on both pieces:

I am still convinced that Schaunard must have his *credo*, because otherwise I would be constrained to have the leads in so important a part. [. . .] For the *brindisi* I tell you again that as it is, it is almost impossible to put to music (I say 'almost' because with enough good will one can even set the tailor's bill to music). You can leave Giacosa's ideas, but give them another form, more quartet-like [. . .]
(CP 136)

But he gradually succumbed to his growing exhaustion and lack of new musical ideas: finding Illica's draft for Schaunard's solo not at all to his liking and merely 'padding', Puccini eventually informed

Ricordi that he had decided to eliminate the piece, 'not wishing to insist' (!) on it; after toying with a *brindisi* in which Schaunard then had the largest share, the composer also capitulated before the insuperable obstacle of disparate metres for the quartet.

The letters justifying this decision vis-à-vis Illica and Ricordi repeat a variety of arguments, the most compelling of which is the realisation that the scene with the reunited Bohemians 'is only put there for contrast, because if we wanted, we could make Mimì appear immediately after the curtain rises' (CP 136) – a teasing reiteration of the stance that infuriated Illica after the Cortile meeting. In response to objections that the cuts would leave Schaunard and Colline with insufficient music, Puccini argues, 'better little *than more* and *unsuccessful*, as would have happened with the water toast, which I didn't feel at all [. . .] Best to go straight to Mimì and use the first scene with the four only for a strong contrast' (CP 143). Illica registered his acquiescence with deft irony. Using precise instructions from Puccini for making the cuts, he transposed the composer's suppression of the *credo* and *brindisi* into the Bohemians' shouting down of Schaunard's attempt to present the 'spirit of Song':

SCHAUNARD   (*solenne*)
             Mi sia permesso
             al nobile consesso ...
RODOLFO, COLLINE   (*interrompendolo*)
             Basta!
MARCELLO   Fiacco!
COLLINE   Che decotto!
MARCELLO   Leva il tacco!
COLLINE   Dammi il gotto!
SCHAUNARD   (*ispirato*)
             M'ispira irresistible
             l'estro della romanza!
GLI ALTRI   (*urlando*)
             No! No! No!

SCHAUNARD   (*solemnly*)
             If the noble company
             will allow me ...
RODOLFO, COLLINE   (*interrupting him*)
             Enough!
MARCELLO   Weak!
COLLINE   What a concoction!
MARCELLO   Get out!
COLLINE   Give me the mug!

SCHAUNARD (*inspired*)
          I am irresistibly inspired
          by the spirit of Song!
THE OTHERS (*shouting*)
          No! No! No!

Given Puccini's persistent interest in the death of Mimì, it is not surprising to find his suggestions and requests becoming increasingly specific as he nears the final stages of composition in the autumn of 1895. Following Act V of Murger's and Barrière's play, the libretto was supposed to have Mimì escape from the hospital, providing a rationale for her threadbare appearance and desire for a muff to warm her hands. Reminding Illica of the separation of Mimì and Rodolfo, Puccini insists on this 'true to life' detail from Murger's play:

You remember that we had noted that Mimì, if she had fled from the Viscount, would not have had such a lively desire for the muff, and that the episode of the muff – as it currently stands – was padding?! You proposed to say, or rather to have her say to Musetta, that she had run away from the hospital. The thing was received by you and me with great enthusiasm, because that way there was a little more that was true to life concerning the end of Mimì. Thus Mimì would have to have presented herself in a shabby dress [. . .] *I insist on*, rather *I absolutely want* (permit me to say it) this modification [. . .]   (CP 136)

A postscript emphasising that 'three things are necessary in Life (of *Bohème*): I [Schaunard's] *credo*, II the *brindisi*, III Mimì (hospital)' illustrates that Puccini did not always have his way, or that he often changed his mind. None of these items appears in the final version of the opera.

In other instances, Puccini prevailed, correcting an unmotivated attempt by Musetta to retrieve the muff, or pleading for 'one more phrase, an expression of affection to Rodolfo' at the moment of Mimì's death: 'I should like her to leave the world less for herself and a little more for the one who loved her' (CP 134; also 137). Musical ideas (the sustained lyrical section in D major from rehearsal nos. 14 to 16) seem to have dictated the 'urgent' request in late November for some verses to bridge the gap between Mimì's relief to be among friends and the ominous revelation 'Ho tanto freddo' ('I'm so cold'). The direction of these musical ideas becomes clearer in a more detailed request to Illica:

Do you have a copy of the fourth act? Yes. Look it over and turn to the page where it says:

Mimì	… mio bel signorino	My fine young gentleman,
	posso ben dirlo adesso:	I can easily say it now:
	lei la trovò assai presto	you found it very quickly
	e a intascarla fu lesto.	and were quick to pocket it.
Rodolfo	Aiutavo il destino.	I was helping fate.
Mimì	[Ful allor che mi dicesti,	[It was then that you told me,
	prendendomi per mano la	taking my hand for the first
	prima volta e stringendomela:	time and squeezing it:
	'Ah, che gelida manina	'What an icy little hand
	se la lasci riscaldar!']	let me warm it!']
	(*Mimì è presa da uno*	(*Mimì is seized with a*
	spasimo, ecc.)	*spasm, etc.*)

What I wrote in brackets is as necessary to me as the air [l'aria]. Will you do me the great favour of sending me two or three or four little rhymed buddhaesque [Giacosan] verses to add? It's very effective for me to repeat in the mouth of Mimì the idea of the 'gelida manina'.　　　　　(CP 145)

These revisions proceed in several complementary directions. Puccini is attempting to make the expiration of Mimì as 'realistic' as possible while still having fragments of discourse that lend themselves to a musical setting: 'It has cost me some effort to make myself adhere to reality and then to *lyricise* somewhat all these *little pieces*. And I succeeded: because I want there to be as much singing, as much *melodising* as possible' (CP 146). Many of these fragments, moreover, refer to the meeting between Mimì and Rodolfo at the end of Act I, and thus lend themselves to musical reminiscences from that act. As the composer was well aware, 'The act is composed almost entirely of logical repetitions, except for the duet "*Sono andati?*" and Colline's "[Vecchia] Zimarra" and little else' (CP 146).

Furthermore, the relative musical 'thinness' of Act IV – whether or not due to the composer's flagging invention – is dramatically apposite: those who criticise *La bohème* for its concluding 'poverty' of melodic invention fail to appreciate the genius of its economy. Mimì's 'flashbacks' not only are appropriate for a realistic portrayal of her death, but, in turning the focus of the concluding scene back to the end of the first act, realise in musical and dramatic terms the implicit circular movement of the work as the scenic parallels between Acts I and IV emerged during the collaboration with Illica and Giacosa. Puccini's intimation that this retrospective closure was not only logical but also very effective has been amply confirmed by generations of theatre audiences.

Although in late November he was still corresponding with Illica about revisions and additions to the libretto, Puccini's composition

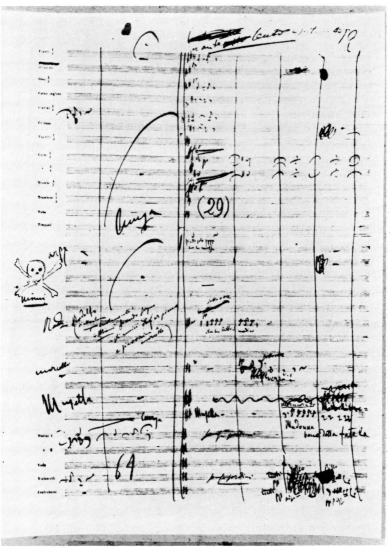

4   The death of Mimì in the autograph score

of the orchestral score proceeded rapidly, owing to the pervasive use of already extant musical ideas from Act I. The autograph records the date of completion as 10 December 1895. At the passage where Mimì expires, Puccini drew broad fermatas in the orchestral score, added the direction 'lunga' (*long* pause), and then sketched a skull and crossbones in the margin next to Mimì's now empty vocal line (see Fig. 4). Those who love Puccini above all for his ability to arouse shameless identification with sentimental subjects would do well to ponder this page, which suggests that he, at least, retained a healthy cynicism and sense of perspective.

Not so the early biographers, who erroneously date the completion of *La bohème* in November, and then vie with each other to 're-create' the final evening's work at Torre del Lago.[18] Fraccaroli, 'recording' Puccini's reminiscences for posterity, recalls two details with a masterly juxtaposition of humour and sentimentality. Two friends of Puccini, who often drank, smoked, and played while the composer worked next to them at the piano, had gradually memorised the libretto, and when Puccini murmured over the piano the line 'Che ha detto il medico?' ('What did the doctor say?'), their voices responded from the gloomy darkness 'Verrà!' ('He will come!'). But later, when Puccini began the death of Mimì, 'alone in the silence of the night', 'I began to cry like a little boy. It seemed to me that I had seen my own child die'. Adami imagines a sombre evening when Puccini wanted to be alone, reaching the final desperate cry of Rodolfo ('Mimì! Mimì!') as dawn broke over the hills: 'a sob tore at the throat of the maestro, his eyes welled up with tears' etc., etc. Marotti and Pagni claim to have been there throughout the night, playing briscola with friends until Puccini announced, 'Silenzio, ragazzi, ho finito!' ('Quiet, boys, I've finished!'). After playing and singing for them the cathartic final scene, 'Giacomo wept also. We surrounded him and silently embraced him.' The 'intimate reminiscence' concludes with a *post hoc* comment of staggering banality: 'Then someone said: "This page renders you immortal."'

But alternately persuasive and laughable as such anecdotes are, they should not blind us to the true story of the genesis of *La bohème*. Sudden bursts of inspiration there may have been, but the overriding impression is of the enormous difficulty of *fin de siècle* operatic composition. The great tradition which had fostered and sustained Italian opera composers for more than two hundred and fifty years was drawing to a close, and Puccini and his loyal, exasperated associates were forced to pick through the remnants, piecing together a work as best they could. The fact that *La bohème* is at all consistent is testimony to their skill, their sensitivity and – perhaps above all – their sheer persistence.

4 The libretto

I

In adapting Henry Murger's scenes of bohemian life for their libretto, Luigi Illica and Giuseppe Giacosa (and, of course, Puccini) were forced to choose from a work with a bewildering variety of characters and episodes, and also to cast a wary eye on contemporary reaction to the artistic and political implications of their decisions. The problem of choice began with the complicated history of Murger's Bohemia. His first 'Scènes', published as short stories in *Le Corsair* between 1845 and 1849, attracted little attention, but the favourable climate for public entertainment after the revolution of 1848 encouraged a stage version, *La Vie de bohème*, written in collaboration with Théodore Barrière.[1] The triumph of the play, which was first performed on 22 November 1849 at the Théâtre des Variétés, earned Murger an offer from the publishing firm of Michel Lévy to write a novel based on his 'Scènes'. The success of that novel, originally *Scènes de la bohème* (1851), later *Scènes de la vie de bohème*, cemented Murger's reputation and established the basis of his international fame.

The existence of the 'Scènes' both as a drama and as a novel presented the librettists with a problem. Unlike Alexandre Dumas *fils*' dramatisation of his own *La Dame aux camélias*, which provided the source for Verdi's *La traviata*, Murger's play provided no immediate basis for a libretto. It was too crowded, combining the bohemian main plot with a subplot in which Rodolphe's uncle, assisted by the droll servant Baptiste, attempts to return his errant nephew to his senses and a pre-arranged marriage with a rich widow. Only the last act (the death of Mimi), which incorporates materials also used in the novel's chapter on 'Francine's Muff', proved viable for the libretto. The play had two further drawbacks. The controversy between Puccini and Leoncavallo over priority to

La bohème, which newspapers and the composers' publishers, Ricordi and Sonzogno respectively, had publicised with such intensity, created expectations of a competition in setting the novel to music. Furthermore, the novel was in the public domain, but the play was still copyrighted (CP 83), and although this did not prevent the librettists from following the play in portraying the death of Mimì, the opera – officially, at least – had to proclaim descent from the novel.

The artistic claims of the libretto also depended upon its association with the novel, which played an important part in the development of Italian bohemianism in the late nineteenth century. In the decades after 1860, a disparate group of northern Italian writers known collectively as the *scapigliati* (unruly ones) – the name derives from a novel by Carlo Righetti, *La scapigliatura e il 6 febbraio* (1862) – stimulated the development of Italian literature from late romanticism to early realism. The *scapigliati* can be characterised generally by their repudiation of contemporary Italian society, its bourgeois taste and morals, and even its classical artistic traditions. This repudiation took a wide variety of stances, ranging from sentimental portrayals of the past to critical nose-thumbing at the present, and frequently employed experimental or non-traditional forms of expression (all features we will encounter in *La bohème*). The *scapigliati* naturally inclined toward foreign sources of inspiration, many of them emphasising 'bohemian' characteristics of late European romanticism – the glorification of artistic existence in opposition to bourgeois philistinism, the identification of art with life, and the pursuit of free subjectivity.

Murger's novel accordingly found a receptive audience in Italy, and was translated twice in the first two decades after its appearance. The first translation, Gian Vincenzo Bruni's *Scene della vita d'artista* (Lausanne, 1859), severely truncated the original, deleting, for example, the famous chapter on 'Francine's Muff'. The novelty of Murger's subject is immediately revealed by the title, which renders the fashionable French 'bohème' with the more generic 'artista', since the Italian equivalent was not to be coined until three years later by Righetti's *Scapigliatura*. A second translation by Felice Camerone was published anonymously in Milan in 1872 by the firm of Sonzogno (later the publisher of Leoncavallo).[2] A reprint appeared in 1890, stimulating interest in the novel that fuelled Leoncavallo's and Puccini's feud; a third printing followed in 1896, capitalising on the premiere of Puccini's opera (1896) and the anticipated appearance of Leoncavallo's (1897).

This influential second translation presented a problem at the same time that it helped to popularise bohemian themes. Inspired by the revolutionary events in the Paris Commune (1871), Camerone espoused a socially engaged form of Bohemianism in his introductory 'Paradoxes':

> *Scapigliatura* is the denial of prejudice, the partisan of the Beautiful and True, the affirmation of individual initiative against quietism. [. . .] Reactionaries persecute *la bohème* because it sounds the call to revolt; hedonists hate it, because it interferes with their digestion; the intelligentsia slander it, because they cannot understand it. [. . .] *La bohème* is destined to pass from the purely artistic field to social conflict. After thought comes action. [. . .] Political *scapigliatura* prepares the mine of revolution in the newspaper, primes it with the powder of agitation, and makes it explode at the barricade.

Camerone's slant seems to have influenced Leoncavallo's bleak portrayal of bohemian existence, but it did not appeal to Puccini, who was already actively hob-nobbing with the upper crust and urged the tamer French original on his librettists at an early stage in the collaboration (CP 83).

Illica and Giacosa therefore continued the *scapigliatura* tradition of twitting bourgeois society and culture, primarily by means of humour, but they drew the line at political engagement. In fact, Camerone's activism originally formed the target of their barbs in a brief scene – subsequently excised – in which Schaunard attempts to present a political platform whose articles trivialise basic concerns of the Paris Commune and nineteenth-century radical thought in general (see Appendix, pp. 141–7). They also distanced themselves more obliquely from Camerone and the events of 1871, as well as those of 1848 and current unrest in industrialised northern Italy, by dating their opera around 1830. To be sure, 1830 was also a revolutionary year in France, but the librettists made no attempt to link the private misery of their Bohemians with the public upheavals of that year. Instead, they began the action after the reinstatement of the monarchy under Louis Philippe, i.e. back-dating the opera to the safety of a distant and counter-revolutionary or 'restoration' past.[3]

In spite of these efforts, a variety of other factors – rumours of Leoncavallo's claims that his opera was more faithful to Murger

(M 158), knowledge that librettist-bashing has always been a cherished diversion in the blood sport of opera, and concern for their own manipulations of *La Vie de bohème* – induced Illica and Giacosa to preface the libretto with an introduction that covers all contingencies, citing their adherence to Murger's characterisation as well as the conflation of Francine and Mimi, faithfulness to details in milieu as well as liberties in the dramatisation of serious and comic episodes, etc. In addition, each act of the printed libretto has its own preface with 'selective quotes' from the novel in order to foster an identification of Murger's *Bohème* with their own.[4]

If we compare Illica's and Giacosa's libretto with their source, making adjustments for the translation of a prose narrative into verse dialogue and musical numbers, it immediately becomes clear that they follow Murger's 'Scènes' in the first and last acts. The list of borrowings for Act I begins with the detail of Marcel drowning an Egyptian on his 'The Crossing of the Red Sea' (Ch. 7), and includes the small episodes in which Rodolphe burns his play act by act (by himself, Ch. 9), Schaunard relates the murder of a parrot (Ch. 17), and the Bohemians dupe their landlord (he is nameless in Ch. 19, but called Benoît in the play). By far the closest and most extensive borrowing, the meeting of Rodolfo and Mimì – especially the beginning moments – derives from the story of the artist Jacques and the seamstress Francine (Ch. 18). Little more than Mimì's name and nickname (Lucille/Mimi, Ch. 14) have been given to the innocent character of Francine in creating the opera's heroine.

Act IV also corresponds generally with Murger's Bohemia. The sentimental reminiscences of Marcello and Rodolfo in the opening scene derive from a similar narrative retrospective in the 'Epilogue to the Loves of Rodolphe and Mademoiselle Mimi' (Ch. 22). After the sudden entrance of Mimì, we have parallel sources, the chapters depicting the deaths of Francine and Mimi (Ch. 18 and 22) as well as Act V of the play, which itself conflates these two stories. The opera generally follows the action of the play: the sudden arrival and collapse of Mimi, her request for a muff, the pawning of Musette's earrings and Schaunard's [!] coat, Musette's concern for Mimi, and her death. Although the novel provides a different ending (Mimi expires days later in a hospital), a central motif of the narrative, her flight from the Viscount, also found its way into the libretto.

Given this extensive list of correspondences, it comes as something of a surprise to discover that Acts II and III have almost no basis in the 'Scènes'. The only chapter that even faintly resembles Act II, 'A Café in Bohemia' (Ch. 11), takes place *inside* the Café Momus and culminates in a billiard game with Barbemuche, suggesting at best a preliminary version of the interaction of characters:

Marcel, suspicious of the origin of Musette's new bonnet [!], was quarrelling with her about it; Mimi and Rodolphe, still in the honeymoon stage, were carrying on a speechless conversation interspersed with strange sonorities. As for Colline, he went from woman to woman with most gracious airs, gallantly stringing together for their benefit elegant extracts culled from the collection of the *Almanach des Muses*.

The penultimate chapter of the book (Ch. 22), which takes place one year later and looks back to this event, describes the bustle of the Christmas Eve *réveillon* only in passing.

Act III appears to be entirely Illica's invention, but the choice of a tollgate ('barrière') as a setting seems quite logical once we understand its historical and literary background. In 1830, the tollgates still marked the transition from city to countryside, and subsequently acquired particular associations during the rapid urbanisation of Paris.[5] Frederick, in Flaubert's *Sentimental Education*, is anxious to enter the city, noticing the melancholy atmosphere less than the crowd that impedes his progress:

A thin rain was falling; it was cold. [. . .] They had to wait a long time at the barrière, for poultry-vendors, carters and a flock of sheep caused an obstruction there. The sentry, with his great-coat thrown back, walked up and down in front of his box, to keep himself warm.   (Pt 2, Ch. 1)

The narrator in Victor Hugo's *Les Misérables*, a more leisurely and perceptive observer, draws attention to the double nature of tollgates:

End of trees, beginning of houses, end of grass, beginning of pavement, end of furrows, beginning of shops, end of ruts, beginning of passions, end of the divine murmur, beginning of the human hubbub; hence, the interest is extraordinary. [. . .] The place where a plain adjoins a city always bears the imprint of some indescribable, penetrating melancholy. There, nature and humanity address you at one and the same moment.   (Pt 3, Bk 1, Ch. 5)

The human activity and the melancholy setting of a barrière provide a singularly appropriate locus for the orchestral evocation of a sad and misty winter day and the ensuing confrontation of characters in Act III.[6]

II

Illica's and Giacosa's alternation between fidelity and freedom in treating source materials results in a striking feature of *La bohème*. Acts II and III, invented independently of Murger's works, bear the closest relationship to traditional musical forms: the former is a *concertato finale*, the latter a progression of numbers from solo recitative to fully developed lyric quartet occasioned by the entrances of additional characters. Acts I and IV, on the other hand, reflect their literary ancestry, establishing a close-knit web of verbal themes. We have included a brief discussion of the central acts in the synopsis chapter (see pp. 17 and 26), and will concentrate initially on the beginning and concluding 'quadri' of the opera.

Acts I and IV take place in the same chilly garret, and are similarly structured. Both consist of two large sections, each with a distinctive atmosphere and idiom, the first presenting the Bohemians, the second concentrating on the love interest between Rodolfo and Mimì. The alternation between what Illica and Giacosa designate in their preface as the 'comic' and 'dramatic' episodes reflects a basic facet of Bohemia, the unmediated extremes of life on the margins of society. The concluding sentence of Murger's preface evokes this liminal existence with the phrase, 'vie charmant et vie terrible' ('delightful and terrible life'), a phrase that Illica and Giacosa isolate in a lapidary exclamation, 'vita gaia e terribile!', both in the general introduction to their libretto and as the end of their preface to Act IV.

The structural parallels between Acts I and IV extend beyond this obvious division into comic and dramatic episodes. Both acts begin *in medias res* with Rodolfo and Marcello engaged in conversation, pursuing characteristic professional activities. In both instances, their considerations are interrupted by the arrival of the two other Bohemians and preparations for dinner. Schaunard, who then attempts unsuccessfully in Act I to narrate his murder of a parrot, has no better luck in Act IV when he commences an after-dinner toast. At one stage of the libretto's genesis, there was also to have been an episode in each act with *scapigliato* social commentary: the bohemian send-up of bourgeois morality with Benoît, and a mock political rally with Schaunard (see pp. 141–7).

Although the latter scene was deleted in the spring of 1895, a mock duel takes its place, concluding the Bohemians' antic dance:

COLLINE	(*offeso*)
	Se non erro,
	lei m'oltraggia.
	Snudi il ferro!
	(*prende le molle del camino*)
SCHAUNARD	(*prende la paletta*)
	Pronti. (*tira un colpo*) Assaggia.
	(*mettendosi in posizione per battersi*)
	Il tuo sangue io voglio ber!
COLLINE	(*fa altrettanto*)
	Uno di noi qui si sbudella.

(*Rodolfo e Marcello cessano dal ballare e si smascellano dalle risa*)

SCHAUNARD	Apprestate una barella!
COLLINE	Apprestate un cimiter!

COLLINE	(*insulted*)
	If I do not err,
	you insult me.
	Unsheathe your blade!
	(*takes the tongs from the fireplace*)
SCHAUNARD	(*takes the shovel*)
	En garde! (*strikes a blow*) Take that!
	(*putting himself in a position to fence*)
	I want to drink your blood!
COLLINE	(*does the same*)
	One of us here will be disembowelled.

(*Rodolfo and Marcello stop dancing and burst into laughter*)

SCHAUNARD	Prepare a litter!
COLLINE	Prepare a cemetery!

This exchange travesties the 'high style' of earlier nineteenth-century Italian operas, with its elevated diction ('se non erro', 'snudi il ferro') and its extremes of passion. One thinks of similar lines in Verdi's *Il trovatore*, where Leonora challenges Count Luna, 'Bleed me to death, drink my blood!' ('Svenami, ti bevi il sangue mio' [IV.1]), or Azucena urges Manrico, 'strike this blade up to the hilt, plunge it in the villain's heart!' ('Sino all'elsa questa lama vibra, immergi all'empio in cor!' [II.1]).

Both the duping of Benoît and this mock-operatic duel serve a function beyond merely poking fun at Italian bourgeois morality or antiquated poetic diction. Each scene immediately precedes an entrance of Mimì and the sudden switch to serious action. As such, it also provides a comic foil for the events that follow. The travesty of old Benoît's lustful pursuits contrasts with the tender beginning of Rodolfo's and Mimì's love; the take-off on the passionate tragedy of grand opera introduces the melodrama of a seamstress's death from consumption. The libretto to *La bohème* thereby self-consciously reflects the general shift in nineteenth-century conceptions of the tragic from Aristotelian norms of character and responsibility to an impersonal process beyond the individual's control.

Accordingly, a principal function of motivic parallels between Acts I and IV is to illustrate the gradual and ineluctable progression of the innocent Mimì's decline. Three series of references during the opera inform us of her condition. When she enters the Bohemians' garret in Act I, she is immediately seized by 'choking' and 'coughing' from the exertion of her climb, tell-tale signs of a respiratory ailment: 'My breath ... those stairs ...' ('Il respir ... Quelle scale ...'). Rodolfo immediately notices his neighbour's pallor, and then responds to her fainting spell with prophetic sympathy: 'How ill she looks!' ('Che viso d'ammalata!'). We are reminded of her illness in Act III by the persistent cough, which marks her entrance and punctuates the musical numbers, and by Rodolfo's frightened description. He informs Marcello (and the eavesdropping Mimì) of his mistress's rapid decline and impending doom, noting with clinical accuracy the signs of advanced pulmonary tuberculosis, a 'terrible cough' and 'red flecks of blood' in her 'emaciated cheeks'. By the time she re-enters the garret in Act IV, we realise that Mimì is finished. No longer able to climb the stairs, as in Act I, she can be seen through the open door, 'seated on the last step of the stairs', and has to be carried inside.

Several other motifs establish a pattern of anticipation and fulfilment between the revelation of Mimì's illness in Act I and her death in Act IV. The most obvious, that of the seamstress's delicate hands (already emphasised in the preface to the libretto), introduces Rodolfo's famous 'Che gelida manina, / se la lasci riscaldar' ('What an icy little hand, / let me warm it').[7] The recapitulation of this verbal motif in the final scene, preceded by Schaunard's aside, 'in half an hour she'll be dead!', announces the beginning of her decline:

MIMÌ	Ho tanto freddo ...
	Se avessi un manicotto! Queste mie mani
	riscaldare non si potranno mai? (*tosse*)
RODOLFO	(*le prendi le mani nelle sue riscaldandogliele*)
	Qui, nelle mie!

MIMÌ   I'm so cold ...
             If only I had a muff! Can these hands of mine
             never be warmed? (*coughs*)
RODOLFO   (*takes her hands in his, warming them*)
             Here, in mine!

Even the change of season from winter to spring and the alternation from night to day in Acts I and IV form a natural progression
that emphasises the impersonal and unalterable course of Mimì's
illness. The innocent longing for a budding rose and the first 'kiss' of
the April sun, which characterises Mimì's autobiographical aria,
fades in Act III to a resigned anticipation of separation from
Rodolfo in 'the season of flowers', when 'one has the sun as a com-
panion'. Ironically, it is the harsh sunlight of spring that reveals their
permanent separation in death, obliterating the moonlit promise of
their love on Christmas Eve. Whereas Act I culminates in a sudden
burst of moonlight through the garret window, suffusing Mimì's
face with its soft 'lunar dawn' and illuminating the poetic ecstasy of
the lovers' first kiss ('Amor! Amor! Amor!'), Act IV concludes with
the harsh intrusion of day through that same window onto the face
of the dead heroine, highlighting the poet's lapse into a speaking
voice and the anguished outburst that concludes the entire opera,
'Mimì ... Mimì ...'

III

The general freedom with which Illica and Giacosa adapted their
source is also reflected in wide-ranging liberties with details of
prosody and diction. The libretto of *La bohème* marks the final
stages of a process that had begun as far back as the eighteenth century, in which the poetic text became subsumed by an increasingly
fluid musical idiom and lost its pretensions as a separate literary
entity. From Metastasio, whose libretti were set by generations of
composers and were even performed as spoken dramas, to Verdi's
poor, browbeaten Piave: the progression could hardly be clearer.
But even in Verdi's operas it is rare to find words that cannot be
arranged into lines of fixed syllabic length and, in musical numbers,
into stanzas of regular stress and rhyme. It was a bold step when, in
Iago's 'Credo' from Act II of *Otello*, Boito experimented with 'versi
rotti', broken verses with no regular pattern of syllabic content or
stress. In Puccini's libretti, however, these 'versi rotti' – or, as

Ricordi is reputed to have dubbed them, 'illicasillabi' – become the norm.

A representative example, both of the remnants of the old style and the shape of the new, comes with the very first lines of Act I:

> Questo Mar Rosso – mi ammollisce e assidera
> come se addosso – mi piovesse in stille.
> Per vendicarmi, affogo un Faraon!

> This Red Sea dampens and freezes me
> As if it were raining on me in drops.
> As revenge, I'll drown a Pharaoh!

According to the rules of Italian prosody, these three lines are just possible – each is an *endecasillabo*, a line in which the final accent falls on the tenth syllable. But the variety of the internal accent, the frequent use of elision, and the manner in which the end word of each line is varied to give a sense of gathering emphasis that is as prosaic as it is powerfully rhetorical (as*si*dera, *stil*le, Fara*on*): all these things are quite at odds with the prosodic expectations for the formal beginning of an opera.

Matters become even more aggressively untraditional a few lines later, where a 'polite', neatly stressed and rhymed quatrain is immediately countered by

MARCELLO   Rodolfo, io voglio dirti un mio pensier profondo:
            ho un freddo cane!

MARCELLO   Rodolfo, I want to tell you a profound thought:
            I'm damned cold!

In spite of its layout, the first of these lines might be scanned as two in the manner of the preceding quatrain ('Rodolfo, io voglio dirti / un mio pensier profondo'), which gives maximum emphasis to the ensuing 'punch' line: 'ho un freddo cane'. More than prosodic rules are broken here: the rough colloquial force of 'ho un freddo cane' would have been unthinkable in the mouth of an earlier nineteenth-century operatic character.

A similar variety marks the diction of the libretto. Colloquial language generally informs the scenes centring on Mimì, most obviously at the beginning of her first encounter with Rodolfo,

MIMÌ   La chiave della stanza
           dove l'ho lasciata?
RODOLFO   Non stia sull'uscio;
           il lume vacilla al vento.

MIMÌ   The key to my room –
              where did I leave it?
RODOLFO   Don't stand in the doorway;
              the light is flickering in the draft.

Similarly realistic diction, albeit with a rapid alternation of details and exclamations, creates the bustling atmosphere of Christmas Eve in the Latin Quarter:

AL CAFFÈ   Presto qua!
             Camerier! Un bicchier! Corri!
             Birra! Da ber!
LA FOLLA   Stringiti a me, ecc.
I VENDITORI Fringuelli e passeri, ecc.
LA MAMMA   Emma, quando ti chiamo!

AT THE CAFÉ Here, quickly!
               Waiter! A glass! Hurry!
               Beer! Something to drink!
THE CROWD   Hold on tight to me, etc.
THE VENDORS Finches and sparrows, etc.
THE MAMMA   Emma, when I call you!

The beginning of Act III also sets a scene and creates an atmosphere: the cries of carters, 'Giddyup!' ('Hopp-la!'), alternate with the greetings of milk-women, 'Good-day!' ('Buon giorno!'), and the cries and gossip of peasant women: 'Butter and cheese! Chicken and eggs! / Which way are you going?' ('Burro e cacio! Polli ed ova! / Voi da che parte andate?') Such determinedly ordinary language, whether used to characterise a particular seamstress or groups of common people, would also have been unthinkable in earlier nineteenth-century opera.

If the colloquial idiom both expresses and determines the character of proletarian figures, an anarchic approach to language reveals the Bohemians' free-spirited independence of social conditions.[8] Their play with words extends from the antiquated 'lippo' (blind), which is coined – so to speak – to rhyme with the image of Luigi Filippo (Louis Philippe) on five-franc pieces, to the pun on 'aringa'/ 'arringa' (herring/harangue) with which Colline introduces a solitary herring as a dish worthy of Demosthenes.[9] The Bohemians also subvert the 'high style' of literary usage by employing it in a trivial context, e.g. when Rodolfo lights candles for dinner, 'Let the splendid hall shine brightly' ('Fulgida folgori la sala splendida'), drawing attention to precisely what the garret is *not*. Both forms of play combine in the spooneristic shift from the elevated to the ridiculous that brackets Benoît's earnest narration of his sexual adventures:

MARCELLO   Ei gongolava arzillo, pettoruto.
BENOÎT   (*ringalluzzito*)
          Son vecchio ma robusto.
RODOLFO, SCHAUNARD, COLLINE   (*con gravità ironica*)
          Ei gongolava arzuto e pettorillo.
MARCELLO   He rejoiced sprightly, haughtily.
BENOÎT   (*elated*)
          I'm old, but sturdy.
RODOLFO, SCHAUNARD, COLLINE   (*with ironic gravity*)
          He rejoiced spraughtily, hightly.

This ludic (and sometimes lunatic) atmosphere also seems to temper the social criticism and class conflict inherent in Murger's material. Marcello and Rodolfo reveal their apparent indifference to power and wealth at the very beginning of the opera by trivialising them: the painter drowns a Pharaoh on his canvas ('an Egyptian' in the novel), whereas the poet metaphorically disparages their cold stove's living 'in idleness like a grand seigneur' ('in ozio come un gran signor'). The Bohemians further reveal their independence of the establishment by duping the adulterous Benoît and the foppish Alcindoro. The focus in both cases on sexual competition enables us to identify with the triumph of enterprising youth over decrepit old age; only subsequently do we realise that the landlord and the Councillor of State also represent bourgeois–political interests, a function underscored at the premiere of *La bohème* and since by assigning both roles to the same singer.

Yet the libretto's humour cuts in both directions, as the conclusion to the episode with Benoît reveals. When the tipsy landlord's description slips into slang, 'thin women mean headaches and often – "horns"' ('le donne magre sono grattacapi / e spesso ... "sopracapi"'), and inadvertently mentions his wife, the Bohemians leap to the defence of injured morality:

MARCELLO   (*terribile*) Quest'uomo ha moglie
            e sconcie voglie ha nel cor!
RODOLFO   E ammorba, e appesta
            la nostra honesta magion!
MARCELLO   (*terrifyingly*) This man has a wife,
            and he has obscene desires in his heart!
RODOLFO   And he corrupts and infects
            our honest dwelling!

This parodic reversal of roles unmasks the landlord's double standard, by which he secretly desires to pursue love as freely as the Bohemians while living behind a façade of bourgeois morality, a façade which they adopt and turn against him. But do the Bohemians secretly long in turn for the comforts of a bourgeois existence? Does their mocking of power and wealth also reveal a fascination as great as their attraction to good food and drink?

Murger certainly thought of his Bohemia as a phase to be outgrown, and concluded his novel with a postlude ('Youth Comes But Once'), which describes the survivors' maturation to successful careers and marriage. There is a hint that Rodolfo has already grown up in his lament in the opening duet of Act IV, 'Ah, Mimì, my brief youth!' Rodolfo confesses in his Act I aria that he has 'a millionaire's soul', but he also reveals to Mimì during their shopping spree in Act II that he has a millionaire uncle in real life, and hopes to inherit his wealth. Similarly, Marcello's argument with Musetta at the end of Act III reveals his conservative, essentially bourgeois attitude toward their relationship:

Musetta	All'altar non siamo uniti.
Marcello	Bada, sotto il mio cappello non ci stan certi ornamenti …
Musetta	Io detesto quegli amanti che la fanno da ah! ah! ah! mariti!
Musetta	We're not united at the altar.
Marcello	Mind you, under my hat certain ornaments don't go …
Musetta	I hate those lovers who act like ha! ha! ha! husbands!

Although Puccini did not realise the suggestion musically, the libretto intimates the underlying harmony between the Bohemians and their society. At the end of Act II, a military tattoo, which the bourgeois crowd acclaims as the emblem of 'the nation's majesty', marches past with orderly precision, led by the drum major, 'the most handsome man in France'. The anarchic Bohemians, joining the procession in order to hide in it, respond with an improvised march of their own, hoisting the beautiful Musetta to their shoulders and acclaiming her 'roguish heart' as the emblem of the Latin Quarter. Far from disturbing the procession, they are acclaimed with noisy ovations before being assimilated by the crowd and disappearing into the distance. Such whimsical resolution of difference and conflict makes *La bohème* an elegy not only for lost love and youth, but for a vanished social utopia as well.

IV

Thanks to their vocal ranges (tenor and baritone) as well as their occupations (poet and painter), Rodolfo and Marcello are instantly differentiated in the first scene of the opera. Mimì and Musetta, both sopranos and mistresses, reveal a less pronounced profile. In the final act of Murger's play, Musette summarises their fates with the observation that both have suffered: 'I [from] an illness that caused me to live, coquetry and pleasure; she [from] a fatal illness, love and honesty' (V.7). The difference between the women results partly from these implied sexual and socio-economic roles as lorette and grisette respectively, but are even more clearly defined in the opera by their association with particular literary types.

Although Musetta remains a lorette (a woman characterised by showy appearance and lack of an occupation, who is supported entirely by lovers), her personality also expresses the pursuit of free subjectivity that subsumes both the artistic and the sexual concerns of Murger's Bohemia. Her most trenchant lines in Acts II and III voice a desire for unrestricted freedom, the egocentricity of which is expressed by the frequency of the first person pronoun: 'I want to do what I please','I want to do as I like!', 'I want complete freedom!', and 'I'll make love with whom I please!' As the last reference suggests, Musetta's overriding concern is for independence in the choice of sexual partners. Unfortunately, her extreme subjectivity also works to subvert itself, since the pursuit of pleasure ultimately makes her a commodity in the realisation of others' desires.

On its apparently public level, Musetta's famous waltz, 'Quando me'n vo'', which basks in 'the flow of desire' that 'surrounds me completely' ('l'effluvio del desìo / tutta m'aggira'), advertises sex indiscriminately, and – not surprisingly – upsets Alcindoro, whose major worry about 'that scurrilous song' seems to be 'What will people say?' At the same time, the song directs a private message at Marcello, who reacts to it as to a siren: 'Tie me to the chair!' Text and subtext, advertisement and declaration of love, are inseparably bound up in the dialectic of Musetta's character. The liaisons that provide her with a better life become, as the prefatory quote from Murger's novel at the beginning of Act II suggests, the stanzas of a song, in which her true love, Marcello, is the refrain ('ciascuno de' miei amori è una strofa, – ma Marcello ne è il ritornello').

Although Mimì shares many affinities with a working-class woman or grisette, she bears an even closer resemblance to a nineteenth-century literary type, the *femme fragile*.[10] Ultimately a reflex of 'the white plague', the epidemic of tuberculosis that pervaded Europe in the last century,[11] this type has influential antecedents in the heroines of E. T. A. Hoffmann and Edgar Allan Poe. Marguerite Gautier in *La Dame aux camélias*(1852) became the model for Violetta in Verdi's *La traviata* (1853), and also helped to engender, thanks to the subsequent influence of Sarah Bernhardt's acting, a host of consumptive and – deliberately – pale imitations in the late nineteenth century. From the mid-1880s through to the beginning of the twentieth century, a broad spectrum of European writers often created female protagonists epitomised by their aesthetically fascinating frailty. Typical features include a delicate, aristocratic bearing, beautiful sickliness, and an innocent sexuality. 'Cool' or 'cold' surroundings – white rooms and clothing, a snowy or moonlit landscape, etc. – provide the appropriate setting that complements a pallid complexion. Incapable of surviving the oppressive rigours of everyday reality, the *fragiles* are frequently compared with flowers (the symbol of beauty and transience), with delicate artifacts such as *fin de siècle* glass and cameos, or with Pre-Raphaelite paintings and medieval madonnas. Most importantly, the slow, 'beautiful' death of these women, usually of consumption, often seems to constitute the sole reason for their existence.

Mimì, whom the librettists describe before the beginning of Act I with a quotation from Ch. 14 of the novel (using their own Italian version rather than either Bruni's or Camerone's translation), represents an adaptation of Murger's heroine to the type of the *femme fragile*:

' . . . Mimì was a charming girl, particularly apt to appeal to Rodolfo and match his plastic and poetic ideals. Age twenty-two, slight, delicate . . . Her face resembled a sketch of an aristocratic figure; its features were of a marvellous refinement . . . '
'The blood of youth coursed warmly and quickly through her veins, giving a rosy tint to her clear skin that had the velvety whiteness of the camellia . . . '
'This sickly beauty allured Rodolfo . . . But what made him madly in love with Mlle Mimì were her tiny hands, which she managed even with household duties to keep whiter than the goddess of leisure.'

Notice the pervasive use of ellipsis: these fragments in fact reproduce only about a quarter of Murger's paragraph, radically taming by means of omission the shrewish and often cruel character of the original Mimi. Murger begins his description, for example, with the statement that 'Rodolphe had first met Mimi when she was the mistress of one of his friends, and he had made her his own', a clear indication of her previous promiscuity – not to mention his future difficulties. The missing text following the first quotation adds that she was 'full of roguery . . . [her eyes] were overcast in moments of ennui or ill-humour by an expression of cruelty that was almost savage, and a physiognomist might have seen in it the indications of profound egoism or great insensibility'. After describing Mimi's delicate hands, Murger adds that they were destined 'to mutilate the poet's heart with their pink nails'.

The librettists' preface renders its 'selections' accurately from the French original, with one exception that immediately illuminates their altered conception of Mimì: Murger's heroine is a 'femme' (woman), Illica's and Giacosa's a 'ragazza' (girl). This introductory reference, minimising her sexual potential, prepares us for the pious and chaste heroine of Act I, who 'doesn't always go to Mass', but 'prays much to the Lord' ('Non vado sempre a messa, / ma prego assai il Signor'), living – unlike a typical grisette, who would have been forced by economic circumstances to share her quarters with a man – 'alone, all alone, there in a little white room' ('sola, soletta, / là in una bianca cameretta'). The ensuing motifs from this introduction, particularly the emphasis on Mimì's aristocratic but pallid and sickly appearance, proclaim her descent from the *femme fragile* more directly. The comparison of her fair complexion with a camellia intimates her affinity with Dumas' heroine as well as suggesting her frailty. Indeed, Rodolfo will come to the anguished realisation in Act III that Mimì, a 'hothouse flower', has 'wilted' under the harshness of their impoverished existence – 'love's not enough, love's not enough!' ('non basta amor, non basta amor!').

Our discussion thus far has concerned issues of sources, structure, themes and characterisation. However, it is not only on this level that the libretto reveals an unusual level of sophistication. A close analysis of the last scenes of Acts I and IV suggests that the interplay of these elements is unusually rich, enabling the relationship between Rodolfo and Mimì to transcend the expectations generated by their origin in the stock types of bohemian lover and *femme fragile.* The double aria and duet that conclude Act I are a marvel of the librettist's craft, first revealing the obvious differences between the poet and the seamstress while suggesting their unconscious affinity, and then proceeding to the sudden discovery of their mutual love.

Rodolfo's famous autobiographical statement, ostensibly designed to inform his neighbour 'who I am and what I do, how I live' ('chi son e che faccio, come vivo'), does not really introduce him (he nowhere reveals his name during this scene), but instead presents 'A Poet' in an artistically appropriate aria of three-line stanzas:

> Chi son? – Sono un poeta.
> Che cosa faccio? – Scrivo.
> E come vivo? – Vivo.
>
> Who am I? – I'm a poet.
> What do I do? – I write.
> And how do I live? – I live.

In simple, straightforward terms, the poet answers his own rhetorical questions with intransitive verbs: existing, writing, and living – without concern for the goals of these actions – constitute a self-sufficient justification for his activities. The identification of art with life, a commonplace in late romanticism and subsequent movements espousing *l'art pour l'art*, comes effortlessly to his lips. The ensuing stanzas describing his artistic existence comprise, appropriately enough, a poetic statement based on one extended metaphor, the richness of the 'merry poverty' in which he squanders rhymes 'like a great lord', dreams with a 'millionaire's soul', and suffers the 'theft' of his jewels by two beautiful eyes. Rodolfo appropriately defines himself as a dreamer of 'rhymes and hymns of love': his aria proceeds in a circle from life to 'chimeras and dreams' and back again from these 'familiar and beautiful dreams' to life, and specifically to the 'sweet hope' directed at Mimì. It is a smooth, calculated gesture, a love poem in search of its own inspiration.

Mimì's answering autobiographical statement is anything but smooth and poetic:

> Sì.
> Mi chiamano Mimì,
> ma il mio nome è Lucia.
> La storia mia
> è breve. A tela o a seta
> ricamo in casa e fuori ...

> Yes.
> They call me Mimì,
> but my name is Lucia.
> My story
> is brief. On canvas or on silk
> I embroider at home and outside ...

She introduces herself passively, citing the nickname others have given her before divulging her real name. Mimì's statement is not stanzaic and more closely resembles prose than poetry; indeed, much of what follows is a rather prosaic description of her occupation and private life. Insecure and inarticulate, she interrupts her narration at its mid-point to enquire, 'do you understand me?' ('Lei m'intende?'), belabouring her 'brief story' in such detail that it expands – verbally, at least – to more than twice the length of Rodolfo's well-wrought introduction. The two parts of her aria begin identically with the statement 'they call me Mimì', and proceed in a revealing repetition from particulars of her chaste existence to the longing to escape from her isolation as a maker of artificial flowers. Mimì's autobiography reaches a conclusion not because of any narrative strategy, as is the case with Rodolfo, but because she runs out of information: 'I wouldn't know what else to tell you about me' ('Altro di me non le saprei narrare').

In spite of the obvious social and intellectual differences separating the poet from the seamstress, their autobiographies establish a mutual dialogue of longing. Each concludes or interrupts the other's introduction by answering 'yes' to a question. After a hesitant beginning, the first half of Mimì's aria builds to an unexpectedly poetic climax that answers Rodolfo's presentation of himself (as a 'poet' writing 'hymns of love', squandering 'dreams and chimeras' that gladly yield to his 'sweet hope') in reverse order, revealing her yearning for the 'sweet magic' of things that 'speak of love', of 'dreams and chimeras', i.e. of 'poetry':

> Mi piaccion quelle cose
> che han sì dolce malìa,
> che parlano d'amor, di primavere,
> che parlano di sogni e di chimere,
> quelle cose che han nome poesia ...
>
> I like those things
> that have such sweet magic,
> which speak of love,
> of springtimes,

which speak of dreams and of chimeras,
those things that are named poetry ...

The concluding half of her autobiography answers the indeterminate longing that Rodolfo reveals at the beginning of the opera by watching the grey skies of Paris, confessing that she also gazes out of her window in anticipation of the first 'kiss' of spring:

> Guardo sui tetti e in cielo,
> ma quando vien lo sgelo
> il primo sole è mio,
> il primo bacio dell'aprile è mio!

> I look out on roofs and into the heavens,
> but when the thaw comes
> the first sun is mine,
> the first kiss of April is mine!

Their mutual affinity dawns on them almost immediately thereafter, as the other Bohemians interrupt from the courtyard below and Rodolfo opens the window to respond, simultaneously 'opening' the way to emotional insight. At that moment, according to the stage direction, *'the moon's rays enter through the open window, thus lighting the room'*. After a brief exchange, in which Rodolfo reveals prophetically that 'I'm not alone. There are two of us' ('Non son solo. Siamo in due'), a further burst of moonlight illuminates Mimì: *'Mimì is still near the window in such a way that the moon's rays illuminate her. Turning, Rodolfo sees Mimì as if wrapped in a halo of light, and he contemplates her, as if ecstatic.'* This isolation of Mimì in an aureole of moonlight within the window-frame, a clear reminiscence of those Pre-Raphaelite madonnas mentioned earlier, forms the last and most vivid in a series of *femme fragile* motifs in Act I. As the object of Rodolfo's intense aesthetic contemplation, she inspires a sudden epiphany of recognition, which is simultaneously confirmed by the voice of Marcello from outside, 'he found poetry' ('Trovò la poesia'), and by the poet's shift to the familiar form of address:

> O soave fanciulla!
> O dolce viso
> di mite circonfuso alba lunar,
> in te, ravviso
> il sogno ch'io vorrei sempre sognar!

O gentle maiden!
O sweet visage
bathed in a soft lunar dawn,
in you, I recognise
the dream I would like to dream forever!

Their voices join in unison for the first time, and they become a complementary pair, she stirring 'extreme sweetnesses' in his soul, his praises descending 'sweetly' to her heart. As if to emphasise their conscious assent to a relationship that began with the accidental touching of hands,

Che gelida manina.
se la lasci riscaldar.

What an icy little hand,
let me warm it.

they exit by formally linking arms (to a nearly identical rhyme scheme):

RODOLFO   Dammi il braccio, mia piccina ...
MIMÌ   Obbedisco, signor!

RODOLFO   Give me your arm, little one ...
MIMÌ   I obey, sir!

It is thus entirely fitting that Rodolfo exuberantly acknowledges the inspiration they have discovered in each other when, in Act II, he introduces himself as 'the poet' and her as 'poetry', adding

Dal mio cervel sbocciano i canti,
dalle sue dita sbocciano i fior,
dall'anime esultanti
sboccia l'amor, sboccia l'amor!

From my brain blossom songs,
from her fingers blossom flowers,
from exultant souls
blossoms love, blossoms love!

V

The death of Mimì at the end of Act IV presented the librettists with the greatest challenge of the collaboration. From the very beginning, the spectre of Verdi's *La traviata* (and anxiety about the extent of its influence) hovered over their deliberations.[12] Giacosa immediately raised the most obvious issue in his initial response to

Illica's scenario, politely observing that the last act 'seems too similar to many others' (CP 82). For some time, Puccini wanted to invite direct comparison with Verdi (as he had with Massenet's *Manon*), beginning the last act, like that of *La traviata*, with the dying Mimì in bed (CP 101, cf. 136). But a year and a half of revisions resulted in a version that met Verdi's challenge in a more subtle manner.

At first glance, death by consumption or pulmonary tuberculosis seems to present limited narrative options. The victim's lungs gradually cease to function, and – in literary portrayals at least – the decline is so regular that its course can be predicted with accuracy. At the beginning of Act III of *La traviata*, for example, Violetta's doctor tells her confidante Annina that the end is 'only a few hours' away. During these moments, the victim's life seems to hang suspended by a thread; and then, breathing simply stops. Verdi's last librettist, the poet–composer Boito, offered an interpretation of the last-act prelude of *La traviata* with his usual sensitivity:

Subtle in the Latin sense of *gracilis, exilis* is really the epithet required to characterise that most moving passage. [. . .] To describe someone who dies of consumption we say *muore di mal sottile* [he dies of the subtle disease]. The prelude appears to say this with sounds, with elevated, sad, frail sounds, almost without body, ethereal, sick, with death imminent. [. . .] the soul of a dying woman tied to her body by the most subtle thread of breath! repeating before death a final memory of love![13]

The action of the last act continues to portray the almost disembodied state of Violetta's 'tranquil soul', descending to the 'prosaic' reminiscence in which she reads Germont's letter and then to a lyrical farewell from life, 'Adieu, lovely, happy dreams of the past'. The unexpected arrival of Alfredo and his father seems to reverse Violetta's decline, and she struggles – through several episodes of rising and collapsing – to return to life, expressing with her dying breath a feeling of singular intensity, the *spes phthisica* or illusion of recovery commonly attributed to terminal consumptives in the nineteenth century:[14] 'An unfamiliar strength / is reborn in me … stirs in me! … / Ah! … Why, I … I am returning to life! / Oh joy!' Violetta's death is all the more poignant because it is so unrealistic (a woman dying of tuberculosis can scarcely breathe, let alone sing a high $b\flat$ at full volume), emphasising with tragic irony the fortitude of a heroine whose redemption has come too late.

Illica and Giacosa proceed in the opposite direction in portraying the death of Mimì; indeed, one is tempted to consider their treatment as a careful inversion of Verdi's. Their scene begins rather than ends with the heroine's collapse and deceptive feeling of strength. Mimì shares Violetta's feeling of being 'reborn' and 'returning to life': 'One is reborn, reborn. / I feel life here again' ('Si rinasce, si rinasce. / Ancor sento la vita qui'). But her hope is undercut throughout the scene by its ironic contrast with the perceptions of others. While Mimì and Rodolfo share a quiet moment, Musetta relates her search for the dying girl, 'I heard it said that Mimì, having fled / from the Viscount, was dying', and the heroine's confirmation of her state, 'She says to me: "I can stand no more ... / I'm dying, I feel it" '. Thus, when Mimì suddenly complains of her cold hands and requests a muff, it is clear to everyone but the lovers that this is 'the last time she'll express a wish'.

While the Bohemians hurry off to purchase a cordial and a muff, Mimì and Rodolfo remain alone in the garret, setting the stage for the heroine's reminiscences. But the intensity of Mimì's 'Sono andati?' seems strangely eloquent for someone who has been so hesitant and inarticulate throughout the opera, and whose immediately ensuing death will involve a rapid loss of consciousness. It scarcely accords, for example, with her naively circular attempt to characterise Rodolfo as a reader of emotions in Act II:

> Ed egli ha letto quel che il core asconde ...
> Ora colui che legge dentro a un cuore
> sa l'amore ... ed è ... lettore.

> And he read what the heart hides ...
> Now he who reads in a heart
> knows love ... and he is ... a reader.

or her helpless request for information at the beginning of Act III, 'Excuse me, can you tell me which is the tavern (*not remembering the name*) ... where a painter is working?' Now, however, Mimì suddenly waxes poetic, expressing herself metaphorically:

> Ho tante cose che ti voglio dire,
> o una sola, ma grande come il mare,
> come il mare profonda ed infinita ...
> Sei il mio amor e tutta la mia vita,
> sei il mio amor e tutta la mia vita!

> I have so many things I want to tell you,
> or one alone, but big as the sea,
> like the sea, profound and infinite ...
> You are my love and all my life,
> You are my love and all my life!

The following lines even draw attention to the heroine's sudden intensity: Rodolfo calls her 'beautiful as a dawn' ('bella come un'aurora'), and Mimì immediately corrects the poet's metaphor: 'You've mistaken the comparison. / You meant: beautiful as a sunset' ('Hai sbagliato il raffronto. / Volevi dir: bella come un tramonto'). This unwonted clarity seems to express another symptom of the *spes phthisica*. According to the carefully researched diagnosis of the Brothers Goncourt in *Madame Gervaisais* (1869), for example, the final moments of consumption often 'call forth in the patient a state of elevation, tenderness, and love, a new urge to see the good, the beautiful and the ideal in everything, a state of human sublimity which seems almost not of this world' (Ch. 93).[15]

In this context, it is not surprising that Mimì's intensity wanes immediately thereafter, revealing the rapid dissolution of her personality as she abruptly begins to recollect fragmentary memories of Act I: 'They call me Mimì; they call me Mimì' ('Mi chiamano Mimì, mi chiamano Mimì'). Visually emphasising the reminiscence by putting on the bonnet purchased in Act II, she recalls the first meeting with Rodolfo, proceeding tenderly but ominously from the 'extinguished light' ('lume spento') to Rodolfo's touching her 'icy little hand' ('gelida manina'). The repetition of this central motif from Act I begins a precipitous decline from memory into mere physical sensation: commenting on how warm and soft ('morbido') the muff feels, Mimì simply dozes off little by little: 'My hands … in the warmth … and … to sleep' ('Le mani … al caldo … e dormire'). The librettists emphasise the heroine's gradual decline to such an extent that the precise moment of death goes unnoticed. A 'spirit lamp' flickers symbolically over Mimì's bed until Schaunard discovers that she has already 'expired' ('è spirata'). The term is clinically precise, and it is not surprising that sopranos have occasionally prepared for the role by observing terminal patients in tuberculosis wards.[16] In keeping with such unheroic realism, Rodolfo responds, not in a lyrical outburst, such as one would expect in earlier nineteenth-century opera, but in a speaking voice, the prosaic nature of which poignantly expresses the poet's discovery of his loss: 'What does that coming and going mean?' ('Che vuol dire quell'andare e venire?')

If the only goal of the final scene of *La bohème* were the realistic demise of Mimì, one might sympathise with critics who denigrate the opera as a simple exercise in calculated sentimentality. To be sure, sentimentality *is* a calculated effect of *La bohème*. Puccini's letters constantly return to the 'goal', the 'Tod von Mimì' ('death of Mimì' – CP 140), emphasising the need to be 'irresistibly moving and very true to life' (CP 121). And his publisher Ricordi, who was most concerned with the commercial success of the work, positively rejoiced in the anticipation of turning the 'whole orchestra floor into a sea of tears' (M 153; cf. M 145). Fortunately, the final libretto both offered and ultimately inspired more than the 'pathetic' soap opera Illica rejected when he protested Puccini's initial desire for a 'lachrymose (and Romantic)' love story (CP 101).

In its final version, the last act of *La bohème* is not confined to Mimì, even if she and her death constitute the central event. Verdi's *La traviata*, in contrast, deals with a woman wrongly judged by common standards of morality, and appropriately focuses on her sublimity of character even in death. But Puccini's opera, as its title implies, also deals with Bohemia, so that the heroine's demise adumbrates a larger loss as well. The beginning of Act IV, with its repetition of setting, seems to announce retrospection as a major theme, a suggestion that is immediately confirmed by the simple, sentimental reminiscences of Marcello's and Rodolfo's duet. Rodolfo is the first to become conscious of his own development from the naive to the sentimental (in the Schillerian sense of the word), lamenting in the absence of Mimì the loss of the 'beautiful days' of 'my brief youth'.

More importantly, that same sense of deprivation later becomes the focus of Colline's farewell to his old coat ('Vecchia zimarra'). Again, a comparison with *La traviata* is instructive. Violetta also symbolises her loss through an object, the portrait that she gives as a memento to Alfredo. At the same time, she bequeathes it to his future bride as 'the gift of one who, among the angels in heaven, is praying for her, for you', thereby subsuming her personal tragedy in the theodicy of divine providence. In *La bohème*, however, we enter a post-romantic, modern world without transcendence. In the absence of a heaven, there remains a pervasive sense of loss that includes the paradise of the past. Colline's aria therefore laments through the farewell to a beloved object the utopian 'happy days' of youth spent in disinterested wholeness, tranquilly disregarding the fragmenting quest for wealth and power that dominates society:

> Mai non curvasti il logoro
> dorso ai ricchi ed ai potenti.
> Passar nelle tue tasche

come in antri tranquilli
filosofi e poeti.
Ora che i giorni lieti
fuggir, ti dico addio
fedele amico mio.
Addio, addio.

You never bent your worn
back to the rich and the mighty.
In your pockets,
as in tranquil grottoes,
passed philosophers and poets.
Now that the happy days
have fled, I bid you farewell,
my faithful friend.
Farewell, farewell.

Colline returns from the pawn shop too late, clutching in his hand the small change of memory, which he deposits helplessly on the table as the drama rushes to its conclusion. In the final bars of the opera, the music of Mimì's 'Sono andati?' will blend with his 'Vecchia zimarra', emphasising the mutual associations of lost love and youth, and their utopian past. Yet they persist in the nostalgia that Puccini's Bohemia evokes and continues to evoke. This wistful longing is perhaps best characterised by the comments of the two heroes at the end of the *duettino* involving the purchase of Mimì's bonnet in Act II. As the 'last words' of the opera's genesis (this section was added after the premiere), they also represent an appropriate final evocation of the work and its legacy to posterity:

MARCELLO   O bella età d'inganni e d'utopie!
　　　　　　Si crede, spera, e tutto bello appare.
RODOLFO　　La più divina delle poesie
　　　　　　è quella, amico, che c'insegna amare!

MARCELLO   O beautiful age of deceits and utopias!
　　　　　　One believes, hopes, and all seems beautiful.
RODOLFO　　The most divine of poems,
　　　　　　my friend, is the one that teaches us to love!

5 The musical language of La bohème

BY WILLIAM DRABKIN

Few people would deny that Puccini's reputation as a composer was made, and has been upheld, in the opera house, and that interest in his music has been largely confined to this establishment and the journalistic world surrounding it. Fifty years after the appearance of the first substantial study of a Puccini opera worthy of the term 'analysis', his musical scores are all but ignored by serious music journals and university analysis seminars, places from which informed critical opinion on other musical matters has long flowed in abundance. The occasions on which his music has been subjected to serious investigation have often pointed up the shortcomings in applying analytical methods or systems which have met with success elsewhere, e.g. the analysis of operatic acts and scenes into smaller structural units associated with, among others, the Wagner scholar Alfred Lorenz,[1] or the search for large-scale tonal unity and motivic organisation;[2] but they have not come up with new approaches, or encouraged further research on the musical content of his operas.

It is not difficult to find critics of Puccini's musical style or dramaturgical methods. Serious writers who have had to face Puccini squarely in their chartings of operatic history have usually found a mixture of good and bad elements in his music: an attitude most eloquently summed up by the ambiguous remark that 'Puccini's music often sounds better than it is, owing to the perfect adjustment of means to ends'.[3] But the best known general assessment of Puccini as an opera composer, Joseph Kerman's in *Opera as Drama*, takes one of his major scores (*Tosca*) as an example of failed operatic composition.[4]

Among the monographs on the composer, which have naturally tended to be more laudatory, Puccini's success has usually been described in terms likely to be unacceptable to the critical reader: melodic genius, attention to orchestral colour, the ability to set up ideal atmospheric conditions for the unfolding of dramatic action.

80

Even the standard English life-and-works survey by Mosco Carner, which is written with all the knowledge, experience and sympathy required of such a piece of scholarship, is dotted with observations on compositional method and the finished scores which the discerning reader may well take to suggest flaws in Puccini's technique or realisation. Referring to the general deployment of the music and dramatic action, for instance, Carner remarks that 'the first act is invariably the best constructed'; a comment which, on reflection, seems as devastating to the integrity of Puccini's art as any I have found in the writings of his most virulent critics.[5] The composer's own pronouncements about his work – that he was above all a melodist, that his genius lay in the working out of 'the little things' in an opera and, perhaps most notorious of all, that he was always concerned with keeping his musical style 'up to date' – cannot have helped matters much, either.

In most discussions of opera composed in the century or so leading up to Puccini – say, from Mozart to late Wagner and Verdi – an important criterion of excellence has been the demonstrability of some sort of *unity*, a system or method operating over the entire range of a score. Following Lorenz's monumental Wagner studies and his lesser-known work on Mozart, there have been numerous attempts to chart the influence of tonal relations over large stretches of operatic music. In an age concerned not only with large-scale tonal unity but also with motivic economy, there have also been important studies of thematic integrity in opera: Donington's monograph on the *Ring* is probably the most spectacular, as well as most sensible, demonstration of interrelationship and interdependence in Wagner's system of leitmotifs.[6] In studies of theme and motif in Italian opera, there have been some admirable essays on recurring themes, particularly in Verdi: their dramatic placement, and the nature of their transformations. But here we have already lost some of the systematisation which had been considered a desideratum of persuasive analysis: the successful account of significant thematic recurrence must necessarily relegate large tracts of music to the function of 'passing time'. An account of the famous 'bacio' theme from *Otello*, for instance, need not concern itself with more than a few minutes of music in the score; and an explanation of this opera in terms of thematic recurrence need not invoke many other important themes from the opera.

Studies sympathetic to Puccini may have fallen into the unity trap by praising his music not for its sheer verve, as Debussy is said to have put it, but for qualities which have conferred the halo of classicism upon early composers: motivic economy and total unity. *La bohème*, for instance, has been admired by both Maisch and Carner for its being underpinned by the key of C major, which is said to govern the tonal organisation of the first act, to return in the fourth act to assume a prominent role, to be transformed towards the end of the act (by Mimì's tragedy) into C minor, and finally to be deflected a semitone upwards to the key of C sharp minor, in which the opera ends. The fact that the opening and closing tonalities of Act II, F and B♭ major, are in a dominant-to-tonic relation is also adduced as evidence of Puccini's 'progressive tonality'. But it is difficult to hear – and just as difficult to observe in the score – a fundamental role for C major in Act I or a sense of 'progression' from F to B♭ in Act II.

At the beginning of the opera the key of C major, however frequently it occurs, is forever moving toward the flat side, by way of the circle of fifths, and usually ends up in B♭ major (from bar 1 of the opera to bar 46 of rehearsal number 1; from no. 3 bar 22 to no. 4 bar 10; from no. 5 bar 1 to no. 6 bar 3). The instability of C major is forecast already by the opening motif in the bass, G–F♯–F, which is initially interpreted as a dominant seventh chord (V_2^4) of C (Ex. 1a), but whose emphasis on F in the first 24 bars is later picked up by the dominant of B♭, whose root *is* F. Indeed, when the G–F of the V_2 chord is 'linearised', i.e. when Puccini assigns a chord to each of these notes, they provide the harmonic impetus for the arrival of B♭ major (Ex. 1b). At the end of the first act the key of C major does make a brief appearance, but it would be a mistake to read into it the resolution of previous tonal arguments. Rodolfo's great aria, beginning with 'Che gelida manina' and culminating in 'Talor dal mio forziere', is set chiefly in the flat keys of D♭ and A♭, Mimì's 'Mi chiamano Mimì' and the ensuing duet ('O soave fanciulla') in the sharp keys D and A; the two pages of the key of C major, which concludes the act, have neither the weight nor the required relationship to the previous keys for us to find sufficient tonal resolution in this key when the act ends.[7]

Similarly, the choice of B♭ at the end of Act II seems governed more by its maximal contrast with the preceding 'Waltz' scene, in E major, than by any affinity to the F major with which the act had opened. With this contrast, Puccini effectively depicts the realities of life which the characters become aware of at the end of the act:

Example 1
[Act I: bars 1 - 2]
a)

[Act I: No. 1, bars 41 - 44]
b)

that all great love scenes and expensive nights on the town must come to an end and that, sooner or later, it is time to pay the bill and go home.

There have been equally valorous efforts to show unity of theme or motivic economy in the score, but these have probably raised more questions than they have been capable of answering. It is well known, for instance, that the final bars of the opera, at which the curtain closes on Mimì's corpse (Ex. 2b), are a repetition – in the same key – of the coda to Colline's 'coat aria' (Ex. 2a); yet it would be being uncharitable to Puccini to regard the literal repetition of theme as underlying some deep symbolic significance in the coat, or in the owner's farewell to it. In an age in which our ears have been trained to listen for unifying devices, it is easy to read more into a score than will be of help in understanding it. Thus the 'coat aria' coda, if we are conscious of its origin when we hear it at the end of the opera, runs an interference pattern against the dramatic substance of the final scene. If, however, we take a more neutral view of it, regarding it as a simple linear elaboration of the final tonic, then its recurrence will sound less prominent. Some evidence for this view is offered by the end of another solo scene, 'Mi chiamano Mimì', in which a major-mode version of this linear elaboration brings the lyrical part of the scene to an end (Ex. 2c).

Example 2

[Act IV: No. 19, bars 23-27]
a)

[Act IV: No. 31, bars 9-12]
b)

[Act I: No. 38, bars 21-22]
c)

The identification of characters with specific themes, which certainly helps to explain much thematic recurrence and development in the opera (and also makes Puccini's technique resemble Wagner's more than Verdi's), has also led to a number of problematic interpretations in the score. And because the relationship between a character and a musical motif is often easier to identify (or defend) than the connection between widely separated harmonies, these problems have actually been raised in discussions of the music. The 'coat aria' coda has been dismissed as a fortuitous resemblance; so has the similarity between the main melodic idea of the 'landlord scene' (Ex. 3a) and the great love-theme heard later in the act (Ex. 3b): 'A strange foreshadowing of Rodolfo's big phrase occurs at No. 20 in Act I. During the scene with Benoît, Marcello and the others twit the landlord about his amorous prowess. Perhaps Puccini was unconscious of the undeniable resemblance.'[8]

Example 3

Example 4 [after Maisch, p. 57]
[Act I: No. 41, bars 1 - 2 (transposed to C)]

Example 5
[Act II: No. 21, bars 17 - 20]

Thematic similarity has often been claimed in support of a dramatic relationship. But sometimes it fails to convince, or it overlooks a much greater similarity whose dramatic significance is questionable. Maisch, for instance, argues for a connection between the great love-theme and that of the opening duet in Act IV, which, he claims, is 'easily recognisable' in Ex. 4a and 4b.[9] But he ignores a more obvious source for the later phrase, the middle strain of Musetta's waltz (Ex. 5).

If some of the more easily perceived thematic relationships in the score are difficult to explain in dramatic terms, then perhaps we are reading into the music – or hearing in it – more than we were intended to, and more than is evidently good for us. We have become familiar not only with Puccini's music but also with the compositional techniques of other, more respected musical dramatists, as well as with a number of methods of modern musical analysis. All of this will make the conditions for 'naively listening' to *La bohème* very difficult to imagine, let alone reconstruct. But if the qualities of greatness we sense in Puccini's art are different from those of his predecessors, then we should not be surprised to find that successful methods of investigating his music may be different from those which have won approval elsewhere.

It is sometimes thought that Puccini represents a half-way house between Verdi and Wagner, a composer rooted in the Italian tradition of vocal melody but strongly influenced by Germanic practice in a number of respects: the use of the orchestra as a binding force over long stretches of music, the consistent association of characters with motifs or themes, and the development of a more chromatic palette when required by the needs of the drama. Therefore it might seem appropriate to re-work some of the traditional methods of opera criticism when dealing with one of his scores. But the resulting 'mixture' in Puccini, whatever its origins, must be understood in its own terms. And the failure so far of attempts to describe Puccini's musical language along even the most progressive lines of opera scholarship must lie in the inapplicability of the analytical precepts developed from that scholarship, not in the music itself. The monuments of Verdi and Wagner research have cast deep shadows over Puccini's scores.

The preceding remarks are not intended as a defence of Puccini's art against his critics, but as an illustration of the difficulties encountered in attempting a positive evaluation. If, as it has been suggested, 'few composers have a more easily identifiable style than Puccini's',[10] it must also be true that few defy accurate description more than Puccini's. We are constantly reminded, for instance, of two cardinal features of his musical language: its rich vein of melody, and its attention to orchestral detail. But these are among the most elusive matters of style, much more difficult to comprehend scientifically than, say, the use of harmony, counterpoint, or rhythm. Music theory is capable of telling us much about harmonic and contrapuntal correctness, and it is beginning to recognise the power of rhythm in clarifying areas of pitch construction. But it has never developed an adequate theory of timbre or instrumentation, i.e. a theory capable of explaining why a musical score could be called 'well orchestrated'. And to demonstrate the way in which a self-contained theme is melodically coherent – as, for example, a detailed Schenkerian analysis may show – is a far cry from showing what makes a theme unforgettable. No self-respecting analyst should regard melodic beauty or perfection of orchestral detail as musically insignificant; but when they seem to loom large in a composer's style, the analyst's task is made all the more difficult: to penetrate the surface of the score, and to discover the true basis of its musical integrity.

It might therefore be appropriate to begin with a consideration of one of the most famous, and typically Puccinian, moments in *La bohème*, Mimì's 'Sono andati?' from Act IV, of which it has been said that 'Puccini would not have been Puccini had he not immortalised Mimì's last moments with one of the most inspired melodies that ever sprang into his head'.[11] Much of the power of the melody is the result of its context: by preceding it with a statement of the opening of the Act I love-theme, Puccini uses one of the simplest musical means of shattering Rodolfo's hope, namely, a continuation in C *minor* of a phrase that the listener will have expected to proceed in the major. Thus the very first note and chord of the theme is highly charged, musically and dramatically, despite its being a simple expression of the key of C minor.

The musical integrity of the next eight bars is based on what at first sight may appear to be the most notorious type of contrapuntal progression, an upper line and bass moving together in parallel octaves for an entire octave descent (Ex. 6). But to describe this bass line as 'doubling the melody' is to miss the point: that the same line is functioning both as a melody and as a bass. There is no other bass line to reckon with.

Here is a clear example of an effective passage in a Puccini score – and the melody could not have been 'harmonised' better by another bass line – which contradicts all that we have been taught by conventional theory about the independence of parts. The key to understanding this theme lies in the compass of the descent, which is precisely one octave, so that – to express it in Schenkerian terms – the melody is outlined by the octave descent 8–7–6–5–4–3–2–1

Example 6
[Act IV: No. 21, bars 5-12]

while the bass arpeggiation I–V–I is filled in by passing notes: C (B♭ A♭) G (F E♭ D) C. The fact that the G in the middle of the arpeggiation supports a I_4^6 chord, rather than a true dominant, is of utmost importance here, for it prevents melody and bass from being genuinely parallel. And the clarity of the bass descent, with the arrival of a G marking a point of relative rhythmic repose (as the end of a four-bar phrase), makes a root-position V^7 in the seventh bar unnecessary.

The inner parts provide a powerful force countering the parallel movement in the outer parts, remaining at or around the same pitch level for as long as possible. It is especially interesting to note that the cellos do not enter until the second bar, and that the judicious use of the harp helps to make the initial C in the viola seem to remain at the same pitch level as well as moving down by a step to B♭.

Example 6, continued

If the above example demonstrates that a melody like 'Sono andati?' cannot be understood simply as a great melody *per se* but in relation to its supporting bass-line and harmonies, then it should perhaps now be easier to demonstrate that Puccini's melodic genius is really a gift for writing great *themes*, i.e. melodies considered together with their accompaniments. There is not a single important unaccompanied melody in the score of *La bohème*, and his melodies are harmonised in different ways only when they serve some specific dramatic purpose, i.e. on the rare occasions when they are treated more like Wagnerian leitmotifs. Conversely, it would be equally wrong to consider Puccini's use of harmony independently of the melodies which they support. The composer has often been accused of harmonic short-breathedness, a tendency to bring phrases quickly to a harmonic close instead of striving towards Wagnerian 'endless melody'. But although it is true that his chords are usually not rich in chromaticism, and that his phrases tend to finish on tonic chords more often than one finds in Wagner, the composer's inclination away from normal triadic accompaniment prevents his music from sounding like a series of short segments, each punctuated by a gesture of finality, in keeping with what is sometimes referred to as his 'mosaic' technique of composition.

In the first famous theme from the opera, that associated with Rodolfo the poet, the harmonic stasis in the first six bars (a descent of 5–4–3–2–1 over a tonic pedal) is mitigated by the crucial placement of a single chromatic note, the E♮ in the fourth bar, which converts an ordinary supertonic chord into a secondary dominant (Ex. 7). This change not only causes the unconventional progression V/V–I, which robs the last tonic chord of its sense of finality, but also sets up the resolution of the V/V as the ultimate goal of the theme in bar 15, the chord of F major. The modification of II to V/V in the first phrase of the theme is paralleled by the same procedure in F major in bars 7–10, and this change of course requires a further expansion of the phrase to accommodate the normal supertonic as part of the cadence in F major (Ex. 8). The simplicity of Puccini's melodies – their diatonicism, their conjunct motion, the frequent long stationary patterns within them – cannot in itself determine their memorability: harmony plays a substantial role in organising them for the listener.

A more sophisticated illustration of Puccini's advanced diatonicism

Example 7
[Act I: No. 1, bars 46-51]

is provided by the great love-theme, first heard at Rodolfo's 'Talor dal mio forziere'. As with most of the themes in *La bohème*, its impact can be felt in the first few bars. Again it is the participation of the bass line which makes the beginning so effective. What might have seemed a pedestrian melody, were it harmonised with ordinary tonic and dominant chords in the first two bars, is given an extra thrust by the supporting 'arpeggiations' (in the Schenkerian sense) in the bass line, A♭–C and B♭–E♭, so that the crucial descent of the melody proceeds in team with the bass (Ex. 9).

In the next bar the same procedure is accelerated, from the minim to the crotchet level, so that from each of the primary chords a third-related chord branches off: note that in both bars 1–2 and bar 3, the 'main' chords flank the secondary branchings. It would be easy enough to label the third chord of bar 3 as a secondary dominant,

Example 8
[Act I: No. 1, bars 52-60]

RODOLFO

pen - so a quel pol - tro - ne d'un vec - chio ca - mi -

net - to ingan - na - to . - re _____ che vi - ve in

poco rit.   a Tempo

o - zio co - me un gran _____ si - gnor!

and thus to 'explain' it as a simple modification of the chord immediately following it. But as a four-part sonority, it has a particular expressiveness of its own, and a tonal ambiguity that enables it to function as a supertonic of a different key, C minor. In the continuation of his theme, Puccini realises this other possibility for the chord, and he exploits its potential further by suspending a note in

the vocal part above it (bar 7, second beat); the marking 'poco allargando' highlights this chord still more, calling the listener's attention to a sonority heard only moments before in a different harmonic context.

There can be no doubt about Puccini's repetition of themes and motifs as a way of organising the score of *La bohème*, and this has sometimes led to unfavourable comparisons with Wagner's use of leitmotifs. But whereas Wagner built the grandest architectural designs from an elaborate *system* of motifs, all of which are derived

– in the literal sense of the word – from the most basic elements of musical language such as common chords and rhythmic figures, and which is applied consistently and completely in his mature works, Puccini's elements of musical identification are much more elaborate utterances, and do not lend themselves to the normal Wagnerian methods of transformation such as change of mode, decomposition, juxtaposition, or contrapuntal combination with other motifs. We have already seen the dangers of imputing transformation of one theme into another in the course of the opera. There are, of course, examples of motifs used in different ways to move the drama along. The theme of the Bohemians from the very beginning of the opera, which is itself based on the repetition of a few motivic cells, lends itself ideally to variation in other contexts: in Act IV, which has rightly been seen as a recapitulation of earlier music from the opera, the Bohemians' theme is appropriately shortened by the omission of some of this repetition.

The theme at the beginning of Act II, which depicts the Latin Quarter festivities, is anticipated in Act I when the four young men decide to dine out on Christmas Eve. This would seem too obvious an example of thematic repetition to be worthy of analytical commentary; but it is instructive in that it clearly points up the difference between Wagner's and Puccini's use of themes. The leitmotifs of the former composer are too short for early, isolated statements of them to be felt as leading up to their main use. In the *Ring*, for instance, the introduction of the 'sword' motif at the end of *Das Rheingold* and the singing of the motif of 'redemption' in the last act of *Die Walküre* (by Sieglinde, although it is later associated with Brünnhilde) are problematic: they cannot really be assimilated into the musico-dramatic design upon first hearing of the cycle. But the extensiveness of the 'Latin Quarter' theme enables Puccini to present it in Act I, at a low dynamic level and with legato articulation, in circumstances under which it will be understood as a premonition of a later statement of the theme – though we have not yet heard the beginning of Act II. The effect is akin to an off-stage statement of a theme followed by its 'on-stage' presentation (i.e. by the pit orchestra), and runs completely contrary to our normal explanation of two playings of a theme: that the second is a repetition or variation of the first.

The fact that Puccini's themes are longer than Wagner's leitmotifs does not prevent them from undergoing any melodic or harmonic

Example 10
[Act IV: No. 2, bars 13-15]

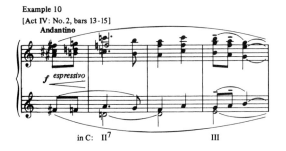

in C: II⁷   III

transformation whatever: rather, transformation is not exploited systematically but is used only sparingly. The two themes from *La bohème* which are given new 'meaning' by such transformation – and not until Act IV – are the love-theme and Mimì's motif. As an introduction to the duet between Rodolfo and Marcello, the love-theme is given a wistfulness by its being harmonised with two minor chords in place of the major tonic and dominant chords. This establishes a mood of regret in which the two Bohemians can lament the absence of their loved ones (Ex. 10). These two chords not only mitigate the effect of the repetition of a familiar theme, but also prepare us for a statement about love that is considerably lower in temperature than any heard earlier in the opera.

Later on, the recurrence of the same theme, at the end of a climactic musical phrase in which Rodolfo and Mimì express their ecstasy in being reunited, is harmonised in another way. From the new harmonic setting, the listener is able to recognise that the characters' happiness is not going to last very long: the harmony, instead of opening out from the tonic to the dominant, now closes up towards the tonic (Ex. 11).

This transformation of the love-theme, timed to mark the beginning of the denouement of the drama, has been preceded by the only instance of a truly Wagnerian development, the reharmonisation of Mimì's motif as the heroine is brought into the garret for the last time (Ex. 12). The references to a Tristanesque sound world with its diminished and half-diminished seventh-chords (and a prominent English horn) are unmistakable, and the special 'symphonically developmental' qualities of the passage have been noted elsewhere. But what makes the passage compelling is that it is the *only* moment in the opera which is developed in this way. Mimì's motif, which is musically as frail as the character it portrays, could be subjected to intervallic distortion or harmonic reinterpretation at

Example 11
[Act IV: No. 15, bars 9-12]

any number of points in the opera. But whereas the failure of a composer to realise the full potential of his musical material might in some circumstances be taken as a criticism of his compositional technique, the very absence of development of Mimì's motif until the final scene of the opera is an essential ingredient of the success of the passage in question.

I should like to end this discussion with one illustration of musical continuity in *La bohème*. As has been stated before, the apparent

Example 12
[Act IV: No. 13, bars 38–45]

shortness of breath in Puccini's harmony – itself a condition of his use of material that strives towards the status of self-contained theme – has led some critics to fault his music, and motivated others to seek another explanation, according to which the ideals of an opera based on the juxtaposition of themes can be seen to be compatible with those of a through-composed score:

Puccini creates continuity not by interweaving his themes but largely by juxtaposition. And this brings us to his characteristic mosaics in which diminutive melodic 'squares', not longer than a bar and often even less, are repeated, varied or treated sequentially, after which the same process is continued with the next 'square'. This technique may have been making a virtue of necessity, for Puccini's melodic invention tends to be short-winded.[12]

The analogy to 'mosaic' technique seems more a way of avoiding a discussion of the binding forces in Puccini's scores than an explanation of their cohesiveness; yet it is certainly in keeping with conventional critical appreciation of Puccini, and probably also with what is generally understood by the composer's self-professed concern for 'the little things'. But a large problem in the understanding of continuity in Puccini is that the normal procedures we have learnt to recognise in music – the interruption of a cadence, elision, 'progressive' harmony (in the real sense of the term) – are not the distinguishing features of the compositional technique of a score like *La bohème*.

I have already given one instance of Puccini's unconventional continuity, the prefacing of 'Sono andati?' by the first four bars of the love-theme. A more extended example of Puccini's skill may be seen in the duet which concludes Act I ('O soave fanciulla'), which is also based on the love-theme and forms a dramatic conclusion to a scene reaching back over two arias and some long stretches of conversation. Here the love-theme is used to introduce itself, so to speak: a four-bar phrase sets up the key of A major, but this is soon reinterpreted as a prelude to another four-bar phrase which aims at a different tonality, E major. When both Mimì and Rodolfo sing together in octaves for the first time ('Ah! tu sol comandi, amor!' / 'Fremon già nell'anima'), the preceding music gives the impression that harmonies underlying this theme have been altered, i.e. that the tonality of E major still governs bar 9 and that the A major chord is a subdominant (Ex. 13). But Puccini proceeds with his theme in its original form, so that after four more bars the listener must be forced to understand everything from bar 9 onwards – retrospectively – as in the key of A major, i.e. that the chord in bar 9 was indeed a tonic. A single bar of uncertainty is enough to carry what might otherwise have been dubbed an excessive repetition of a familiar tune. It is a passage like this which reminds us of the judgment that, in Puccini, 'the musical utterance is kept at high tension, almost without repose, as though it were to be feared that if the audiences were not continually excited they would go to sleep'.[13] I hope that this illustration might be accepted as evidence that, for Puccini, the art of musical continuity lies in something more sophisticated than giving his listener a periodic poke in the ribs.

The activity we call 'musical analysis' is nowadays defined in broad terms, and encompasses a far wider range of investigative methods

Example 13
[Act I: No. 41, bars 1-12]

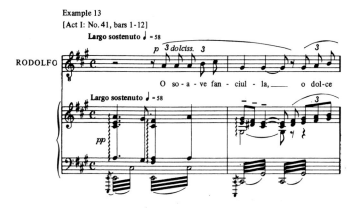

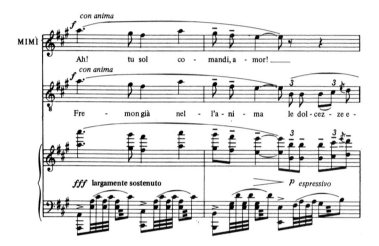

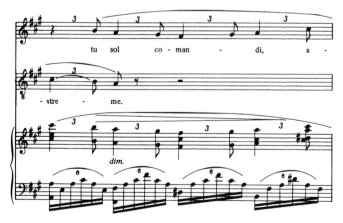

Example 13, continued

than ever before. Yet most attempts at it are still directed toward finding unity in musical works of art, or at least strong evidence of the application of a system. In even as modern, wide-ranging and perceptive a study as Kerman's *Opera as Drama*, the search is for universal truths more than for an understanding of individual masterpieces: in the end, one remembers the names of the composers Monteverdi, Gluck, Mozart, Verdi and Wagner better than the titles of operas by other composers: *Fidelio, Carmen, Boris Godunov*.

If Puccini failed, in his collected work, to establish a valid aesthetic of opera composition, or to live up to those of his great predecessors, then the enormous success which many of his stage works have enjoyed must be the result of an extraordinary ability to focus on the problems relating to the single art-work, without the benefits of a governing system or of elements of what one may wish to call a steadily maturing 'personal style'. On close inspection, we might even find that, for instance, 'Un bel dì' works along very different lines from those of its precursor in *La bohème*, 'Sono andati?'; indeed, the results of this essay may not be of much help in explaining the musical rightness of a *Butterfly*, or a *Tosca*. But if we concern ourselves less with discovering unity in Puccini's scores, or consistency in the application of a system, or even features common to many of his operas, and instead follow Tovey in the search for *integrity* in the individual art-work, we shall probably be in a better position to discover the elements of mastery which inform a score like *La bohème*.

6 *Puccini at work: a note on the autograph score*

The autograph score of *La bohème* stands as awesome confirmation that Puccini was an obsessive reviser and polisher of his work – a fact fully in evidence already from his dealings with librettists. Bound in four large, unwieldy volumes, the score is a palimpsest of rare proportions and complexity. There are at least six kinds of paper, some or all of them reflecting different stages of composition, with single leaves, or occasionally much larger gatherings, 'tipped in' sometime after the basic layer was written. In some places, the reader must deal with as many as three independent paginations. At each stage corrections are numerous, and hardly a page goes by without substantial evidence of revision. But in spite of this extensive reworking, the score is far from being a complete record of the composition history of *La bohème*, and before considering it in detail, we must examine something of the larger context of the work's musical genesis.

So far as we can tell, the music of Puccini's mature operas underwent three main creative stages. The first was a 'continuity draft', written on the minimum number of staves, usually containing no more than the essential musical lines, the harmony, and an approximate indication of the accompanimental texture. We have been able to trace only a small fragment of the *La bohème* 'continuity draft': a single folio of the passage immediately preceding Mimì's 'Sono andati?' in Act IV, and of the opening bars of Colline's 'Vecchia zimarra' from a little earlier in the same act (the verso of this folio is reproduced as Fig. 5).[1] The date, '12. 12. 90cinque' (12 December 1895) and the fact that Puccini signed the folio and decorated it with a humorous self-portrait, suggest that it was given away as a memento, possibly during the celebrations that followed the completion of the autograph score (the final page of which is dated 10 December 1895). There are many interesting details on these two pages, and a complete transcription and commentary

5 Sketch of a passage from Act IV

would be a most useful addition to our knowledge of Puccini. What may impress the reader most forcibly, however, is the essentially finished state of the material. Most of the alterations Puccini would subsequently make involve small details: one sees less evidence of a 'creative' struggle, more of an 'executive' one. This strengthens the impression that the former activity occurred primarily as the libretto took shape. But there is one striking feature, namely that the passage leading up to 'Sono andati?' (and presumably the aria itself) was sketched a tone higher than the final version. The decision to transpose it occurred while the passage was still in sketch form; on the first page the three bars leading up to no. 20 are altered and the passage from no. 20 marked *in sol*. Whether this represents a 'surface detail' is of course a matter of some debate; certainly the ease with which Puccini could effect such major transpositions must say something about his whole attitude to tonality. We shall return to this topic shortly.

The second compositional stage was the autograph score, in which Puccini attempts to arrive at a 'definitive' text. And in the case of earlier nineteenth-century opera composers such as Verdi, the story of the musical text would largely end there; any future alterations (those for instance made after the first performance) would be recorded in the autograph, which thus remained the authoritative record of the composer's work. But, as with so many late nineteenth- and early twentieth-century artists, Puccini was evidently allowed by his publisher to regard page proofs of the piano vocal score, perhaps also of the orchestral score, as a further opportunity to make large and small revisions, with the result that in many places the eventual published work diverges widely from the autograph. In some cases, revision of the proofs ran parallel to composition of other parts in the autograph. We know, for example, from Ricordi's unusually complete publication records (held in their so-called *libroni*) that engraving of the vocal score of *La bohème* began on 4 September 1895, long before the autograph was completed (in December 1895).[2]

Unfortunately, the *Bohème* proofs which mark this crucial third stage of composition are not available for study, and perhaps no longer exist. We do, however, have a fascinating glimpse into what they might contain. In the week of *La bohème*'s premiere in Turin, Ricordi's Milanese house journal, the *Gazzetta musicale di Milano*, published as a musical supplement a piano-vocal score of Musetta's 'Quando me'n vo' '.[3] As we see from Fig. 6, this version differs in several important respects from the final text, most noticeably by having no countersubject in bars 3 to 4ff., by including a bar of 4/4 at the start of p. 3 (in the final version this pause is marked by a *ritenuto*), and by lacking the closing vocal flourish up to high *b*.

There are also a host of minor performance details which differ from the version we know today. Some of these may have greater claims to authenticity than the current musical text, and underline the fact that we badly need a 'critical edition' of the opera. Given the current state of the sources, there remains some doubt whether such an edition can be successfully completed. If our knowledge of Puccini's proof revisions to later operas provides a reliable guide, the retouchings to 'Quando me'n vo'' may be slight in comparison to other passages in the score.[4]

To sum up, it would seem as though each of the three compositional stages we have isolated would, if only they were available, offer the commentator interested in musical genesis an embarrassment of riches. In the present circumstances, we can do no more than mention briefly a number of areas in which the autograph score (our one complete source) casts particular light on Puccini's working methods and, by extension, his priorities as a musical dramatist. In each case, the points raised involve matters basic to the composer's language: his attitude to large-scale tonal planning; his concern with dramatic pacing; and finally his complex, ambivalent reaction to the relationship of words and music.

Our first example, mentioned briefly by William Ashbrook in his monograph on the composer,[5] involves another case of transposition, this time from the latter part of Act I. In the autograph, the passage from rehearsal no. 26 (Rodolfo: 'Si sente meglio') to no. 31 (Rodolfo: 'Chi son?') was originally written a half-step lower, thus making the opening section of 'Che gelida manina' in C major rather than D flat major. There may well have been pragmatic reasons for the change – an accommodation to the tessitura of the singers, for example – but there are also two interesting long-range consequences. On the one hand, Act I both begins and ends in C major, and the arrival of that key in the closing moments of the act coincides with a recapitulation of 'Che gelida manina'. If the main statement of 'Che gelida' had remained in C, it might encourage us to regard that key as one of special importance in the act. On the other hand, the entire opera ends in D flat (written C sharp), a key also articulated through a recapitulation of 'Che gelida manina'. This, it might be argued, creates an even larger tonal symmetry or cross-reference (one backed up by numerous motivic and dramatic parallels) between the close of Act IV and the meeting of the two lovers in Act I. But, both in this case and in that of the sketch transposition, the crucial point is that there are equally valid possibilities.

6   Early printed version of Musetta's 'Quando me'n vo' '

_cul _ te bel.tà. Così l'ef _ flu _ vio del de _ sì _ o... m'ag-

_gi _ ra,............... fe_li _ ce mi fa,............ fe_li _ ce

mi fa!........ E tu che sa _ i...........

... che me mo-ri e ti strug - gi, ... da me tan-to ri-

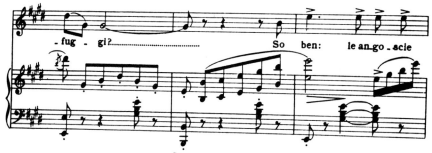

-fug - gi? .... So ben: le an-go-scie

tue non le vuoi dir .... non le vuoi dir, so

ben .... ma ti sen - -ti mo-rir!

It is probably fruitless to search for large-scale tonal constructs in Puccini, but it does not necessarily follow that he was indifferent to such matters; indeed, tonality undoubtedly functions as an important force on a more occasional level, and could be manipulated with some subtlety. The present example is a good case in point: by transposing the passages in Act I and Act IV, the composer did not obliterate (or create) essential tonal relationships; he merely replaced one set of possible connections and reverberations with another, thus altering slightly our perception of the entire work.

In documenting the struggles Puccini had with dramatic pacing, a matter that obsessed him throughout his career, the autograph can often be very helpful, as the presence of different paper types sometimes allows us to establish which portions of the score are late additions. By far the most complex case is Act IV, particularly toward the end, where there are hardly two or three consecutive folios of the same type, suggesting that Puccini constructed the act in a piecemeal fashion. The considerable number of letters from Puccini to his librettists concerning last-minute changes to Act IV further confirms this. The second act is also challenging, showing as it does a gradual and (one would guess) painful expansion; we have already seen how this section, originally planned as a grand *concertato finale* to Act I, eventually became a fully-fledged act. As we shall see below, the revisions continued even into later printed editions of the score (see pp. 119–20). Act I is the most uniform of the four in paper type, and thus apparently in conception, but it still contains interesting insertions, one of which may serve to illustrate the general principles involved. In an early layer of the autograph, the Bohemians' 'Dividiam!' (no. 22 bar 10) led immediately to Rodolfo's 'Io resto' (no. 23), with the entire passage beginning at Marcello's 'Là ci son beltà' added later in different paper. Puccini clearly felt that more time was needed to effect the essential 'modulation' of mood from bohemian riotousness to the sentimental meeting of the two lovers. It is therefore understandable that the additional passage is, for the most part, harmonically static: this emphasises the slowing pace and links it with a series of tension-releasing cadential prolongations which underpin the crucial dramatic transition.

But the insight the autograph offers into Puccini's attitude to word setting is perhaps most revealing. From letters to Giacosa and Illica, we know that there were occasions on which Puccini conceived music without reference to any particular words in the

Example 1
[Autograph f. 124r (erased)]

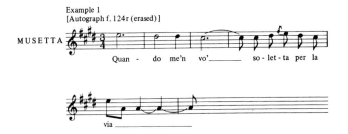

MUSETTA

Quan - do me'n vo'_____ so - let - ta per la

via _____

libretto. The correspondence shows two moments in which the composer made up his own doggerel verse as an indication to his hapless librettists of precisely the types of lines he required.[6] By far the most famous and oft-quoted anecdote on this subject is reported by Puccini's friend, sometime librettist, and early biographer, Giuseppe Adami:

[. . .] in his musical work, he [Puccini] feels an impetus and excitement that Giacosa does not feel. He has his 'busy hours in which the hand is slow to follow the mind'. Having found situations and scenes, if the verses are lacking, he sets the situations to music, as he always did, as he always will do. The words will come later and can adapt to already fixed rhythms.

From time to time he makes a trip to Milan. He needs the verses for Musetta. He has already composed the famous waltz. He sings it again and again to Giacosa, pacing up and down his studio in Foro Bonaparte like a Napoleon who must overcome every obstacle, including that of the obstinate musical ear of his great collaborator. To make things clear, he writes the metre he wants:

'Look, you must do me some verses that correspond to these words: *Cocoricò, cocoricò, bistecca ...*' The poet turns pale, shudders, groans. But the next day Musetta's lines are adapted precisely to the music:

'Quando me'n vo – quando me'n vo – soletta ... '

Giacomo pockets the verses. He smiles, satisfied:

'Well then. Now we're there ... As you see, it was really so simple.'[7]

It is easy to see the popularity of this tale; it wittily and succinctly illustrates Puccini's exigencies when he had fixed musical ideas and needed words to 'clothe' them. Perhaps a little too much so: the autograph makes it plain that Adami – not for the first time – sacrificed accuracy at the altar of narrative force. At the start of 'Quando me'n vo'' Puccini originally set the first line of the text with no repetition of the verbal incipit (Ex. 1). Only at some later time did he decide to repeat the opening phrase of text, presumably to give Musetta's line a greater feeling of breathlessness

Example 2
[Act II, No. 21]

MUSETTA

Quan - do me'n vo'_____ quan - do me'n vo so -

let - ta per la via

and skittishness (Ex. 2). Adami's essential point remains, of course: this was a passage in which the words were written for music, rather than directly inspiring it.[8]

A more lengthy and extreme example of the same process occurs in the Mimì–Marcello duet at the beginning of Act III. An extended section of Mimì's part was recast at the autograph stage, but with the original version still clearly legible. If this first version is placed side by side with that of the vocal score the musical differences are relatively slight until the final moments, when Mimì's grand climax, high *c* and emphatic cadence are replaced by a much more abrupt descent into parlando (Ex. 3). Much more important, however, is the fact that the relationship between the words and music has been fundamentally altered, as each phrase of the libretto has been 'moved on' by one bar. This shows a remarkable indifference on the composer's part to one level of close interaction between verbal and musical gesture.

Furthermore, the nature of the change stimulates us to make some stylistic observations: it is only because of the extreme rhythmic flexibility of Puccini's musical language that such 'accommodations' can be made convincingly, that there is even the possibility of adjusting words and music so grossly while still preserving convincing verbal declamation. It would be a bold person who contended that the second text setting is any less persuasive than the first. Indeed, the very fact that such mechanical changes were made should cause us to ponder precisely where Puccini's musical and dramatic priorities lay. Certainly, as we all know, he was fanatically concerned with the words. The libretto, as we have seen earlier, was a fundamental – perhaps *the* fundamental – creative stage; but the struggle was basically one of discovering structure, of establishing the precise relative durations – the ordered juxtapositions that make good drama. When it came to

Example 3

individual lines of text, this concern for words – if we are to learn from Ex. 3 – seemed to vanish.

It is well to end this brief survey on such a cautionary note. Our final impression from the autograph score is that Puccini magnificently vindicates Edison's adage about the relative amounts of inspiration vs. perspiration required by a creative genius. Puccini perspired. And in one sense this can be profoundly shocking. *La bohème* is, for many of us, an opera so familiar that we cannot remember a first hearing, perhaps not even a first performance. It seems always to have existed, full-grown. The autograph's patchwork quilt of experiments, rejections, additions and refinements challenges this view on every page, forcing us to react critically and analytically to a work as familiar as it is elusive.

7 A brief stage history

BY WILLIAM ASHBROOK

A comprehensive stage history of *La bohème* from its *prima assoluta* in Turin on 1 February 1896 would involve a labour to make Hercules quail. The result, assuming that all the evidence could be retrieved, would more than fill this volume. *La bohème* is one of the most frequently performed of all operas, and these performances range from productions in the leading opera houses around the world to the efforts of the most modest 'pre-professional' workshops. A selective – and necessarily somewhat arbitrary – overview of the stage history of *La bohème* is all one can attempt in the present circumstances; such a survey has the merit, if not of completeness, at least of revealing a good deal about the practice, the prejudice and the taste of those on both sides of the footlights, and can chart the emergence of the work as an apparently indestructible segment of the basic repertory. The following, then, will concentrate on two elements of the opera's reception: first, the initial performances in various Italian centres – the crucial phase that established its success; and second, the ways in which *La bohème* came to function within the repertory, taking as examples its early history at Covent Garden in London and the Metropolitan in New York.

I

The world premiere of *La bohème* took place exactly three years later than Puccini's previous opera, *Manon Lescaut*, and in the same theatre, the Teatro Regio of Turin (see Figs. 7, 8 and 9). What is more, Cesira Ferrani, who had been Puccini's first Manon, was again on hand to create the leading female role.[1] Behind these apparent coincidences one can discern the calculations of Puccini's publisher, Giulio Ricordi, ever concerned to achieve the most fortunate circumstances for launching a new and potentially valu-

7 Original set for Act II by Riccardo Salvadori

8   Costume design for the first Mimì
(Adolf Hohenstein)

9   Costume design for the first Rodolfo
(Adolf Hohenstein)

able property. Puccini, operating on the principle that nothing leaves one so vulnerable as success, was less sanguine about the prospects of this second assault on Turin: he disliked the acoustics of the Regio and felt he was tempting fate by giving two consecutive *prime* on the same stage (CP 137). The difference of opinion between publisher and composer extended even to matters of casting. Puccini had apparently insisted on an illustrious (and expensive) group of singers; Ricordi warned against depending on superstars and 'plunging opera into bankruptcy':

Yes, there was a time when everything depended on virtuosity of the throat, and one had to have specialists: for *Sonnambula* and *Norma*, etc. Today opera needs a homogeneous cast, the more intelligent the better! It is not the artist who is responsible for the success of the opera, but the opera itself. [. . .] Let us put together a cast that is homogeneous, willing, and animated by enthusiasm, and we will obtain what is needed.   (CP 142)

As we shall see, both approaches proved successful: at some points in its history, *La bohème* has indeed been sustained by the patronage of virtuoso singers; but it has also proved durable as a 'company' work, in which the strengths of the ensemble help to mitigate any individual weaknesses.

Puccini approached the premiere with some trepidation. To be sure, the Regio had a dynamic new conductor in the young Arturo Toscanini, but neither the expectations of the audience nor the cast of the opera were propitious. Toscanini had opened the Regio's season with the first Italian performance of *Götterdämmerung*, and audiences inured to evenings of Wagnerian gravity and length must have felt a little shell-shocked when *La bohème* had them back on the streets in a little over two hours. Moreover, the cast was not ideal: the Rodolfo was having vocal difficulties, even with most of his role transposed down; the Marcello, brought in at the last minute to replace an inept predecessor, was in Puccini's opinion a 'dog'; and the outstanding Musetta of subsequent productions, Rosina Storchio, had not yet been found (CP 142, 156).

Given these handicaps, the mixed reception of the opera is not surprising. Puccini was called out for only three curtain calls after the end of Act I – Act II pleased even less. But the public responded warmly to the conclusion: 'Mimì's death scene, listened to with the most ardent attention and in the greatest silence, created the most favourable impression. The public jumped to its feet in great enthusiasm. Puccini presented himself five times. Total, fifteen curtain calls'.[2]

The critics in particular did not disappoint Puccini's sense of foreboding. Perhaps the most severe judgment came from Carlo Bersezio in the *Gazzetta piemontese*:

La bohème, since it makes no great impression on the soul of its audience, will leave no large imprint on the history of our lyric stage. And it will be well if the composer, considering it as the error of a moment, will proceed vigorously ['gagliardamente'] on his proper path, and if he will persuade himself that this has been a brief detour in the road of art.[3]

Reviewers who journeyed to Turin for the occasion from other Italian cities were, on the whole, less harsh with the new opera, but we should bear in mind that their presence was – to some extent at least – arranged by Ricordi, whose house journal, the *Gazzetta musicale di Milano*, served as a propaganda machine for the works published by his company. A letter to the librettist Illica from

Rome, where Ricordi was supervising rehearsals for the second production of the opera, hints that there had been some sort of cabal
against *La bohème* at Turin (CP 157), and Puccini voiced less veiled
suspicions to one of his early biographers.[4] Certainly, there was a
marked difference of opinion between the critics and the audience,
as several of the former noted. The Milanese correspondent of
Fanfulla, whose two early reactions to *La bohème* head Ricordi's
initial symposium of reviews in the *Gazzetta* (6 February 1896), is
representative of favourable opinion, and his second piece is clearly
written with a view to defusing the hostile remarks of some Turinese
critics with a polemic of his own:

Between the two litigants, I say that the public is right. Free from precon-
ceptions and from systems, from methods and schools, and from all those
other scientific devilries which have nothing to do with fantasy or inspiration, the public of the Teatro Regio, which, as I telegraphed yesterday,
warmly and enthusiastically applauded Puccini's new opera, today shrugs
its shoulders at reading all those fine and incomprehensible things that our
gentlemen critics write: and they will return this evening to fill the theatre
and applaud [. . .]

A considered retrospective of the *prima*, attributed to Toscanini,
expresses a similar view:

Not one of those critics had understood that *La bohème* was a completely
new opera, as much in the orchestra as on stage. They were not aware they
had heard a masterpiece and demolished it without thinking about it. It
could not have been otherwise, for, although they were at heart worthy
men who – I believe – acted in good faith, they were still a little too much
tied to existing traditions. Puccini took it very badly; it left him like a rag.
Luckily, the public, which was not one of the easiest to win over, had understood quickly and well, and set things to rights. In the end it is always the
judgment of the public that counts.[5]

The accuracy of Toscanini's estimate was demonstrated even during
the first run of performances at the Regio. A poster for Sunday,
22 March 1896 announced: 'definitely the last popular performance
at reduced prices and of the season' – the twenty-fourth in less than
two months.[6] Puccini certainly felt that the public had vindicated
him in spite of the critics: 'What a marvellous outcome in Turin!
Twenty-four performances – what will Bersezio and Co. say?'
(CP 159).

   La bohème's second round of performances took place in Rome
at the Teatro Argentina. The conductor of the *prima* on 23 February
was Edoardo Mascheroni, and the cast included Angelica

Pandolfini (Mimì), the twenty-year-old Rosina Storchio (Musetta), Giovanni Apostolu (Rodolfo) and Maurizio Bensaude (Marcello). The critical reaction, duly reprinted in Ricordi's *Gazzetta*, was generally favourable, yet there was a consensus that Act II (at the Café Momus) was markedly less satisfactory than the other three. A representative example of this dissatisfaction was reported by Gino Monaldi on 24 February in *Il popolo romano*, a review that subsequently reappeared in the *Gazzetta*:

Only the second act does not manifest this artistic fusion [of musical thought and stage business], and it is broken up here and there by the episodic nature of the action – all colourful and descriptive. But the fault is not so much that of Puccini as of his librettists, who have tried, without estimating the difficulty of it, to reproduce upon the stage the sights of the so-called Latin Quarter. [. . .] Puccini, overwhelmed and beset by certain effects of scenic realism has taxed his imagination, which has responded and produced – even with success – such moments as Musetta's *valzer*, the chorus of Parpignol and the military music at the end: most genial musical effects. But the music of this act, taken altogether, remained nevertheless unequal to the visual aspects of the scene.[7]

Monaldi may have realised that this second act – in the form in which it then existed – was unusually short, even shorter than the version we know today. Puccini had originally planned a *duettino* between Rodolfo and Mimì for the Café Momus scene, and then excised it (see p. 44); undoubtedly the reaction of the Roman critics spurred him to consider changes (CP 159), and ultimately to insert another number, the 'bonnet' episode, just before Musetta's first entrance.[8]

But before the problem could be corrected there was the pressure of forthcoming productions: first at the San Carlo in Naples on 14 March 1896, then at the Teatro Carolino in Palermo on 13 April, the latter with Leopoldo Mugnone (a favourite of Puccini) as conductor. It is not clear whether Puccini was present for the Neapolitan opening, but he certainly supervised the Sicilian production (CP 160, 161). To the best of my knowledge, the 'bonnet' episode was first included in Act II for this occasion, which was also (perhaps not fortuitously) the first to arouse that response of unbridled enthusiasm that the Italians call *fanatismo*; innumerable curtain calls prolonged the performance until one in the morning, and when the audience refused to leave, Mugnone was forced to repeat the last scene, even though some of the orchestra had already left and the singers had changed to street clothes. These performances in Palermo set the seal on the future of *La bohème* in Italy.

Thirteen and a half months after its introduction, and after further productions in various Italian cities, *La bohème* finally came to La Scala. The delay suggests that Ricordi felt a need for caution in approaching the theatre with which his firm had the closest connections. Puccini attended the first performance on 15 March 1897. The conductor was again Leopoldo Mugnone, with Angelica Pandolfini repeating her Roman Mimì, Camilla Pasini, the first Musetta from Turin, and Fernando de Lucia, who had sung Rodolfo in Naples; the Colline, Gennaro Berenzone, was another veteran of the Roman performances. The conclusion seems obvious: both Puccini and Ricordi had regarded the performances of 1896, at least in part, as a means of identifying the most desirable elements to form a cast for the all-important production at La Scala. There was a total of sixteen performances before the season ended in the middle of April.

Before considering the fortunes of *La bohème* outside Italy, it is instructive to examine certain aspects of the opera's Italian career in the next quarter-century, roughly up to the time of Puccini's death in 1924. At the Regio in Turin, where the work was first performed, *La bohème* was mounted in 1898, again conducted by Toscanini, for a further round of fifteen performances. Ten years were to elapse before it was repeated in a single, apparently disastrously miscast performance led by Tullio Serafin. In December 1916 there were five further performances, benefits for the army, and in some of them Bonci sang Rodolfo under Mugnone's direction. Then the opera had to wait until 1927 to be staged again, after which the frequency of its appearances increases.

We can observe a similar pattern at La Scala. After its introduction in 1897, the opera returned in 1900–1 to open the Carnival season, with Toscanini directing Caruso in his debut on that stage. That 'edition' achieved a total of ten performances. *La bohème* did not appear on the *cartellone* of La Scala again until 3 January 1916, when Gino Marinuzzi led nine performances in which the Mimì was Rosina Storchio, and Bonci and de Lucia shared the role of Rodolfo. In 1923 there were six further performances. The following December it was staged again, this time preceded by a concert in Puccini's memory conducted by Toscanini. At La Scala, too, the frequency of performances accelerated following the composer's death.

This pattern also holds for certain other theatres north of the Apennines. At the Teatro Comunale in Bologna, for instance, *La bohème* was first heard on 4 November 1896, where Toscanini directed a run of twenty performances. There is no further trace of the opera until 1916, when Bologna was one of the stops on the Marinuzzi–Bonci tour to raise money for disabled soldiers. A third production began on 8 December 1924, shortly after Puccini's death. The statistics for the Teatro Regio of Parma are similar. *La bohème* opened on 28 January 1898 and continued in a run of thirteen performances featuring Salomea Krusceniski as Mimì. It returned that autumn and again in the 1903–4 season, after which there was a hiatus until 1925.

A different attitude toward the work prevailed in southern Italy. At the San Carlo in Naples, for example, *La bohème* was staged in thirteen different seasons during Puccini's lifetime, and returned for twenty-two seasons in the ensuing thirty-five years. Although the Teatro Petruzzelli in Bari played much shorter *stagioni* than the San Carlo, *La bohème* was also mounted with regularity. The opera was sung there in 1903, its inaugural year, and returned in 1905, 1907, 1910, 1916, 1918, 1920, and 1923. The next performance took place on 7 February 1925 as a memorial to Puccini, with Act III prefaced by the *marcia funebre* from Catalani's *Loreley*.

This discrepancy between the frequency of *La bohème*'s revivals in the north and south of Italy before 1924 is puzzling, particularly since it disappears after Puccini's death. One can only conjecture. Perhaps the opera initially lost ground amid the more adventurous and cosmopolitan repertory of the north, whereas it immediately became a mainstay in the more conservative, predominantly Italian repertory of the south. The less prosperous southern audiences may also have felt a special bond with Puccini's impecunious Bohemians; this in turn might explain the favourable early reception of the opera in North and South America, where a significant number of the audience were immigrants from southern Italy. It may be that in the north of Italy there was also some resentment of Puccini's royalties and mode of living, whereas after his death he came to be considered part of the country's cultural heritage. Economic conditions during the depression, World War II and after undoubtedly contributed to *La bohème*'s increased popularity, forcing houses to mount 'safe' operas certain to draw large audiences in order to defray the costs of more esoteric ventures. Whatever the causes, *La bohème* is now one of the most frequently staged operas in all parts of Italy. To cite one random piece of evidence: at the Teatro Regio in Parma, by 1979 it had reached second place behind *Aïda* in total number of performances.

II

The first production of *La bohème* outside Italy took place in Buenos Aires on 16 June 1896 with further premieres in Alexandria, Moscow and Lisbon in early 1897. But the opera was slow to establish itself in England, Germany, Austria, and France, making its initial success in secondary theatres (with translated librettos) before arriving at major houses. The first English performance of *The Bohemians* occurred on 27 April 1897 in Manchester, with Puccini in attendance. This Carl Rosa Company production included Alice Esty (Mimì), Bessie Macdonald (Musetta), Robert Cunningham (Rodolfo) and William Paull (Marcello); it reached Covent Garden the following October with a slightly different cast.[9] German audiences were first introduced to *Die Boheme* on 22 June 1897 at Krolls Theater in Berlin, with Puccini on hand; the Austrian premiere took place on 5 October, at the Theater an der Wien and prompted a scathing review by Eduard Hanslick (see pp. 133–5). Leoncavallo's rival opera had been accepted first by the more august stage of the Hofoper, and it was not until 1903 that Gustav Mahler granted access to Puccini's version in a production that included Selma Kurz (Mimì) and Franz Naval (Rodolfo). Finally, *La Vie de Bohème* was launched at the Opéra-Comique on 13 June 1898 under the supervision of Puccini, who hated Paris (CP 185) but must have been delighted by his opera's reception. Conducted by Alexandre Luigini and led by a cast that included Julia Guiraudon as Mimi and Alphonse Maréchal as Rodolphe, the production made a profound impression (see the review of Camille Bellaigue, pp. 135–7). So successful has *La bohème* been at the Opéra-Comique that it celebrated its thousandth performance in May 1951.

The premiere of *La bohème* in England, as we have seen, was given by a travelling company (the Carl Rosa) rather than by that country's most prestigious opera house. The same is true for the United States: the American premiere took place on 14 October 1897 at the Los Angeles Theater, performed by the Royal Italian Grand Opera, a group that was also responsible for the opera's first New York performance on 16 May 1898 at Wallack's Theater in Herald Square. To establish the work in the major houses of both countries there was need of a stout champion – a function soon fulfilled in the ample person of Nellie Melba. To be sure, Puccini's opera would ultimately have asserted its presence in both English and American repertories, but there is no gainsaying that she accelerated the process by her early fondness for, and steadfast loyalty to, the role of Mimì.

Melba introduced *La bohème* in Italian to Covent Garden audiences on 1 July 1899 in association with Zélie de Lussan (Musetta), Alessandro Bonci (in his London debut as Rodolfo), Mario Ancona (Marcello), Charles Gilibert (Schaunard) and Marcel Journet (Colline); the conductor was Luigi Mancinelli. Melba sang in almost all subsequent performances during her extended tenure at the theatre, resisting suggestions that she share a role she had studied under Puccini's personal supervision and regarded as her personal property.[10] Between 1899 and 1928 Melba sang the opera with a host of tenors, from de Reszke and de Lucia to McCormack and Martinelli, but her most memorable partner was the young Enrico Caruso, who had made his La Scala debut as Rodolfo in December 1900 and joined her for the first time during the winter season at Monte Carlo in 1902.

The Melba–Caruso triumph in Monte Carlo fuelled expectations at Covent Garden, where the duo sang their first *Bohème* on 24 May, creating a sensation that remained undiminished through several subsequent seasons and established the popular reputation of the opera in England.[11] Even professional singers were astonished. John McCormack recalled that when he first heard Caruso sing Rodolfo's opening phrases, 'my jaw dropped as though hung on a hinge. Such smoothness and purity of tone, and such quality; it was like a stream of liquid gold'. Mary Garden described Melba's high *c* at the end of Act I:

It left Melba's throat, it left Melba's body, it left everything, and came over like a star and passed us in our box, and went out into the infinite. I have never heard anything like it in my life, not from any other singer, ever. It just rolled over the hall of Covent Garden. My God, how beautiful it was!

Since then I always wait for that note when I hear the first act of *Bohème*, and they reach and reach for it, and they scream it, and it's underneath and it's false, and it rolls down the stairs, and it never comes out from behind that door, never. That note of Melba's was just like a ball of light. It wasn't attached to anything at all – it was out of everything.

The collaboration was not all serious, though, not with a practical joker like Caruso and a business-like potential victim. Once, while singing 'Che gelida manina' to Melba, he pressed a hot dog into her hand, continued the aria while she shrieked and spluttered, and finally paused to whisper, 'English lady, you like sausage?' On another occasion, he surreptitiously replaced the chewing gum she used between acts to keep her mouth moist – with a wad of tobacco.

In its early career at Covent Garden, *La bohème* clearly came to be regarded as a star's, if not a prima donna's opera. Melba sang Mimì there every year from 1899 through 1914 (except 1909 and 1912); she appeared again in the first post-war season (1919) and returned for a final appearance in 1923. Her impact (and Caruso's) can be seen from the house's performance statistics: only four performances in 1902 and 1903 (Caruso did not appear that year); but eleven in 1904, twelve in 1905, sixteen in 1906. During the 1905 season, *La bohème* featured prominently in other ways, closing the summer season, and opening as well as closing the autumn season; in addition, Act III was included on 8 June for a gala performance ordered by King Edward and Queen Alexandra for the King of Spain, and on 12 July for a 'Grand Benefit Matinée'. When Melba returned to London on 22 May 1913 after a year's absence (a date that also marked the twenty-fifth anniversary of her Covent Garden debut), the gala featured *La bohème*. Melba opened the summer season as Mimì in 1914, and again in the first post-war season in 1919. Although the summers of 1920 and 1922 also began with this opera, circumstances had changed. After Melba's tenure, *La bohème* rapidly changed to a utility opera, with large, interchangeable casts, and a relatively permanent place in the repertory – it has rarely missed more than one season up to the present day.

The history of *La bohème* in the United States, as we have seen, also begins with performances by a travelling company. Here, too, Melba and Caruso were instrumental in securing the work's acceptance. Melba made her first American appearance with the Metropolitan on a pre-season tour in Los Angeles on 9 November 1900. She was heard as Mimì twice in Los Angeles, and once each in Denver, Kansas City and Minneapolis before participating in the premiere of *La bohème* at the Met on 26 December. While on tour and on at least one occasion in New York, Melba sought to develop an audience for the unfamiliar score by employing the Mad Scene from *Lucia* as an addendum. Clearly, *La bohème* was regarded as a prima donna's opera at this phase of its career. That status would remain for a while: when Melba left the Metropolitan, her successor as Mimì was Marcella Sembrich. In the meantime, Caruso also contributed to the work's growing reputation: his own success in New York is generally considered to have begun with his first appearance as Rodolfo on 5 December 1903, and Rodolfo remained his principal Puccini role in America for the next three years.[12]

Incidentally, Melba was largely responsible for one of the oddest episodes in the stage history of this opera. When she returned to New York in the early months of 1907, it was not to appear at the Metropolitan, but at the Manhattan Opera House, managed by the enterprising Oscar Hammerstein. The first sign of a problem had emerged the previous spring when Hammerstein had announced both the engagement of Melba and that, among other roles, she would be singing Mimì. On 19 October 1906 George Maxwell, the New York agent for Ricordi's firm, filed an injunction to prevent Hammerstein from performing *La bohème*, claiming that the Metropolitan had exclusive rights to it in the United States. This was obviously a case of the theatre putting pressure on the publisher, for in March 1906 it had seemed that the Metropolitan possessed no such exclusivity and that Hammerstein could produce the work as long as he paid a royalty of $150 a performance.[13] In light of this, Hammerstein decided to ignore the injunction until his season was over. What made possible Melba's appearance in *La bohème* at the Manhattan on 1 March 1907 is told by Irving Kolodin in his history of the Metropolitan.

This was one performance [Cleofonte] Campanini did not conduct. Conried [then the manager of the Metropolitan] claimed exclusive rights to the Puccini scores, and this one was given with the orchestral parts 'remembered' by an unidentified scholar. To avoid reprisals against him in Italy, Campanini sat in a box while [Fernando] Tanara conducted.[14]

Also during 1907, the cause of Puccini's operas in general was given considerable impetus when Conried imported the composer – with Ricordi's blessing – to oversee the introduction of *Madama Butterfly* on 11 February. This season also saw the introduction of *Manon Lescaut* to the Met repertory to join *La bohème* and *Tosca*, the latter having been a regular since 4 February 1901. The larger share of the repertory assigned to Puccini caused no diminishing of performances of *La bohème*: in fact, this was the first season the company presented it as many as seven times in New York; there were an additional seven on tour, all featuring Caruso as Rodolfo.

From this Metropolitan season on, there occurs a change in the approach to casting *La bohème* that parallels the pattern at Covent

Garden. Ever since 1903, the year of Caruso's New York debut, the roles of Mimì and Rodolfo had been almost the exclusive property of Sembrich and Caruso. Although Caruso sang most of the seven Metropolitan performances in 1906–7, Sembrich was his partner only in the first two. Her replacements were Bessie Abott, Lina Cavalieri and Geraldine Farrar, the latter two making their first local appearances as Mimì. The tendency to vary the casting of *La bohème* would increase over succeeding seasons.

With the perspective of time, certain patterns begin to emerge. *La bohème* has never been regarded as sufficiently imposing an opera to open a season at the Metropolitan, although one act of it was included in the mixed bill that initiated the 1954–55 season. In some years, it would be given once or twice around Christmas and sometimes as a New Year's matinée to attract audiences at a time when attendance might drop off. Because of its brevity, it was sometimes given as part of a double-bill, and on more than one occasion was preceded by Stravinsky's ballet *Petroushka*. When the baritone Antonio Scotti ended his thirty-three-year career at the Metropolitan with a final appearance in Leoni's *L'oracolo*, that one-act score was appended to *La bohème*. Other short operas of limited appeal, such as John Laurence Seymour's *In the Pasha's Garden* and Menotti's *The Island God*, were occasionally attached to Puccini's score to bolster their attractiveness. In short, *La bohème* came to be regarded as a utility opera that could serve a variety of functions: it could on rare occasions be highlighted as a special event, as for the debut of Giovanni Martinelli in 1913 or for the return of Lucrezia Bori in 1921; but it could always be brought out to fill an evening when some important revival or novelty was in preparation. Small wonder, then, that *La bohème* remained in the repertory of the Metropolitan without interruption until 1959–60, and that since then it has never been absent for more than a single season at a time.

A glance at the casts of *La bohème* at the Metropolitan during these years of almost unbroken activity reveals some surprises. During Toscanini's tenure with the company (1908–15), for example, he conducted *La bohème* only twice, during the 1910–11 season, as a special compliment to Puccini, who was in New York for the world premiere of *La fanciulla del west*. The other four performances of *La bohème* that season were led by Vittorio Podesti. One might have expected that Toscanini, who had conducted the first performance of the opera, would have paid more attention to it in subsequent years, but his successors as first-string Italian conductors at the Metropolitan – Moranzoni, Serafin and Panizza – were also content to leave *La bohème* to the attention of others, such as Gennaro Papi, Vincenzo Bellezza and Cesare Sodero. The extent to which *La bohème* became a utility opera at the Metropolitan emerges from a comparison of two seasons, chosen at random. In 1926–7, there were seven performances, with four Mimìs (Alda, Rethberg, Bori and Maria Müller) and four Rodolfos (Gigli, Lauri-Volpi, Martinelli and Mario Chamlee). In 1953–4, although this season was two weeks shorter than that of 1926–7, the Metropolitan saw its way clear to present *La bohème* no fewer than fifteen times. That year one could choose between the Mimìs of Hilde Gueden, Nadine Conner, Lucine Amara and Licia Albanese, or the Rodolfos of Eugene Conley, Brian Sullivan, Giulio Gari or Jan Peerce.

And what of the future? *La bohème* shows no sign of diminishing in importance, and has taken a new lease on life by way of films and television, proving itself to be one of the most 'photogenic' of the great repertory pieces. It has also weathered well in the Age of the Producer, and has emerged with some dignity from modern-dress productions, textual updatings, and even a backdrop of symbolic projections. It goes on undaunted by a New York production that presents it in the idiom of modern musical theatre, with singers from the area of popular music. All in all, there seems little doubt: *La bohème* is virtually indestructible. So long as the concept of an operatic repertory survives, Puccini's great opera will remain among the most performed and best loved.

8 *Three early critics and the Brothers Mann: aspects of the La bohème reception*

'Fra i due litiganti io dò ragione al pubblico' ('Between the two liti-gants, I say that the public is right'), wrote one critic about the premiere of *La bohème*,[1] referring to the clear division between critical and public reaction to the opera. It is true that the first Turinese audiences had some difficulties with the score, in particu-lar with the second act which (in the original version) seems to have passed by at too hectic a pace; and, as Puccini's staunch advocate and protector Ricordi was quick to make public, by no means all the critics were hostile.[2] Nevertheless, a division between critics and public there undoubtedly was, and it has continued to the present day. Of the enduring popular success of *La bohème* there can be no doubt: performance statistics show us that it is (though by a fairly narrow margin) the most performed of Puccini's operas, and this means one of the three or four most popular works in the entire repertory.[3] One looks in vain for a body of informed criticism to respond to this success. In fact, most critics who bother to discuss Puccini at any length take a negative view, often deliberately placing themselves against the public, and adopting a *de haut en bas* tone. In compiling an account of the *La bohème* reception, the temptation to indulge exclusively in these (often highly amusing) demolition jobs – to write, as it were, a kind of *Destruktions-geschichte* – is great.

It should come as no surprise that most of Puccini's distinguished fellow composers had little time for his music. In spite of frequent and not unsuccessful attempts to 'come up to date' in matters of orchestration, the essentials of his musical language continued to be firmly grounded in the nineteenth century. Stravinsky was wickedly caustic; Richard Strauss's detailed plans (in 1945) for the repertoire of a future German opera house contained not a single Puccini opera; Debussy was dismissive on several occasions, specifically about Puccini's temerity in attempting to tackle a subject so

129

unassailably French as Murger; one of Webern's biographers reports the following anecdote: 'Klemperer suddenly fired the question at Webern: "What do you think of Puccini?" Webern quietly replied: "Nothing whatever!" '[4] To some younger Italian contemporaries, the name Puccini seems to have assumed honorary status as a four-letter word. Support did come, though, from surprising directions: Mahler (when newly appointed as conductor at the Vienna Hofoper) much preferred Puccini's *Bohème* to Leoncavallo's (the management's choice), and was prepared to get into trouble by saying so. It is only fair to admit, though, that Mahler was considerably less impressed by Puccini the man, in particular by his insistent social pretentions.[5]

We can regret, at least in the English-speaking world, that a potentially strong and articulate supporter, George Bernard Shaw, had stopped writing regular music criticism by the time *La bohème* reached London. Shaw's piece on *Manon Lescaut* certainly provides hints of what his reaction to *Bohème* might have been. His discussion of the earlier opera's first act, for example, singles out an aspect that would be developed even further in *Bohème*:

[. . .] in *Manon Lescaut* the domain of Italian opera is enlarged by an annexation of German territory. The first act, which is as gay and effective and romantic as the opening of any version of *Manon* need be, is also unmistakably symphonic in its treatment. There is genuine symphonic modification, development, and occasionally combination of the thematic material, all in a dramatic way, but also in a musically homogeneous way, so that the act is really a single movement with episodes instead of being a succession of separate numbers, linked together, to conform to the modern fashion, by substituting interrupted cadences for full closes and parading a Leitmotif occasionally.

And if (as so often) Shaw's musical judgements are debatable, in particular his view of what 'symphonic' might mean, his basic instincts could hardly have been sharper than at the close of his review: 'Puccini looks to me more like the heir of Verdi than any of his rivals.'[6]

But the fact that Shaw was discussing Puccini at a time before the composer's international success had been consolidated is significant. A balanced view seemed no longer possible after *La bohème*, when the marked differences of opinion noted above began to surface. It is in this sense symptomatic that the four early commentators we have chosen to quote from extensively (all, so far as we know, published in English for the first time) are balanced only in relation to one another – as two 'negative' and two 'positive' reactions. None can be called in any sense disinterested. However, our reasons for choosing them were not confined to matters of alignment. Each of them advances an aesthetic position, each reacts to the *idea* of Puccini as much as to his musical achievements. Perhaps this was inevitable in the early years of the century; the fact that it continues today is of course far less excusable.

Fausto Torrefranca's *Puccini e l'opera internazionale*, published when the composer was in mid-career, is a polemic of rare severity, a full-length book whose approach to its subject is almost entirely critical.[7] There are few subtleties, the author employing a style that would today be called 'hard-hitting'. As he says in the preface, Puccini was chosen because 'he seems to me the composer who personifies with greatest completeness the decadence of today's Italian music, and who represents its cynical commercialism, its lamentable impotence, its celebration of the international vogue'. Torrefranca's spleen extrudes in many other directions: Debussy, Richard Strauss, Mascagni, even Verdi – all come in for censure. And the book's anti-feminism is laughably extreme: 'Women undoubtedly lower literary and artistic levels [. . .] because feminine activity is still little less than a "translation" of elements of art and thought already developed by masculine brains' (p. 4). Puccini is, naturally, a typical example of an 'artista femminile'. It soon becomes clear that Torrefranca's main positive term of reference is Wagner, and much of the general theorising about opera can be traced to that source. There are, inevitably, a few absurdly simplistic comparisons, such as that between the music that accompanies the burning of Rodolfo's play in Act I of *La bohème* and the magic fire music from *Die Walküre*. Indeed, such is the range of the author's invective that no single quotation could quite do him justice. The following extracts apply to specific passages from *La bohème*, and are thus particularly germane to our present purpose. The first addresses characterisation:

[. . .] Puccini has neither the power nor the wish to pause over his characters for what they are, but merely for what they do. And in this he is at the opposite pole from all the great Italian opera composers, including Verdi. I shall give proof of this forthwith: through one of the characters with which he is said to have been most successful – Rodolfo.

Rodolfo is a poet, all well and good; but before he says it to Mimì, nobody tells us, still less are we told by the music of the duet. Rodolfo is more of a poet in the second act, in 'Quest' è Mimì' and 'Nel [*sic*] mio cervel sbocciano i canti', than in the first act, in 'Talor dal mio forziere' or 'Fremon già nell'anima'. In the first act there is the bombast of a finale, in the second the spontaneity of an episode: and thus there is more poetry. The former begins from high notes, the latter from less high notes, the former dies away immediately in low notes, in the latter the emotion succeeds in broadening the rhythm and sustaining it in the verses that follow. [. . .]

And yet there is a point, in the first act, in which it would have been possible to present, in the most opportune manner, this colourless figure of Rodolfo. [. . .]

The moment is when, after his friends have gone, Rodolfo sits at the table to poeticize. But the maestro hasn't yet got it through his head that Rodolfo is a poet! The forthcoming love duet is very close at hand, and it doesn't seem right to the opera composer to delay its arrival. But if my opinion doesn't convince you, perhaps since you are also anxiously awaiting the 'gelida manina' duet, Rodolfo could have been presented to us earlier, as he contemplated Paris. But when Marcello asks him 'Che fai?' ['What are you doing?'], he responds, as though his imagination is bubbling over: 'Nei cieli bigi vedo [*sic*] fumar dai mille comignoli Parigi' ['In the grey skies of Paris I see the smoke from a thousand chimneys'], to music that would go equally well with 'Per questa sera vorrei dei maccheroni' ['And for this evening I'd like some macaroni'], or 'Penso che oggi ancor digiuneremo' ['I think today that we'll again be starving'], or with anything else. Try it and say I'm wrong, if you dare!

In these few bars the words are squeezed like scraps of meat into a sausage skin. The accented words, though fleetingly so, are: *bigi, mille, Parigi*. *Cieli* and *fumar*, which would have attracted the attention of a true musician, escape the musical sense of Puccini, because though poetry has its rights, dance has its ineluctable logic, from which neither images nor metrics can hold it.   (pp. 74–5)

The emphasis of these final paragraphs is taken up, with renewed zest, in a later passage discussing the death of Mimì:

[. . .] the words that he has accented: *dormire, restare, dire, mare*, have something expansive, durable, indefinite which relates well to the grave and diffuse progress of the funereal canzonetta. But the pity is that Puccini didn't know how to go any further: gathering up the imaginative unity of those verses, he did not succeed in giving them full musical expression.

The music, as usual, is too strophic, too symmetrical and, in trying to pull everything together in a long heart-throb, finishes by suffocating all those minute and unexpected little palpitations through which we especially recognise melodic expression that has real life.

And when the instruments comment on the death of Mimì by singing again 'Ho tante cose che ti voglio dire' ['I have so many things I wish to tell you'], we seem to feel in these words, re-invoked by the pure, simple melody, a complete expression of the composer's impotent nostalgia.

(pp. 112–13)

What is immediately striking is that many of Torrefranca's specific criticisms are the same as those habitually advanced today: Puccini's melodic idiom is too restricted to allow genuine characterisation; in spite of surface variations, the music is over-symmetrical and rhythmically predictable; he cynically disregards dramatic truth in order to incorporate musically effective set pieces; he continually teeters on the verge of full expressiveness, and somehow never drops over the edge – a modern commentator refers to a 'kind of perpetual pregnancy in the melody'.[8] But in one important respect Torrefranca differs from recent criticism: it is clear that his most basic objection is to the *realism* of the opera, the attachment to detail ('grey', 'thousand', 'Paris') rather than to evocative, vague, 'poetic' images ('skies', 'smoke'). The absence of a grand emotional gesture at the moment of Mimì's death, of 'full musical expression', becomes, ultimately, a sign of 'impotent nostalgia'. This seems to have been a genuine stumbling block, something which, over and above polemical positions, reflected a significant newness in Puccini's operatic language. Our second commentator was no more forgiving in the face of this novelty.

One thing is certain: no one could accuse Eduard Hanslick of a blinkered Wagnerian perspective. Nearing the end of his long career when *La bohème* came to Vienna in 1897, he still retained a vigorous appetite for polemic. His extended essay on the opera is worth quoting at length, and not only as a magnificent example of sustained, non-comprehending invective.[9] It also furnishes us with an extreme but nevertheless logical conclusion to Hanslick's earlier ideas on the progress of Italian opera, in particular his unease at the direction Verdi had taken in his last operas. For a man who found the third act *concertato* of *Otello* (by far the most traditional passage in the score) that opera's finest piece, and felt that the opening of the final scene had a 'penchant for graphic representation [that] borders on the bizarre', *La bohème* was to prove a trial indeed:[10]

[. . .] That these composers [i.e. Puccini and Leoncavallo] have just now seized upon this play with such eagerness typifies contemporary taste, which also subscribes to *verismo* – relentless realism – in opera. The few earlier operas that deal seriously with affairs between wanton courtesans and weak youths ('Traviata', 'Carmen', and lately 'Manon') have at least dressed them in picturesque national or historic garb, or set them in romantic surroundings and thus raised them out of the lowest regions of everyday wretchedness. With 'Bohème', our composers take the last step toward the naked, prosaic dissoluteness of our time: heroes in loud-checked trousers, gaudy ties and crumpled felt hats, cigarette butts in their mouths, their companions in bonnets and scanty shawls. This is new, a sensational break with the last romantic and artistic traditions of opera. Thus the breathless competition between two already renowned composers over this as yet untried, piquant lure. [. . .]

[*La bohème*] appeared in the Theater an der Wien immediately after the celebrated Franceschina Prevosti had sung 'Traviata' there six times in succession. The coughs of the dying Violetta still nested painfully in our ears when Puccini's Mimì began to cough herself to death on the same stage. [. . .] A long, painful death, quite horribly drawn out and endowed with every pathological misery, to which is added the naked poverty and helplessness of the surrounding artist-proletarians. That Mimì's battle with death directly follows their farcical quadrille is characteristic of a libretto that achieves its effect mainly by juxtaposing the most glaring contrasts. As soon as one scene has slapped us in the face with its brutal gaiety, the next bores slowly and painfully into our hearts with its mental anguish and the fear of death. If the audience really finds pleasure and edification in operas of this sort, so much the better for them and the theatre director. I do not feel the slightest stirring of gratitude.

Music actually plays a secondary role in this opera, even if it does intrude pretentiously and noisily in isolated passages. If, before a performance, one reads the first four or five closely printed pages of the text, one wonders if it is not really a comedy rather than an opera libretto. This insatiably garrulous dialogue, which revolves humourlessly and unfeelingly around the most ordinary things – *this* – is supposed to elicit music, inspire a composer? It is impossible for music to function here as an equal, independently creative art; it can only serve as background, priming for everyday conversation. This is the penultimate stage of music on the decline; the next and last stage is undisguised melodrama. Actually, in 'Bohème' we already hear from these figures less of a singing than a speaking over characteristic orchestral sounds; moreover, with the quick tempo of such enormous masses of words, it is an indistinct, unintelligible speaking. Understandably, with this flood of garrulous dialogue entire pages of the score – to borrow a term from acoustics – have to, and actually do, consist of nothing but 'dead spots'. From time to time, transient melodic thoughts free themselves from these dead spots; something begins to resound and sing in the midst of recitative – but how long does that last? Such oases, where feeling is concentrated and melody takes on form and expands, are found most often and at their purest in the role of Mimì. On the whole, melodic invention is extremely scanty. All kinds of fine instrumental detail and cleverly allusive wit glitter more abundantly throughout the orchestral score. These irritants, which almost crowd out musical creativity and forms, are actually part and parcel of our latest school, the latest Italian school. What Puccini completely lacks is a quality that makes Murger's descriptions so attractive: humour. [. . .] Everything is broken up into the smallest bits and pieces; the power to comprehend and unite, without which there is no genuine effect in music, is totally lacking. [. . .]

How quickly the young Mascagni has found adherents! Especially with his rhythmic and harmonic oddities, melodic unnaturalness and caprice.

From Mascagni comes the dominant, incessant change of rhythm in 'La bohème' – the unmediated modulation or, more precisely, the leap into the remotest keys and the almost childish overcrowding with directions for performance. The basic feeling of the whole, continually broken up, is thus dissipated in purely nervous details. [. . .] But this is just insignificant pleasantry compared with Puccini's harmonic atrocities. In the most diverse scenes there arise columns of ascending and descending parallel fifths of such obtrusive ugliness – preferably blared 'marcatissimo' by trumpets – that one asks oneself in vain, what the composer wanted to accomplish with these rude monstrosities? The text does not offer the remotest motivation for them, for with these ghastly fifth-rods Puccini beats the conversation of the friends in the garret as well as the crowd scene in front of the café, and even the customs officers at the barrière. It is impossible to interpret this clever cultivation of ugliness as a 'witty' protest against the harmony of our great masters; it is nothing more than a crude musical insult. The unmotivated use of ugliness just because it is ugly, as well as the insolent predominance of the most banal dialogue, are a result of the naked realism that has now also invaded opera. Criticism remains powerless against such trends. [. . .]

One point in Hanslick's defence: his prolonged diatribe against the parallel fifths is not the outmoded complaint of a cranky old man. Almost every critic, whether for or against the opera, mentioned the orchestral passages that begin Acts II and III, with their prominent descending triads or fifths. Though innocuous to our Debussy-trained ears, such writing was at the time highly unconventional, and the prominence Puccini gave these passages must have seemed a deliberate challenge to traditional harmonic practice. It is more remarkable – at least considering our present-day, rather one-sided view of Hanslick as a man guided by obsessive anti-Wagnerism – that the critic fails to draw attention to those aspects of the score that are overtly Wagnerian: the use of leitmotifs, or of the half-diminished chord. Again, as with Torrefranca, the dominant impression is of deep unease with the 'naked realism' of the opera – its sudden juxtapositions, its lack of continuous musical argument, the colloquialism and free prosody of the libretto. This, one senses, was just as threatening to Hanslick's aesthetic stance as were Wagner's mature music dramas; and especially so, because Puccini was clearly a continuation of a national school (represented fundamentally by middle-period Verdi), on which he had pinned such high hopes.

One approaches the French reception of *La bohème* with trepidation. Murger was something of a national monument by this time, and the French are notoriously possessive of their cultural heritage. However, the essay on the Parisian *Bohème* of 1898 published in the *Revue des deux mondes* turns out to be one of the most perceptive and sensitive early reactions to the composer.[11] Camille Bellaigue, our third critic, was certainly well-versed in recent Italian music; he was a close friend of Arrigo Boito, and served as adviser to the French translation of *Falstaff*, an opera which, as a staunch anti-Wagnerian, he had hailed as 'a masterpiece of *Latin*, classical genius!'[12] Unlike Torrefranca and Hanslick, Bellaigue chose to meet the innovative aspect of the score in a direct and positive manner. In a passage describing the death of Mimì, for example, Bellaigue cites details strikingly similar to those mentioned by our earlier critics, but draws radically different conclusions simply because he fully accepts, and even rejoices in, the new realism:

[. . .] The reality [the music] searches for, at least that which for the most part it finds, is not often the reality that is hidden, intimate and, one might say, ideal, that makes for the depths of life or of the soul. M. Puccini's music willingly attaches itself to concrete, palpable reality, to the outward and to appearances, to its exterior and insignificant signs. Such attachments must be common in Italy, as two musicians, MM. Puccini and Leoncavallo, have coincided in choosing a subject such as Murger's novel, whose least impressive aspect is the analytical or psychological. This surface reality, which is to profound truth what decor or costume [. . .] are to thought or feeling, M. Puccini's music expresses marvellously, giving us its acute and constant sensation. And how does the music manage this? Sometimes by renouncing itself, by not fearing to sacrifice itself to word or to action, or to theatrical display and purely scenic effects. What makes the final scene of *la Vie de Bohème*, the death of Mimì, so moving? A music from which music is almost absent; in which speech (I am thinking of the very last pages) replaces song, in which even silence has perhaps more importance and effectiveness than sound, up until the moment when two or three chords from the brass, suddenly bursting forth, move us with a physical shock, arresting us brutally before the reality of the corpse much more than before the mystery of death.   (pp. 470–71)

But it is in the final paragraphs that Bellaigue sounds his deepest note. From an understanding and acceptance of the attempts at realism, which – as we have seen from Torrefranca and Hanslick – was a problem all contemporaries had to face, he moves to an appreciation of Puccini's music which will hold for many today. Bellaigue strives to pinpoint (as few have done since) the manner in which *La bohème* transcends its technical limitations; and he does so primarily by appealing to the multiple layers of nostalgia the opera brings to the surface: for bohemian Paris; for carefree, ardent youth; and, perhaps most crucially, for the great days of Italian vocal lyricism:

In the last act of *la Vie de Bohème*, among so many musical reminiscences, listen to the new phrase, perhaps the most beautiful of the entire work, that of the dying Mimi, alone with Rodolphe, and murmuring to him her love in her last sigh, crying it to him in her last sob. Listen to the main part of Act III: two duos, a quartet, so many easy, rather loose cantilenas, but from which suddenly springs forth an accent of tenderness or of sorrow, of life and of truth. Finally, in the first act listen to how one of Rodolphe's phrases expands. Listen to the violins singing with full bows, the tenor with full heart, and the music rising, always rising up to those trembling, seemingly bewildered notes, from the instruments and the voice. However much you try to protest, perhaps in the depths of yourself, against your too easy and too physical pleasure, your pleasure will be the stronger. Do not be ashamed, because these accents go far, further than the situations, feelings or characters. And they also come from afar: from the old, illustrious land where melody is born, where, fallen and impoverished though it may be, it still survives and does battle. Loved for itself, for itself alone, Italian melody remains the sign or memory, enfeebled but still affecting, of something great, almost sacred. Down there 'they are still singing', and when one of their songs, a song that belongs to them, that *is* them, reaches our ears, is it our fault, our great fault, if we feel, as the poet said, our Italy beats in our hearts, if an ineffable sweetness of life penetrates us and inspires within us a vague desire for tears? (p. 474)

Considering the immense popularity of *La bohème*, references and evocations of the opera in literature are surprisingly difficult to find. There is one passage which many will know, as it comes from one of the most celebrated sections of a novel famous for its involvement with music. In 'Fullness of Harmony' from Thomas Mann's *The Magic Mountain* (*Der Zauberberg*, 1924), the acquisition of the latest model phonograph by the Berghof Sanatorium provides the hero, Hans Castorp, with an opportunity to indulge his passion for music. Given the nature of the setting (Castorp has been admitted as a patient in the sanatorium) – the hero's fascination with the movement of the phonograph, which functions 'almost like breathing', and with records featuring the 'swelling, breathing, articulating human voice'–the selection of excerpts from *La bohème* creates a considerable ironic undercurrent. Among the records he listens to is a version of the Act I duet between Rodolfo and Mimì:

[. . .] And there could be on earth nothing more tender than the next number he chose: a duet from a modern Italian opera, a simple, heartfelt mingling of emotion between two beings, one part taken by a world-famous tenor who was so well represented in the albums, the other by a crystal-clear and sweet little soprano voice; nothing more lovely than his '*Da mi il braccio, mia piccina*' [*sic*] and the simple, sweet, succinct little melodic phrase in which she replies. Hans Castorp started as the door opened behind him. It was the Hofrat, looking in on him; in his clinical coat, the stethoscope showing in his breast pocket, he stood there a moment, with his hand on the door-knob, and nodded at the distiller of sweet sounds. Hans Castorp, over his shoulder, replied to the nod, and the chief's blue-checked visage, with its one-sided moustache, disappeared as he drew the door to behind him. Hans Castorp returned to his invisible, melodious pair of voices.[13]

Since Thomas Mann places the events of the novel in the years between 1907 and the beginning of World War I, it may be possible to identify the singers to whom he alludes but teasingly refrains from identifying. The 'world-famous tenor so well represented in the albums' would certainly be Enrico Caruso, who recorded the duet four times during this period. Only two of these recordings were published, and we leave it to record enthusiasts to speculate as to whether Castorp's 'crystal-clear and sweet little soprano voice' might be Nellie Melba (Vic. 95200) or Geraldine Farrar (IRCC 61B).[14]

Thomas Mann's novelistic evocation of Puccini and *La bohème*, however relevant it may be to the central concerns of *The Magic Mountain*, is tantalisingly brief. In the case of Mann's older brother Heinrich, our fourth commentator, the involvement went far deeper. Heinrich Mann (1871–1950), although recognised elsewhere as a prolific novelist and social critic, is known in English-speaking countries almost exclusively for his early novel *Professor Unrat* (*The Blue Angel*, 1905), and that through the film adaptation with Marlene Dietrich and Emil Jannings (1930). A long-time connoisseur of Italian culture and life, Heinrich Mann discovered Puccini early, and expressed his familiarity with the composer in writings that span nearly half a century. The plot of an early novel, *Die Jagd nach Liebe* (*Pursuit of Love*, 1903) reveals a clear indebtedness to *Manon Lescaut*; *Die kleine Stadt* (*The Little Town*, 1909) pays homage to the young composer in the character of a conductor. But the most remarkable tribute to Puccini occurs in Mann's autobiography, *Ein Zeitalter wird besichtigt* (*Review of an Age*, 1947), in a chapter called 'Geistige Liebe' ('Spiritual Love'). Our excerpt begins with his discovery of Puccini, a discovery whose description eloquently evokes the broad public appeal the composer so rapidly achieved. In the concluding section, Mann analyses with considerable subtlety the reasons why Puccini was such a seminal influence; in doing so, he identifies a further dimension of the nostalgia that Bellaigue had analysed with such insight in 1898. In Puccini, and perhaps in *La bohème* above all, our pleasure is valedictory: for bohemian Paris; for carefree, ardent youth; for the great days of Italian vocal lyricism; and finally, after the catastrophe of two world wars, for a vanished age. It seems a fitting note on which to end.[15]

An opera composer, in his day the most popular everywhere. One joins the countless multitude, one shares the melodious passion – the last – of an age which would secretly lose almost everything, the facts of its existence, its reactions to intellectual events. Perhaps the intimation that there would soon be no more opportunity for profound enthusiasms allowed me to seize this one.

I was not aware of anything as I journeyed uphill from Florence to Fiesole in November 1900 (unforgettable date!) on the back platform of a slow horse-drawn tram. I travelled or walked there every day; this time a hurdy-gurdy played along the way. In order that no banality was wanting, it was a hurdy-gurdy that acquainted me with Maestro Puccini. Until then, I had never known of his existence, nor heard 'La bohème'.

The few bars that the wind carried toward me induced me to jump off the tram. I stood there and let myself be transported. The most attractive acrobat, exhibiting her nimble limbs on a carpet in the dust, would scarcely have been able to captivate me for so long. This was my first encounter with a perfect interpreter of the passionate feeling for life in those days: with his melting sweetness, his élan, his longing for death.

On a country road I heard the grand Act I aria of Rodolfo. In a wine-tavern in Riva – I still know that the innkeeper's name was Marchetti – the orchestra played 'Io muoio disperato', 'Tosca' Act III, for the first time. When the piece came to an end, my neighbour, the Segretario comunale, rose to his feet along with me. He, who had not yet spoken to me, said: 'Questo è proprio divino'. It was, and the man's tone of voice testified to his poignant rapture.

I heard 'Madama Butterfly' *avant la lettre*, in the house of a Florentine priest of San Lorenzo. The opera had not yet been performed, but someone had read the score and played from memory for a long time: I was immediately transported to a state of perfect love, as previously on the country road and at Marchetti's. By now I have seen and heard all these operas for many years in the theatres of many cities – seeing them has also intensified their impression. The position of the four figures around the bed of the deceased Mimì is fixed in my mind like a classical picture [. . .]

Note: I have always felt him to be the originator, not only of the most passionate song, but also of the heightened feeling of his age. It is something consequential to make a single 'little town' sing – the conductor Enrico Dorlenghi does this in my novel of the same name [*Die kleine Stadt*]. Maestro Puccini did it for a world, before all its song vanished. My young conductor, his glowing desire to invent music for an entire people, is my view of the developing Puccini – otherwise I would not have written the novel. [. . .]

Spiritual love finds its satisfaction in a modest (not entirely modest) obscurity. Only very late – he had scarcely three years left – was my name mentioned to him.

Strangely enough, he had come to Oberammergau: the curiosity of the old practitioner about stage effects went that far. The representative of a Berlin newspaper told him that he had a special admirer in Germany. Puccini had the name repeated and shook his head: 'Jamais entendu'. Whether he did so justifiably or not, out of arrogance, humility, irony – when I learned of it, it made me happy.

Then he died 'the difficult death', as Nils Lyhne calls it. Cancer of the larynx or whatever – the real agony was not that. Hope and frustration over his uncompleted 'Turandot' pursued him from his writing desk, where he drew the smoke of the last cigarettes into his diseased throat, to Brussels, to the operation that everyone could perform for him – it was always in vain. He said to his nurse: 'It is very difficult for an artist to die with an unfinished work'.

A year later I saw the production at the Vienna Opera. A whole evening of Puccini, and no melody. With 'The Girl of the Golden West' he had begun to become harsh and unpleasant. Come along or let it be; feel – as I do – how life loses its enchantment, or retain your illusions: it's all the same to me. His most profound enchantment is in the last analysis our recognition that it was little, and that it is harsh. 'I profondi amori fanno le profonde miserie' – Scarpia, in 'Tosca', Act I.

We would never have celebrated life if it did not make us bitter and homicidal at the end. Princess Turandot, young and untested, kills her suitors, as the eccentric Gozzi wanted. The existence of a Puccini follows a better trajectory, from bliss to bitterness, from the power of melody to death, which celebrates itself in its own way. [. . .]

I heard 'Turandot' only that one time and – even if I had previously experienced less than I actually did – it seemed like the departure of a beloved personality. Its poignant depths did not remain foreign to me while on the surface it radiated an intoxicated feeling for life, and I wonder if I would have fallen suddenly in love with the composer of 'La bohème' if I had not secretly known about his deadly last heroine in advance. Thus we know that our happiness is fragile, that an era has run its course, and been judged.

At the first performance [of 'Turandot'] at La Scala, the conductor Toscanini lowered his baton in the last act. Facing the audience, he said: 'Qui finisce la partitura del maestro Puccini'. Here ends – a great deal. [. . .]

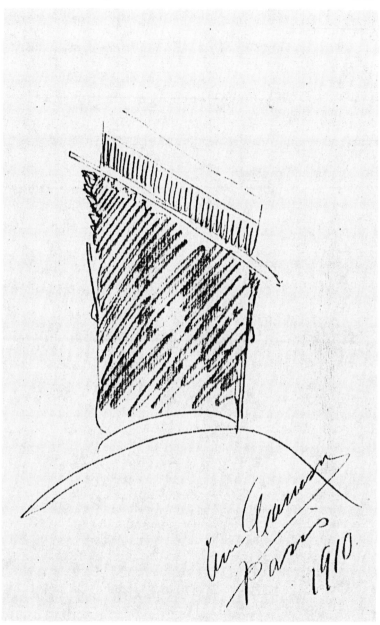

10 A caricature of Puccini in a sketch by the tenor Caruso

Appendix: bohemian politics and the act that disappeared

BY F. REGINA PSAKI, ARTHUR GROOS, ROGER PARKER

Although *La bohème* confounds the usual generalisations about the quality of art produced by collaboration, the Puccini–Illica–Giacosa–Ricordi team consumed, like most committees, large amounts of time and paper. In the protracted battle to find a satisfactory portrayal of that 'gay and terrible life', they inevitably left behind many traces and rejected pieces of work – enough material, according to Illica, 'for another ten operas'. Most of the surviving material remains unpublished. The following chapter makes available two documents illustrating the creation of the opera: (1) a political scene *à la bohème* which they eliminated from Act IV in order to expedite the arrival of Mimì; and (2) the entire Cortile act (originally Act III), an evening party in the courtyard below Musetta's flat, which they deleted midway in the genesis of the opera, thus drastically altering its development. The first of these documents is, so far as we know, presented for the first time in English translation; the second appears for the first time in a rendering that preserves the lineation of the Italian original.[1]

I

Luigi Illica's reminiscences of Giuseppe Giacosa, published shortly after the latter's death in 1906, conclude with the scene edited and translated below. Although Illica precedes the text with an encomium of his colleague's ability as *tailleur*, emphasising his skill in transforming the patchwork of revision into a seamless whole, the context of a memorial to Giacosa may also imply that the scene was a favourite of the poet's. The episode certainly represents an important document of the reception of Bohemianism in Italy, particularly in the wake of Felice Camerone's provocative political statements in the preface to his Italian translation of *La bohème* (see pp. 56f.). Contrary to the assertions of some critics, this scene

142

reveals that the team of Puccini, Illica and Giacosa also recognised a relationship between the private lives of their Bohemians and larger social issues of the time, but distanced themselves from activism such as Camerone's by emphasising their characters' anarchic independence of politics.

The correspondence suggests that this episode was deleted in the spring of 1895. On 6 April, Puccini wrote Giacosa a plea in doggerel to include the 'little scenes' of Act IV in his revisions. The poet's extended outburst on 25 June concludes with the promise to finish Act IV within a few days (CP 123). Giacosa thus seems to have excised our 'little scene' at about this time, since final cuts that autumn were undertaken by Illica. In the final version of the libretto, this episode of bohemian politics has been telescoped into Colline's brief assertion that the King has appointed him a Minister of State, which is cut short by Schaunard's attempt to propose a toast (later suppressed in its turn, in order to hasten the arrival of Mimì).

Although the humour of Schaunard's confrontation with his 'constituents' is timeless, the particular items in the platform (sexual, political and economic reform) seem to reflect concerns that had been intensified by the events in the Paris Commune in 1871. Each item on Schaunard's agenda, however, is undercut by the ironic gap between the 'true revolution' implied by the political slogan and the ensuing trivialisation which reduces it to 'genuine Bohème': (1) 'sexual reform' . . . of the gender of an Italian noun; (2) 'reform of the Diplomatic Corps and the Official World' (international and internal affairs respectively) . . . by the cancellation of debts; and (3) 'economic reform', particularly 'free exchange of assets' (a 'red flag' topic in debates of the period) . . . accomplished 'just like that'. The scene takes a turn in the opposite direction when Schaunard's liberal rhetoric raises the Bohemians' suspicion that he is really an *agent provocateur* of conservative government, evoking another basic political tension of the nineteenth century. The humour thus cuts across both extremes of the political spectrum, effectively defusing the political issues Camerone and others wished to see in Murger's subject matter.

SCHAUNARD (*candidato politico in piedi sul tavolo*)
Elettori ... commosso ...
accetto il delicato
mestier del deputato ...
(*Una lagrima, un sospiro*)
Altro ... dire ... non posso! ...
(*Bisbiglio di incoraggiamento e di simpatia*)
SCHAUNARD (*atteggiamento da martire*)
A tanto pondo il dosso
Schaunard, già come Atlante,
piega, accetta esitante
e ringrazia ... (*un singhiozzo*)
R. C. M. (*flebili*)   ... commosso.
RODOLFO Fuori il programma! ...
C. e M.   Fuori ...
SCHAUNARD Primo comma, Elettori!
Riforma sessuale:
'Le portinaie cessano
d'essere al femminile!'
(*Si delinea il successo. Applausi*)
M. C. R. (*approvano*)
Son di sesso maschile!
SCHAUNARD Secondo: Revisione
del Corpo Diplomatico
e del Mondo Ufficiale:
'Le croci non si mettono
che sotto ai vecchi debiti!'
(*Il successo è sicuro. Applausi frenetici*)
GRIDA   Vera rivoluzione!
(*Il successo è quasi fantastico e cresce sempre più a vista d'occhio,
per Colline a vista d'occhiali*)
SCHAUNARD Terzo: lo scambio libero
di tutti i patrimonii:
(*A Marcello*)
Schizzi un ritratto
a un sarto? Un *tout de même!*
MARCELLO Son soddisfatto!
M. e R. Autentica Bohème!
COLLINE (*diffidente e dissidente*)
In queste idee si esagera
un po' troppo lo zucchero ...
RODOLFO (*Insospettito, guardando Schaunard*)
Del naso ha dell'agente
provocatore!
MARCELLO   Sente,
pouah, di governo!
SCHAUNARD (*intromettente*) prego
la parola ...
COLLINE (*furioso*)   La nego!
R. e M. Abbasso i corruttori!

SCHAUNARD   (*as a political candidate, standing on the table*)
　　　　　Constituents ... moved ...
　　　　　I accept the delicate
　　　　　office of representative ...
　　(*A tear, a sigh*)
　　　　　I can ... say ... no more! ...
　　(*Murmur of encouragement and sympathy*)
SCHAUNARD   (*striking a martyr's pose*)
　　　　　Bending his back to such a weight,
　　　　　Schaunard, even as Atlas did,
　　　　　accepts hesitantly
　　　　　and thanks ... (*a sob*)
RODOLFO, COLLINE, MARCELLO   (*weakly*)   ... He's moved.
RODOLFO   Out with the programme! ...
COLLINE AND MARCELLO　　　　　　　　Out with it ...
SCHAUNARD   First article, Constituents!
　　　　　Sexual reform:
　　　　　' "Concierges" will henceforth cease
　　　　　to be in the feminine!'
　　(*Signs of approval. Applause*)
MARCELLO, COLLINE, RODOLFO   (*approving*)
　　　　　They are of the masculine sex!
SCHAUNARD   Second: Revision
　　　　　of the Diplomatic Corps
　　　　　and the Official World:
　　　　　'Crosses will only be put
　　　　　under old debts!'
　　(*His success is assured. Frenetic applause*)
SHOUT　　　　　　　　　　　　　　　True revolution!
　　(*The success is almost unbelievable, and increases before everyone's
　　eyes – in Colline's case before his spectacles*)
SCHAUNARD   Third: free exchange
　　　　　of all assets:
　　(*To Marcello*)
　　　　　You sketch a portrait
　　　　　for a tailor? Just like that!
MARCELLO   Fine with me!
MARCELLO AND RODOLFO   Genuine Bohème!
COLLINE   (*mistrusting and dissenting*)
　　　　　These ideas
　　　　　are a little too saccharine ...
RODOLFO   (*suspicious, looking at Schaunard*)
　　　　　He has the nose
　　　　　of an *agent provocateur*!
MARCELLO　　　　　　　　　　　　He reeks,
　　　　　ugh, of the government!
SCHAUNARD   (*intervening*)　　　　　Please,
　　　　　　　　a word ...
COLLINE   (*furious*)　　　　　I forbid it!
RODOLFO AND MARCELLO   Down with corruptors!

SCHAUNARD   Dissi …
COLLINE   Alla porta!
M. e R.   Taccia!
SCHAUNARD   (*colpito nella parte più sacra dei suoi principí, afferra la carta che conteneva l'arringa e grida dignitoso ma disgustato*)
      Amabili Elettori,
      volete un piatto in faccia?

SCHAUNARD   I only said …
COLLINE   To the door!
MARCELLO AND RODOLFO   Shut up!
SCHAUNARD   (*kicked in the most tender area of his principles, grabs the paper which contained the herring, and shouts, dignified but disgusted*)
      My dear Constituents,
      do you want a plate in your faces?

II. The Cortile act

The Cortile [Courtyard] act, one of the most fascinating documents in the genesis of *La bohème*, represents the largest cut and thus the most consequential decision in the protracted process of creating a satisfactory libretto. Its entrance into and exit from the work in progress are relatively well documented, enabling us to obtain some idea of the original scenario, as well as of the exigencies that produced the libretto we know today. In addition, it provides a means of comparing the Puccini–Illica–Giacosa *Bohème* with that of Leoncavallo, which also contains a Cortile act based on the identical episode in Murger's novel.

The idea of including a party and dance scene in the opera first occurs in an early letter from Puccini to Illica about copyrights and the need for rapid progress. As an afterthought to the more pressing business, the composer vetoes a previous suggestion by the librettist: 'Mabille doesn't seem to me to be an innovation: I think better of another idea devised today with Sig. Giulio' (CP 83). Puccini here refers to the famous Mabille Ball in Paris, which existed in the garden of the same name from 1843 to 1875, and which a mid-century source describes as: 'shining with light, ringing with joyous sounds, with farandoles, with shouts, songs, and music. This garden is the market-place of easy love affairs, the Paradise, the El Dorado, the Promised Land of sensitive women and generous young men'.[2] As he suggests, the Bal Mabille would not have provided any novelty to opera audiences already familiar with dozens of ballroom scenes in nineteenth-century opera (one thinks of Verdi's *Un ballo in maschera* or – the real 'competition' – *La traviata*). Nonetheless, a vestige of Illica's original plan remains in Act I, when the Bohemians mention to Benoît that he has been caught 'in amorous sin' at Mabille. The reference seems to have been inserted by Illica to prepare the later scene at the Bal Mabille itself, since in the corresponding passage of the novel the unnamed landlord unwittingly reveals that his affair (with Phémie, Schaunard's mistress) is carried on in a private room.

Although we cannot be certain that the 'other idea' Puccini had devised with Ricordi concerned the Cortile act, this section of the libretto soon becomes the focus of activity. On 28 July 1893 Giacosa asks Ricordi to see the act again (CP 89), while Ricordi asks Illica for the 'Latin Quarter' and the 'Cortile' as soon as the 'proposed revisions' have been completed (CP 88). Giacosa's versification proceeded smoothly, judging from the unusual lack of complaints in his correspondence. He appears to have completed the basic work sometime between July and October 1893, since on 2 October he reminds Ricordi that the Cortile lacks only a 'few verses' (CP 91), a conviction repeated four days later with the complaint that Puccini should apply himself to the Cortile act, 'which I sent almost finished, and give me time for Act II [Barrière]' (CP 92).

A general paralysis, induced by Puccini's as well as Giacosa's reservations concerning the viability of the entire *Bohème* project, and protracted difficulties with other acts inhibit the working sessions throughout the autumn. Sometime that winter there occurred in Ricordi's office one of the sessions later described by Illica, the famous 'Cortile meeting', in which the entire act was deleted. Illica's lengthy and fascinating letter (CP 101), tentatively dated February 1894, and written in response either to the original excision or a confirmation of that decision the previous Sunday, proposes ways for dealing with the 'enormous wound inflicted on the libretto by the cutting of the Cortile'. As we have seen, many of these suggestions raise issues that move the libretto in the direction of its present format.

The source for the Cortile act is a brief but charming episode in Ch. 6 of the novel ('Mademoiselle Musette'), which describes the unusual result of Musette's invitation to a party at her flat in the rue de la Bruyère:

Monsieur Casimir Bonjour could not have been more surprised on the day he learned about his election to the Institute than were Marcel and Rodolphe when they arrived at the house of Mlle Musette. This was the cause of their astonishment: Musette, who had for some time been quarrelling with her lover the Councillor of State, had been abandoned by him at a very critical moment. She had been pursued by her creditors and her landlord; her furniture had been seized and brought down to the courtyard, to be taken away and sold the following morning. Despite this incident, Mlle Musette did not for a moment entertain the idea of slipping away from her guests, and did not cancel the soirée. She solemnly had the courtyard arranged as a salon, put a carpet on the pavement, prepared everything as usual, dressed to receive her company, and invited all the other tenants to her little fête, to the splendour of which heaven graciously contributed the lighting.

This *divertissement* enjoyed enormous success: no party of Musette's had ever occasioned so much liveliness and gaiety. They were still dancing and singing when the agents came to carry away furniture, carpet, and couches, and the company was finally forced to retire.

Musette saw them all off, singing:

> They'll talk for a long time, la, ri, ra.
> About my Thursday party,
> They'll talk about it for a long time, la, ri, ri.

Marcel and Rodolphe were left alone with Musette, who had climbed back up to her flat, where there was nothing left but the bed.

This delightful scene constitutes a small and insignificant episode in a kaleidoscopic novel filled with many such events. The fact that the libretti of both Puccini and Leoncavallo originally expanded the episode into an entire act inevitably raises again the question posed by their *contretemps* of March 1893. Those familiar with Puccini's methods of pursuing and acquiring potential libretti may be inclined to believe Leoncavallo's reported accusation of plagiarism; those familiar with Leoncavallo's persecution complex may be inclined to believe that Puccini recognised coincidentally the possibilities of the material. Whatever the case, both men seized the opportunity to add a highly individual variation to the conventional party and dance scene of opera. Both shift the focus from Musette to the soirée by having the furniture moved during the course of the act, creating *in extenso* the party which is only implied in the novel, and building to a typical operatic climax involving the principals and a chorus.

But beyond this common process of transforming narrative description into operatic action, each composer proceeded in a different direction. Leoncavallo, the more socially engaged of the two, departs from the novel in order to emphasise the socio-economic opposition between the Bohemians and society. He changes Musette's lover from a Councillor to a rich banker, with whose wealth the impoverished Marcello cannot compete ('Io non ho che una povera stanzetta' – 'I only have a poor little room'), adds a scene in which the concierge is bribed, and has Rodolfo's anguished aria at the end of the act accuse Mimì of having 'sold herself' to the Viscount ('Mimì s'è venduta'). The Cortile act concludes with a general mêlée between the spirited revellers (who twice break out in choruses of the 'Bohemian Hymn') and the bourgeois inhabitants of the building, who shout for quiet and finally resort to violence. Musetta exacerbates the conflict by improvising her soirée not on a Thursday (as in the novel), but on 'April 15th, 1838', what Murger calls 'the cruel Quarter-day', when the rent is collected and insolvent tenants evicted. (It is unlikely that Leoncavallo knew that 15 April 1838 actually fell on Easter Sunday – certainly no day for revelry in the bourgeois Paris of the period.)

Puccini, on the other hand, adheres more closely to the novel. Schaunard invites Musetta's fellow tenants in 8 rue de la Bruyère, 'upstairs and down, every class, age, sex, and way of life', creating an event reminiscent of a modern 'block party'. The carefree atmosphere thus establishes a harmonious background against which the Bohemians achieve greater profile. The unattached Schaunard and Colline, for example, first arrange the courtyard for the party, and then participate in characteristic ways – the musician Schaunard conducting the band and calling out the figures of the *quadrille*, and the philosopher Colline consoling Rodolfo and meditating on the wines from the Councillor's cellar. More importantly, Puccini's concern with character differentiation allows for further comparison of Musetta and Mimì, and especially for the contrastive development of the two sets of lovers. Musetta, abandoned by her Councillor, is reconciled with Marcello, while Mimì, who has just been introduced to the Viscount, leaves Rodolfo after enduring his rages of jealousy.

The lively dialogue and careful attention to the structure as well as the constellation of characters combine to make this a potentially splendid act for *La bohème*. Yet the fact remains that the Cortile was deleted within a year of the opera's inception. Although its principal advantage lies in explaining the separation between Rodolfo and Mimì (something insisted on by Illica [CP 101]), this innovation simultaneously blurs the basic distinction between Musetta and Mimì, the lorette and grisette, the *femme fatale* and the *femme fragile*. The attempt to 'disguise' Mimì's character-change in the scene with the students by dressing her symbolically in a gown of Musetta's only calls attention to the problem. Even more important for the deliberations in Ricordi's office may have been the overriding liability of duplication within an already extensive libretto. The musical high-jinks of the large crowd scene, for example, duplicate the type of events already planned for the Café Momus, and the contrastive treatment of the couples already dominates the end of the Barrière act (assuming that this material was not placed there after the Cortile was deleted). Perhaps even more striking, the librettists clearly intended that Musetta should have a solo early in the Cortile act, which would increase its (already considerable) similarity to the present Act II. The fact that the opening verses of this solo are prosodically identical to 'Quando me'n vo'':

> Quando me'n vo' soletta per la via,
> . . .
> Ecco, l'autunno annebbia già le vie! ...

may of course be accidental, but it underlines the difficulty Puccini would have had in fashioning a further aria of sufficiently contrasting character.

Not everything from the Cortile act was lost to *La bohème*. For example, Rodolfo's remorse over the ineluctable death of the 'hothouse flower' Mimì reappears at the end of the Barrière act, and the parodic dance and duelling scene that immediately precedes the entrance of Mimì in Act IV includes the suggestion that the Bohemians attempt a *quadrille*. Finally, when Musetta introduces Mimì to the students, she offers an early form of what has become for many the most famous line of the opera: 'Mimì è chiamata, / ma il suo nome è Lucia' ('She is called Mimì, but her name is Lucia').

Cortile di una casa in Via Labruyère N. 8

A destra portone d'ingresso e portico. A sinistra scala che conduce all'appartamento di Musetta. Presso il portone la loggia del portinaio Perdrigeaux. Altre scale conducono ai piani superiori. E' notte. Chiarore di luna.
Dietro il cancello della portineria si ferma la compagnia dei bohèmi.
Marcello indica a Rodolfo, Mimì, Schaunard, Colline la scala che conduce all'appartamento abitato da Musetta.

MARCELLO
Musetta abita là!
SCHAUNARD
    Neppure l'ombra
d'un portinaio!
COLLINE
    Entriam!
TUTTI (*tranne Marcello*)
     Siamo invitati!
MARCELLO (*indica*)
Ecco! ... in fondo al cortile ... Quella scala.
  (*per avviarsi*)
Vi saluto.
RODOLFO (*trattenendolo*)
    Marcel ...
GLI ALTRI
     Vieni anche tu!
MARCELLO
Sapete a successore chi m'ha dato
Musetta? ...
GLI ALTRI
    Ebbene?
MARCELLO (*con immenso disprezzo*)
     Un consiglier di stato!
  (*grida e gesti d'orrore degli altri*)
Non bevo nel bicchier d'altri il mio vino.
  (*si allontana con dignità*)
Gli altri lo guardano allontanarsi crollando il capo. Entrano nel cortile.
Perdrigeaux scende dalla scala di Musetta con un lume in mano ed incontra i bohèmi.
PERDRIGEAUX
Signori, chi cercate?
RODOLFO (*imbarazzato*)
    Veramente ...
COLLINE
Siamo invitati! ...
SCHAUNARD
    Ed è la signorina
Musetta ...

Courtyard of a house at 8 rue de la Bruyère

To the right a large door and portico. To the left a stairway leading to Musetta's flat. Next to the entrance the room of the concierge Perdrigeaux. Other stairs lead to the upper floors. It is night. Moonlight.
The group of Bohemians stops at the concierge's gate. Marcello indicates to Rodolfo, Mimì, Schaunard, Colline the stairway leading to Musetta's flat.

MARCELLO
Musetta lives there!
SCHAUNARD
          No trace
of a concierge!
COLLINE
          Let's go in!
ALL   (*except for Marcello*)
          We're invited!
MARCELLO (*pointing*)
There! ... across the courtyard ... Those stairs.
   (*turning away*)
Goodbye.
RODOLFO (*stopping him*)
          Marcel ...
THE OTHERS
          You come too!
MARCELLO
Do you know who Musetta has given me
as a successor? ...
THE OTHERS
          Well?
MARCELLO (*with great scorn*)
          A Crown Councillor!
   (*shouts and gestures of horror from the others*)
I don't drink my wine from another man's cup.
   (*walks away with dignity*)
The others watch him go away, shaking their heads. They enter the courtyard. Perdrigeaux comes down Musetta's stairs with a light in his hand and meets the Bohemians.
PERDRIGEAUX
Gentlemen, who are you looking for?
RODOLFO (*embarrassed*)
          Actually ...
COLLINE
We're invited! ...
SCHAUNARD
          And is Mlle
Musetta ...

PERDRIGEAUX
    Ah! certo voi volete dire
Madama De Musette!
SCHAUNARD
                    E' ver, perdono.
RODOLFO
Madama De Musette oggi riceve?
(*Gran baccano di voci dall'appartamento e dalla scala di Musetta*)
PERDRIGEAUX
Gnorsì! Sta ricevendo degli uscieri.
(*Alcuni uscieri scendono a precipizio dalla scala di Musetta*)*
USCIERI (*sbuffanti ansanti*)
E' jena! ... E' tigre! ...
E' serpe! ... e' gatta
furente! ...

Scatta! ...   MUSETTA (*al*   PERDRIGEAUX (*agli uscieri e a*
S'imbizza ...   *balcone*   *Musetta*)
Strepita! ...   *inviperita*)   Tacete! ...
Furore   Quando con   Silenzio!
  schizza! ...   gentildonna,   Decoro!
S'avventa!   signori, s'ha a   La casa! ...
  Impazza! ...   trattare,   La porta!
Pantera! ...   anche un   (*agli uscieri*)
  Vespa! ...   usciere deve   partite!
Leonessa   sapersi   La porta! ...
  in furia! ...   regolare,   Tacete! ...
Lupa che   perchè una   La casa! ...
  allatta! ...   citazione,   Il decoro! ...   I BOHÈMI
Istrice! ...   signori uscieri   (*spinge gli*   (*intervengono,*
  Arpia! ...   miei,   *uscieri verso la*   *prendendo le*
Furiosa! ...   non esclude per   *porta*)   *difese di*
  Matta! ...   altro   Venite!   *Musetta*)
Modo e maniera   la buona   Ha ragione!
di pignorare   educazione!   Ha ragione!
di sequestrare   L'agire con   Ragioni ne ha
con lei non c'è!   violenza   da vendere!
    non tollero,   Certo ...
      screanzanti   Certo ...
    uscieri, in casa   Un po' d'edu-
      mia!   cazione! ...

PERDRIGEAUX (*parla,*
trascinandoli via, sottovoce agli
uscieri)
Subito all'alba indetta
sia l'asta! ...

MUSETTA (*ravvisando gli amici,*
esclamazioni di gioia dal balcone)
Schaunard! Rodolfo! ... Colline e
Mimì.

*In questo punto, nel testo originale, vi è la seguente annotazione:
'Puccini può far sentire delle risate di inquilini'.

PERDRIGEAUX
Ah, you must mean
Madame De Musette!
SCHAUNARD
Of course, pardon me.

RODOLFO
Is Madame De Musette receiving today?
(*Great uproar from Musetta's flat and stairway*)
PERDRIGEAUX
Yessir, she's receiving some bailiffs.
(*Some bailiffs tumble down Musetta's stairs*)*
BAILIFFS (*panting and gasping*)
A hyena! ... A tigress! ...
A serpent! ... A wildcat! ...

BAILIFFS
She snaps! ...
Rages ...
Shouts! ...
Spits
fire! ...
She pounces!
Goes mad! ...
A panther! ...
A hornet! ...
A lioness
in fury! ...
A she-wolf that
nurses! ...
A porcupine! ...
A harpy! ...
A fury! ...
A maniac! ...
With her,
there's no way
we'll ever seize
and confiscate!

MUSETTA (*on the balcony, enraged*)
When dealing
with a gentle-
woman, kind
sirs, even a
bailiff should
know how to
behave,
because a
warrant, my dear
bailiffs, does
not exempt you
from good
manners! I will
not tolerate
brute force in
my house, you
uncouth
bailiffs!

PERDRIGEAUX (*to the bailiffs and Musetta*)
Be quiet! ...
Silence!
Decorum!
The house! ...
The door!
(*to the bailiffs*)
Leave!
The door! ...
Be quiet! ...
The
house! ...
Decorum! ...
(*pushes the bailiffs toward the door*)
Come!

THE BOHEMIANS (*they interrupt, taking up Musetta's defence*)
She's right!
She's right!
She's absolutely
right!
Surely ...
Surely ...
Show some
manners! ...

PERDRIGEAUX (*speaking sotto voce to the bailiffs as he drags them away*)
Set the auction for daybreak tomorrow! ...

MUSETTA (*recognising her friends, exclamations of joy from the balcony*)
Schaunard! Rodolfo! ... Colline and Mimì.

---

*At this point, in the original text, there comes the following annotation:
'Puccini can make heard some laughter from the tenants'.

Dai facchini
farò intanto sgombrare! ...
Sia questa la vendetta! ...
(*esce con gli uscieri*)

(abbandona rapidamente il balcone. Entra in scena e corre ad abbracciare Mimì con slancio pieno di effusione)

MUSETTA
    Ah! finalmente
dei volti da cristiano!
Schaunard, Colline, e voi Rodolfo,
stringiamoci la mano ...
(*Ritorna Perdrigeaux con quattro facchini e con questi sale all'appartamento di Musetta*)
E noi ancora un bacio, o mia Mimì!
RODOLFO
Ah, siete tale e quale,
allegra ancora come un carnevale ...
SCHAUNARD
Vi siete conservata,
il mangiar bene non v'ha punto cambiata!
COLLINE
Pulcra, formosa, kala! ...
Vi sta a pennello un abito di gala.
MIMÌ   (*toccandole l'abito*)
Quale abito perfetto!
La gonna val dieci scudi, lo scommetto!
E il busto! ... Ardito e snello! ...
MUSETTA   (*che ha guardato intorno cercando*)
Ov'è Marcello?
(*tutti tacciano imbarazzati*)
        (*capisce dal loro silenzio, ed esclama con dolore*)
Pur se sapeste quanto m'è costato
L'aver pensato a lui e aver spedito
quel mio invito! ...
(*i bohèmi non hanno cuore di consolarla*)
Ecco, l'autunno annebbia già le vie! ...
Voi, di Firenze, addio, larghi cappelli,
vesti indiscrete e fisciù trasparenti
che non mentite, e maniche imprudenti! ...
Addio, bel sole! Addio, canto d'augelli ...
Musetta ha già le sue malinconie.
PERDRIGEAUX   (*dal balcone, ai facchini che hanno portato giù un canapè e delle sedie*)
Giudizio, e fate piano.
(*I facchini posano nel cortile il canapè e le sedie*)
MUSETTA   (*distrattamente si siede sul canapè. Ai facchini:*)
        Grazie!
MIMÌ   (*la imita*)
        Grazie!

Meanwhile I'll have (*quickly leaves the balcony.*
the porters clear things away! ... *Enters the stage and runs to embrace*
Let this be our revenge! *Mimì with a burst of emotion*)
(*exits with the bailiffs*)

MUSETTA

Ah! finally
some Christian faces!
Schaunard, Colline, and you Rodolfo,
give me your hands ...
(*Perdrigeaux returns with four porters and goes with them up to Musetta's flat*)
Give me another kiss, dear Mimì!

RODOLFO
Ah, you're just the same as ever,
still happy as a holiday ...

SCHAUNARD
You're in good shape,
eating well hasn't hurt you in the least!

COLLINE
Pulcra, formosa, kala! ...
A ball gown suits you perfectly.

MIMÌ (*touching the gown*)
What a perfect gown!
I bet the skirt is worth ten scudi!
And the bodice! ... Tight and bold! ...

MUSETTA (*who has been looking around, searching*)
Where is Marcello?
(*they all fall silent, embarrassed*)
(*she understands their silence, and exclaims sorrowfully*)
If you only knew what it has cost me,
to have thought of him and sent
that invitation! ...
(*the Bohemians don't have the heart to console her*)
Look, autumn mists already darken the streets! ...
Farewell, broad Florentine hats,
revealing dresses and transparent fichus
that don't deceive, and daring sleeves! ...
Farewell, beautiful sun! Farewell, warbling birds ...
Musetta's feeling melancholy already.

PERDRIGEAUX (*from the balcony, to the porters who have carried down a couch and some chairs*)
Careful, and no noise.
(*The porters put the couch and chairs down in the courtyard*)

MUSETTA (*absent-mindedly sitting down on the couch. To the porters:*)
Thank you!

MIMÌ (*imitating her*)
Thank you!

MUSETTA   (*continuando, sentimentale*)
Sale dai campi odore d'erbe morte …
Gli alberi, i rami stendon scheletriti …
(*Rodolfo, Schaunard, Colline le si avvicinano.   Intanto i facchini sono saliti
a prendere altri mobili*)
Pensano le signore a fare inviti
per prepararsi il verno un po' di corte …
Oh allora … ai vecchi tempi è ritornato
il mio pensiero! …
               E allora vi ho invitati …
PERDRIGEAUX   (*ai facchini che sono ridiscesi portando una poltrona ed
altre sedie*)
Da bravi … adagio! …
         (*i facchini dispongono poltrona e sedie: i bohèmi siedono*)
RODOLFO   (*sedendo*)
                  Grazie!
SCHAUNARD   (*c.s.*)
                     Grazie!
COLLINE   (*c.s.*)
                        Grazie! …
(*sono tutti seduti intorno a Musetta – i facchini vanno e vengono portando
giù i mobili*)
MUSETTA
Ma appena lesse il Consiglier di Stato
fra gli invitati un certo nome … allor
apriti terra! … Che furia e furor!
E di pagar l'affitto ha rifiutato.
               (*pausa*)
Ecco in che modo ho uscieri e citazioni
ed invitati – e non ho più saloni.
(*si guardano in faccia. Poi ad un tratto tutti prorompono in una grande,
allegra, rumorosa risata*)
RODOLFO   (*levandosi in piedi, con entusiasmo*)
Salone non avete?
Ma guardate!
Questo cortil, sapete,
è una gran serra senza vetriate,
e Musetta e Mimì sono i suoi fiori.
Che volete di più? …
Un po' di luce … vino e compagnia.
MUSETTA
E poi: festa da ballo!
TUTTI
               E così sia!
(*Si alzano con entusiasmo, corrono pel cortile collocando i mobili e
trasformandolo in sala da ballo. Perdrigeaux che si era soffermato sul-
l'ultimo gradino della scala per godere dell'imbarazzo, rimane atterrito a
quella gioia.*)

MUSETTA (*continuing, sentimentally*)
The scent of dead flowers rises from the fields ...
The trees spread out their skeletal branches ...
(*Rodolfo, Schaunard, Colline gather round her. Meanwhile the porters have gone up to take more furniture*)
Ladies think of sending invitations
to assure themselves of a little company in winter ...
Oh then ... my thoughts returned
to the old days! ...
    And then I invited you ...
PERDRIGEAUX (*to the porters, who have come back down carrying an armchair and other chairs*)
Very good ... careful! ...
  (*the porters put down the armchair and chairs: the Bohemians sit down*)
RODOLFO (*sitting down*)
     Thank you!
SCHAUNARD (*ditto*)
      Thank you!
COLLINE (*ditto*)
       Thank you! ...
(*all are seated around Musetta. The porters come and go, bringing down furniture*)
MUSETTA
But as soon as the Crown Councillor
read a certain name among the guests ... then
all hell broke loose! ... What ranting and raving!
And he refused to pay the rent.
    (*pause*)
And that's how I have bailiffs and warrants
and guests – and I no longer have a salon.
(*they look at each other. Then, suddenly, they all break out in huge, joyful, noisy laughter*)
RODOLFO (*standing up, enthusiastically*)
You have no salon?
But look!
This courtyard, you know,
is a large greenhouse without glass,
and Musetta and Mimì are its flowers.
What more do you need? ...
A little light ... wine and friends.
MUSETTA
And then: a ball!
ALL
    So be it!
(*They jump up enthusiastically and run around the courtyard arranging the furniture to make a ballroom. Perdrigeaux, who has stopped at the last step of the stairs to enjoy their discomfiture, is horrified at their high spirits.*)

SCHAUNARD
Presto!

COLLINE
   Il tappeto!

SCHAUNARD
In circolo le seggiole!

MUSETTA
Il selciato è discreto.

MIMÌ
Io ballo volentieri!

COLLINE
Ecco là dei doppieri!

RODOLFO (*a Musetta*)
Vado pei suonatori e le candele
e qui ritorno subito! (*parte correndo*)
(*Musetta e Mimì da un lato
chiacchierano fra loro, ridendo e
scherzando, senza badare agli altri.
Poi tornano a baciarsi molto
affettuosamente.*)

MUSETTA
Quante volte, Mimì
t'ho qui desiderata
e t'ho aspettata
sempre ... ogni dì ...

MIMÌ
E veduta m'avresti! ...
Ma sai! ... (*arrossisce mostrando a
Musetta la sua veste meschina*)
      Sol questa
di tutte le mie vesti
che non ebbi ... mi resta! ...
(*Sorride, ma poi con tristezza
soggiunge:*)
Con Rodolfo, all'asciutto
si è sempre di denari
ed or anche d'amore ...
all'asciutto ... (*sospira*)
      di tutto!
(*mostra ancora la veste*)
Or se si balla, qui,
ah! ... (*dispettita*)
    dalla veste mia
capiranno ch'io sia
e diranno: – E' Mimì! ... –

MUSETTA (*sorridendo e baciandola*)
Non capiranno niente! ...

(*Schaunard e Colline mettono in
ordine il cortile, mentre Perdrigeaux
va dall'uno all'altro infuriato e
sbalordito.*)

PERDRIGEAUX
Signori, che si fa?

SCHAUNARD
Avreste il mal di fiele?

PERDRIGEAUX
Ballare forse credono,
signori?

COLLINE
    Gnorsì!

SCHAUNARD
     Già.

COLLINE (*indicando Musetta*)
Finchè l'asta non va
sono suoi questi mobili!

SCHAUNARD
Musetta è la padrona
qui, fino a domattina.

PERDRIGEAUX
M'ascoltino!

SCHAUNARD
     ... Idea nobile!
In fondo al porticato
il paravento.

PERDRIGEAUX
Miei signori!

SCHAUNARD
Quick!
COLLINE
   The carpet!
SCHAUNARD
Chairs in a circle!
MUSETTA
The pavement is smooth.
MIMÌ
I'm happy to dance!
COLLINE
There are some candlesticks!
RODOLFO (*to Musetta*)
I'll get the musicians and the candles
and be right back! (*running off*)

(*Musetta and Mimì, to one side, are chattering, laughing and joking, without paying attention to the others. Then they kiss each other affectionately again.*)

MUSETTA
How often, Mimì
I have wanted you here
and I have waited for you
always ... every day ...
MIMÌ
And you would have seen me! ...
But you know! ... (*blushes, showing Musetta her shabby dress*)
       This is the last
of all the dresses
I ever had ...
(*smiles, but then adds sadly:*)
With Rodolfo, one is
always short of money
and now even of love ...
we're short ... (*sighs*)
       of everything!
(*again pointing to her dress*)
Now, if I dance here,
ah! ... (*angrily*)
   from my dress
they will know who I am
and will say: – It's Mimì! ...
MUSETTA (*smiling and kissing her*)
They won't see anything! ...

(*Schaunard and Colline put the courtyard in order, while Perdrigeaux goes from one to the other, infuriated and amazed.*)

PERDRIGEAUX
Gentlemen, what are you doing?
SCHAUNARD
What's galling you?
PERDRIGEAUX
Are you perhaps planning to dance, gentlemen?
COLLINE
      Yessir!
SCHAUNARD
       Certainly.
COLLINE (*pointing to Musetta*)
Until the auction starts
this furniture is hers!
SCHAUNARD
Musetta is the mistress
here, until tomorrow morning.
PERDRIGEAUX
Listen to me!
SCHAUNARD
     ... A fine idea!
At the far end of the portico,
the screen.
PERDRIGEAUX
Gentlemen!

Signora sembrerai
e un qualche bel studente
ricco conquisterai ...
ho un abito che fatto
pare per te!
MIMÌ   (*con gioia*)
   Ed è bello?
MUSETTA
Sì, cara mia, bellissimo! ...
MIMÌ
Bellissimo! ...
MUSETTA   (*è interrotta da Schaunard,*
cui consegna le chiavi) SCHAUNARD   (*a Musetta*)
  ... Marcello!   Le chiavi mancano della cantina.
(*Entra Rodolfo con un pacco di candele, trascinandosi dietro Marcello e*
seguito da alcuni suonatori ambulanti. Schaunard e Colline vanno e vengono
carichi di bottiglie che depongono su di un tavolo.)
RODOLFO   (*a Musetta*)
Signora, dal droghiere
ho incontrato questo mio vecchio amico.
Credetemi, è, vi dico,
un vero cavaliere!
(*va ad accendere le candele*)
(*Perdrigeaux corre sempre come un pazzo di qua e di là, ma nessuno gli*
bada. Va alfine a rinchiudersi nel suo stambugio sbattendone l'uscio.)
MUSETTA   (*a Marcello, con fare da gran dama*)
L'amico degli amici è amico mio.
E' un onore per me ...
MARCELLO   (*imbarazzato*)
     E' un onor mio ... eziandio.
(*Musetta conduce Mimì dietro il paravento. Al trambusto che succede nel*
cortile si aprono delle finestre e fanno capolino vari inquilini maschi e
femmine.)
GLI INQUILINI
– Nel cortile che accade?
– O che baccano è questo?
– Di notte è ben molesto
 il non dormir!
–   Ballare
vogliono a quel che pare!
– Curiosa cosa
 davvero è questa!
– Se invitan, muto vesta!
– Addio riposo e letto!
– Han flauto e clarinetto!
SCHAUNARD   (*vedendo gente alle finestre, si cava il cappello, fa un grande*
inchino, poi grida agli inquilini:)
Madama De Musette invita a danza

You will look like a lady
and will captivate some rich
and handsome student ...
I have a dress that looks
made for you!
MIMÌ *(joyfully)*
      Is it beautiful?
MUSETTA
Yes, my dear, very beautiful! ...
MIMÌ
Very beautiful! ...
MUSETTA *(interrupted by Schaunard,*
to whom she gives the keys)   SCHAUNARD *(to Musetta)*
      ... Marcello!   We need the keys to the wine cellar.
(Enter Rodolfo with a bundle of candles, dragging behind him Marcello and
followed by some street musicians. Schaunard and Colline come and go,
loaded with bottles which they put down on a table)
RODOLFO *(to Musetta)*
Madame, at the grocer's
I met this old friend of mine.
Believe me when I tell you
he's a true cavalier!
(goes to light the candles)
(Perdrigeaux is still running hither and thither like a madman, but no one
pays him any attention. Finally he shuts himself in his room, slamming the
door.)
MUSETTA *(to Marcello, with a dignified air)*
A friend of my friends is a friend of mine.
It's an honour for me ...
MARCELLO *(embarrassed)*
      It is I who am honoured ... really.
(Musetta leads Mimì behind the screen. During the ensuing commotion in
the courtyard, some windows open, and various tenants, men and women,
peek out.)
TENANTS
– What's happening in the courtyard?
– Oh, what's all this noise?
– It's very annoying not to sleep
   at night!
–   It seems as though
   they are planning to dance!
– This is really
   very strange!
– If they invite us, I'll get changed!
– Farewell rest and bed!
– They've got a flute and clarinet!
SCHAUNARD *(seeing people at the windows, takes off his hat, makes a*
deep bow, then shouts to the tenants:)
Madama De Musette invites to dance

tutta la casa di via La Bruyère – Otto –
Tutti invitati sono – sopra e sotto –
Ogni ceto, ogni età, sesso ed usanza.
GLI INQUILINI   (*dalle finestre*)
E' cortese! è gentile
quel signore dal naso
grosso, che dal cortile
sì nobile parlò.
– Grazie! Grazie! Scendiamo!
– Grazie! Grazie! Veniamo!
– Grazie, grazie. Accorriamo!
– Grazie, grazie! Voliamo!
(*Poco a poco il cortile si riempie degli inquilini: intanto Rodolfo cogli amici
ha acceso alcune lampade, una quantità di candele in modo da formare
un'illuminazione vivissima. Poi stappano bottiglie ed offrono da bere agli
invitati. Un gruppo di giovanotti, studenti, vedendo Musetta che esce dietro
il paravento, le vanno incontro complimentosi. Fra gli studenti è il
viscontino.*)
STUDENTI
Madama, qui vedete a voi davanti
aspiratrici adoratrici schiere;
siam vostri servitori spasimanti,
al posto concorriam del Consigliere.
Madama, ai vostri piè le nostre brame,
ai vostri piè, Musetta, i nostri cuori:
la cattedra aspiriam dei vostri amori,
e … fateci ripetere l'esame.
MUSETTA   (*agli studenti*)
In cattedra è tornato il professore
ordinario, Marcel fatalità;
ma un'altra insuperbisca all'alto onore
di piroettare coll'Università.
(*Corre a prendere Mimì che esce dietro il paravento vestita elegantemente
con una veste di Musetta. E' imbarazzata e impacciata nel gestire, nel
muoversi, nel camminare; però si guarda, compiacendosi. Musetta la
presenta.*)
Mimì è chiamata,
ma il suo nome è Lucia.
(*a Mimì*)
Perchè così impacciata? …
(*agli studenti*)
E voi? … Che fate? … Or via,
coraggio, ed invitatela!
(*uno studente si offre*)
Bravo! (*lo presenta a Mimì*)
      E' il visconte Paolo!
Oh, fortunata mia presentazione!
(*sottovoce al visconte*)
Complamente libera!

the entire house of 8 rue de la Bruyère.
Everyone's invited – upstairs and down –
Every class, every age, sex and way of life.
TENANTS   (*from the windows*)
He's courteous! he's polite,
that man with the big
nose, who spoke so nicely
from the courtyard.
– Thank you! Thank you! We're coming down!
– Thank you! Thank you! We're coming!
– Thank you, thank you. We'll hurry!
– Thank you, thank you! We'll fly!
(*Little by little the courtyard fills with tenants: meanwhile Rodolfo and his friends have lit several lamps and a great many candles, providing brilliant illumination. They then uncork the bottles and offer drinks to the guests. A group of young students, seeing Musetta emerge from behind the screen, moves towards her admiringly. Among the students is the Viscount.*)
STUDENTS
Madame, here you see before you
crowds of adoring aspirants:
we are your ardent servants,
vying for the Councillor's position.
Madame, at your feet we lay our yearning,
at your feet, Musetta, our hearts:
we aspire to the instruction of your love,
and ... make us repeat the exercise.
MUSETTA   (*to the students*)
The endowed professor, Marcello my destiny,
has returned to his chair:
but let another preen herself for the high honour
of pirouetting with Academe.
(*She runs to take Mimì, who emerges from behind the screen elegantly dressed in one of Musetta's gowns. She is embarrassed and awkward in gesture, movement and walk; but she looks at herself, pleased. Musetta introduces her.*)
She is called Mimì,
but her name is Lucia.
(*to Mimì*)
Why so awkward? ...
(*to the students*)
And you? ... What are you doing? ... Come on,
Take courage, and ask her!
(*a student steps forward*)
Bravo! (*introduces him to Mimì*)
          It's Viscount Paolo!
What a lucky introduction!
(*sotto voce to the Viscount*)
She's absolutely free!

(*sottovoce a Mimì*)
Ricco! Gentile! Giovane! ...
(*vedendoli ancora un po' impacciati prende il braccio di Mimì e lo infila sotto a quello del visconte Paolo*)
Or completate la combinazione!
(*Il viscontino va con Mimì al braccio a prender posto per la quadriglia che nel mezzo del cortile sta organizzando Schaunard. Gli studenti salutano Musetta e si allontanano vedendo avvicinarsi a lei Marcello.*)

MARCELLO
Signora, non danzate.
MUSETTA
Nessuno m'ha invitata.
MARCELLO
Se osassi ...
MUSETTA
    Mi invitate?
MARCELLO (*ombroso*)
Rifiutate?
MUSETTA
Sono civetta, vana, velenosa,
accettando farei cosa noiosa.
MARCELLO
Musetta ...
MUSETTA
Ebben?
MARCELLO
    Musetta! ...
MUSETTA
      Ascolto.
MARCELLO
        Ancora?
MUSETTA
Che cosa ...
MARCELLO
    Via!
MUSETTA
    Insistete nell'invito?
Siccome un ballo a tutti si concede,
ecco il mio braccio e se il signore
   crede
ballar con me, balliamo la
   quadriglia.
(*Marcello la stringe con entusiasmo*)

RODOLFO (*si aggira fra la gente
cercando Mimì, poi s'avvicina a
Schaunard*)
Mimì hai veduta?
SCHAUNARD
    No!
(*lo spinge fuori dal quadrato dove
sta mettendo a posto le coppie*)
Via dal quadrato!
(*corre a prendere anzi la prima
coppia che vede e la mette a posto*)
    Qui,
signori miei!
(*sono appunto Mimì e il viscontino
Paolo. Passano vicinissimi a
Rodolfo. Mimì nasconde abilmente
il volto. Rodolfo la guarda senza
ravvisarla e dice:*)
RODOLFO
    Non so
dove andata è Mimì!
(*si allontana*)
SCHAUNARD (*grida*)
Un'altra coppia! Or via! ...
(*Colline accorre tenendo al braccio
una grassotta borghese piuttosto
attempata*)
RODOLFO (*fermandoli*)
Mimì l'hai tu veduta?
COLLINE (*in fretta*)
Affatto!
(*va a prender posto*)
RODOLFO
    Dove sia

RODOLFO (*ferma Musetta e Marcello come ha fermato Colline*)
Mimì veduta avete?   non so! ... Io l'ho perduta! ...

(*sotto voce to Mimì*)
Rich! Noble! Young! ...
(*seeing they are still a little stiff, she takes Mimì's arm and links it to Viscount Paolo's*)
Now go and make up the dance!
(*The Viscount goes with Mimì on his arm to take a place in the quadrille which Schaunard is organising in the middle of the courtyard. The students take their leave of Musetta and move away as they see Marcello approaching her.*)

MARCELLO
Madame, you're not dancing.
MUSETTA
No one has asked me.
MARCELLO
If I should venture ...
MUSETTA
        To invite me?
MARCELLO   (*moodily*)
You refuse?
MUSETTA
I am a flirt, vain, and spiteful,
It would be boring to accept.
MARCELLO
Musetta ...
MUSETTA
Well?
MARCELLO
    Musetta! ...
MUSETTA
        I'm listening.
MARCELLO
          Still?
MUSETTA

What ...
MARCELLO
    Come on!
MUSETTA
    You persist in the invitation?
Since everyone's allowed a dance,
here's my arm, and if the gentleman
  wants
to dance with me, let's dance the
  quadrille.
(*Marcello embraces her enthusiastically*)

RODOLFO   (*moving through the crowd looking for Mimì, then approaching Schaunard*)
Have you seen Mimì?
SCHAUNARD
        No!
(*pushing him out of the square where he is placing the couples*)
Out of the square!
(*runs to take the first couple he sees and puts them in place*)
    Here,
my friends!
(*they are in fact Mimì and the young Viscount Paolo. They pass very close to Rodolfo. Mimì adroitly hides her face. Rodolfo looks at her without recognition and says:*)
RODOLFO
      I don't know
where Mimì has gone!
(*moves away*)
SCHAUNARD   (*calling*)
Another couple! Let's go! ...

(*Colline runs up with a plump, middle-aged bourgeoise on his arm*)
RODOLFO   (*stopping them*)
Have you seen Mimì?
COLLINE   (*in haste*)
Not at all!

(*goes to take his place*)
RODOLFO
    I don't know
Where she is! ... I've lost her! ...

RODOLFO   (*stops Musetta and Marcello as he stopped Colline*)
Have you seen Mimì?

MUSETTA   (*indicando*)
Eccola là.
RODOLFO   (*non la riconosce*)
Là ... dove?
MUSETTA
Al braccio di quel bruno!
RODOLFO   (*ravvisandola*)
Oh! Dei!
SCHAUNARD   (*ai suonatori*)
Una quadriglia! I cavalieri qua,
conducete le dame.
RODOLFO   (*non crede ai suoi occhi. Le si avvicina e la chiama*)
Mimì!
(*Mimì si svolge*)
E' lei! ...
(*a Mimì con ira*)
Che fate?
SCHAUNARD   (*sempre in faccenda colle coppie dei ballerini*)
Attenti!
MIMÌ
Danzo!
RODOLFO   (*entra in mezzo alle coppie*)
Che v'ha detto
d'abbigliarvi così?
SCHAUNARD   (*impazientito*)
Rodolfo, via!
MUSETTA E MARCELLO
Via! S'incomincia.
RODOLFO
Al diavol la quadriglia!
(*a Mimì*)
Non voglio che balliate.
TUTTI
Via, Rodolfo!
RODOLFO
Mimì ballar non deve!
MIMÌ   (*stizzita*)
Invece ballerò!
TUTTI
Rodolfo via!
RODOLFO   (*afferra Mimì per un braccio*)
Così tu mi rispondi?
MIMÌ   (*getta uno strido*)
Ahimè!
TUTTI   (*interponendosi*)
Vergogna!
– Rodolfo!
– E' pazzo!
– Via!

MUSETTA   (*pointing*)
                   There she is.
RODOLFO   (*not recognising her*)
There ... where?
MUSETTA
                   On the arm of that dark young man!
RODOLFO   (*recognising her*)
                                   Oh! Gods!
SCHAUNARD   (*to the players*)
A quadrille! The gentlemen here,
lead the ladies.
RODOLFO   (*not believing his eyes. He approaches her and calls to her*)
                   Mimì!
                       (*Mimì turns*)
                       It's she! ...
                       (*angrily to Mimì*)
What are you doing?
SCHAUNARD   (*still preoccupied with the pairs of dancers*)
                                   Watch out!
MIMÌ
                           Dancing!
RODOLFO   (*going amongst the couples*)
                                   Who told you
to dress up like this?
SCHAUNARD   (*impatient*)
                       Rodolfo, get out!
MUSETTA AND MARCELLO
Out! We're starting.
RODOLFO
                       Damn the quadrille!
(*to Mimì*)
I don't want you to dance.
ALL
                       Rodolfo, out!
RODOLFO
Mimì must not dance!
MIMÌ   (*annoyed*)
But I will dance!
ALL
                   Get out, Rodolfo!
RODOLFO   (*seizing Mimì by the arm*)
Is this how you answer me?
MIMÌ   (*shrieking*)
                           Oh!
ALL   (*interrupting*)
                           For shame!
– Rodolfo!
           – He's mad!
                   – Away!

– E' una donna!

– Lasciatela danzare.

   – E' un ubriaco!

MARCELLO
Acchetati.

COLLINE   (*trascinando via Rodolfo*)
  Prudenza!

SCHAUNARD   (*rimette a posto i ballerini e fa cenno ai suonatori di incominciare*)
   S'incomincia!

SCHAUNARD (*dirige i suonatori e dà i comandi per le figure della quadriglia*)	COLLINE (*riesce a condurre Rodolfo presso il tavolo – lo forza a sedersi e gli versa da bere*)

       RODOLFO
       Dammi da bere! Ancora! ancora!
       ancora!
       La bile ho che m'affoga, ora!

Pantalon   Oh, le donne!
Chaîne anglaise   Eccola là. (*accenna a Mimì*)
       COLLINE
Balancé à vos Dames   T'accheta!
       RODOLFO
         Ecco la vana
Tour de mains   leggiadra creatura! … E come adesca
       quel fringuellin di primo pelo!
           Ride!
       Si pavoneggia! E parla, la sfacciata!
       Parla, parla e sorride!
          E sai perchè? …
Chaîne des Dames Perch'ella sa così di torturarmi
       E sa di farmi piangere …
       (*soffocando un singhiozzo*) essa
        ride! …
       Da bere … ancora … sempre! …
       Ed or … ed or …
       COLLINE   (*cerca calmarlo*)
Demi-quene du chât   Suvvia!
       RODOLFO   (*colto da un'idea*)
         Scriver le voglio.
Demi-chaîne   COLLINE   (*leva di tasca un vecchio libro e strappa il primo foglio bianco*)
       Ecco la carta!
Révérence   RODOLFO
         Grazie!

– She's a woman!
– Let her dance!
– He's a drunkard!
MARCELLO
Calm down.
COLLINE (*dragging Rodolfo away*)
Be sensible!
SCHAUNARD (*restoring the dancers to their positions and signalling the players to start*)
Let's begin!

SCHAUNARD (*conducting the players and giving commands for the figures of the quadrille*)	COLLINE (*succeeds in leading Rodolfo toward the table – forces him to sit down and pours him a drink*)
	RODOLFO
	Give me a drink! More! more! more!
	My own bile is choking me, now!
Pantalon	Oh, women!
Chaîne anglaise	Look at her there. (*pointing to Mimì*)
	COLLINE
Balancé à vos Dames	Calm down!
	RODOLFO
	Look at the vain
Tour de mains	charming creature! … And how she lures
	that fledgling on!
	She laughs!
	She prances! And talks, the shameless thing!
	She talks, talks and smiles!
	And do you know why? …
Chaîne des Dames	Because she knows she can torture me that way
	and knows it makes me cry …
	(*stifling a sob*) she laughs! …
	A drink … more … again! …
	And now … and now …
	COLLINE (*trying to calm him*)
Demi-quene du chât	Come now!
	RODOLFO (*struck by an idea*)
	I want to write to her.
Demi-chaîne	COLLINE (*taking an old book out of his pocket and tearing out the first blank page*)
	Here's some paper!
Révérence	RODOLFO
	Thank you!

Pastourelle
Le cavalier avec sa Dame en avant
et en arrière

Le cavalier à sa place

En avant trois

Le cavalier seul

Demi-ronde

Demi chaîne

COLLINE   (*gli dà una matita*)
                    Scrivi!
RODOLFO
                                    Grazie!
(*Rodolfo scrive. Colline beve.
Marcello e Musetta infervorati in un
dialogo lasciano la quadriglia e si
avanzano. Schaunard indispettito
vorrebbe trattenerli ... poi, ridendo,
mette assieme un'altra coppia di
ballerini, e comincia un'altra figura
della quadriglia.*)
MARCELLO   (*a Musetta*)
Ah! la tua voce mi fa morire.
No, non fissarmi così! Più bella
tu ti sei fatta! Parla, e sentire
fa la carezza di tua favella.
Ha la tua voce d'una canzone
leggiadra il ritmo – se parli è canto
la tua parola – se ridi è incanto ...
E ... dì ... sei libera?
MUSETTA
                        Se fra le stelle
del paradiso fossi seduta,
se avessi udito tue labbra belle
chiamar: – Musetta – sarei venuta!
Sarei volata da te, Marcello,
dal mio Marcello sarei volata
e per volare ... avrei spennata
l'ala ad un angelo, l'ala a un augello.
(*si guardano sorridendo, e
passeggiano sempre parlandosi*)
RODOLFO   (*lacera indispettito il
foglio*)
Un foglio ancor!
COLLINE
                        Non ho più frontespizi!
(*la quadriglia porta innanzi la
coppia di Mimì col viscontino. Mimì
risponde continuando il suo
discorso*)

COLLINE (*giving him a pencil*)
Write!
RODOLFO
Thank you!
(*Rodolfo writes. Colline drinks.
Marcello and Musetta, engrossed in
intimate conversation, leave the
quadrille and come forward.
Schaunard, annoyed, would like to
detain them ... then, laughing, he
joins together another couple of
dancers, and begins a new figure of
the quadrille.*)

Pastourelle

Le cavalier avec sa Dame en avant
et en arrière

MARCELLO (*to Musetta*)
Ah! your voice makes me die.
No, don't stare at me like that!
You've become
even more beautiful!
Speak, and let me hear

Le cavalier à sa place

the caress of your words.
Your voice has the rhythm of

En avant trois

a graceful song – when you speak,
your words
are music – your laugh is an
enchantment ...
And ... tell me ... are you free?
MUSETTA
If among the stars
of heaven I had been seated,
if I had heard your beautiful lips

Le cavalier seul

calling 'Musetta' I would have
come!
I would have flown to you,
Marcello,

Demi-ronde

to my Marcello I would have flown
and to fly ... I would have plucked

Demi chaîne

the wings of an angel, the wings of a
bird.
(*they smile at each other, and walk
on, still talking*)
RODOLFO (*angrily tearing up the
page*)
Another page!
COLLINE
I have no more frontispieces!
(*the quadrille carries Mimì and the
young Viscount to the front. Mimì
answers, continuing her
conversation*)

Finale

Grand chassé-croisé

En avant deux
Chassé à droite et gauche

Traversé – Chasse à droite et à
gauche

Traversé –

Grande Chaîne.

[MIMÌ]
....
Se le vesti mi piacciono?
O tutte bianche, o in nero!...
Liscie... basta una rosa!...
E un nastro so appuntarmelo
da parere vezzosa...
Se ho una veste di seta
allor... Dio mio!
(*la quadriglia riconduce lontano la
coppia di Mimì col viscontino*)
RODOLFO (*guardando Mimì che
danza e chiacchiera col viscontino*)
Essa parla e sorride! – Lo studente
sorride e ascolta! Ingannatrice! Oh!
come
esce soavemente la menzogna
dalla sua bocca, ed io per non
sentirla
gliela chiudevo con un bacio
pazzo!...
(*rimane colla testa nelle mani, gli
occhi fissi, immoto – indifferente a
tutto*)

SCHAUNARD (*finita la quadriglia indica ai ballerini e spettatori le bottiglie
di vino poste in bell'ordine in fondo alla scena*)
Ed ora assalto ai vini.
(*tutti accorrono. L'allegria è al colmo. Gli invitati bevono, cozzano i
bicchieri. Sarà intanto spuntata l'alba. Colline va a parlare animatamente
con Mimì. Si affacciano al cancello d'ingresso alcuni rigattieri. Perdrigeaux
li scorge, corre ad aprire e li abbraccia commosso.*)
RIGATTIERI (*a Perdrigeaux*)
Via La Bruyère?
Asta di mobili?
E' questa, diteci,
la casa?
PERDRIGEAUX (*con gioia*)
      Sì!
RIGATTIERI
Quando incominciasi?
L'incanto affrettisi!
Dove procedesi
all'asta?
PERDRIGEAUX
      Qui!
(*accenna ai rigattieri di aspettare un momento sotto il portico; poi corre a
svegliare i facchini che s'erano addormentati sulla scala di Musetta, ed ordina*)

[MIMÌ]
....
Do I like clothes?
Either all white, or all in black!...
Plain... one rose will do!...

Finale

And I know how to arrange a ribbon
to make myself look pretty...

Grand chassé-croisé

If I have a silk gown,
then... My Lord!
(*the quadrille carries Mimì and the*

En avant deux

Viscount away again)

Chassé à droite et gauche

RODOLFO (*watching Mimì, who
is dancing and chattering with the
Viscount*)
She speaks and smiles! – The
student

Traversé – Chassé à droite et à
gauche

smiles and listens! Deceiver! Oh!
how
sweetly the lie leaves
her mouth, and I, in order not to
hear,

Traversé –

used to close it for her with a wild
kiss!...
(*remains with head in hands,
staring, motionless – indifferent to*

Grande Chaîne.

everything)

SCHAUNARD (*the quadrille over, indicates to the dancers and the spectators the bottles of wine neatly arranged at the back of the stage*)
And now an attack on the wines.
(*all come running. The merriment reaches its peak. The guests drink, touch glasses. Meanwhile, dawn has broken. Colline goes to speak excitedly with Mimì. Some second-hand dealers look through the entrance gate. Perdrigeaux sees them, runs to open the gate, and greets them emotionally.*)
DEALERS (*to Perdrigeaux*)
Via La Bruyère?
Furniture sale?
Tell us, is this
the house?
PERDRIGEAUX (*joyfully*)
        Yes!
DEALERS
When does it start?
Let the auction begin!
Where does the bidding
take place?
PERDRIGEAUX
        Here!
(*motioning the dealers to wait a moment under the portico; then running to wake up the porters who had fallen asleep on Musetta's stairs, and ordering*

loro di prendere i mobili e di radunarli in fondo al cortile. La luce della mattina si fa più intensa.)
Colline (*sorseggiando beatamente un bicchiere ed indicando le etichette delle bottiglie*)
Il consigliere
aveva una cantina poliglotta.
(*beve*)
Questo è sanscrito puro.
Schaunard (*immerge un biscotto in un bicchiere colmo di Champagne*)
Nel bicchiere
ve' il franco idioma come s'imbiscotta!

Colline (*costringe a bere Rodolfo*)
Bevi!
Rodolfo (*tragico*)
Fosse veleno! ...
Schaunard (*versandosi del Borgogna*)
Il dialettale
sapore afforza stranamente il vino! ...
(*tutti ridono e cozzano il bicchiere contro quello di Schaunard*)
Marcello (*siede in disparte con Musetta, indifferenti a quanto succede intorno loro, su di un divano*)
... a un *tilbury* – a un *coupé*
mi sobbalzava il cuore ...
Musetta
... se vedevo un cappello
di felpa ... ecco è Marcello!
Perdrigeaux (*coi facchini, viene a prendere il divano*)
Permesso!
(*i due senza badare si alzano e vanno a sedere altrove, continuando il loro discorso*)
Marcello
... una biondina,
un'agile gonnella ...
Ecco ... Musetta è quella.
Colline (*stappa alcune bottiglie, versa a tutti, poscia ponendo le labbra al suo bicchiere, assaggia ed esclama entusiasmato*)
Che classicismo in questo provenzale!
Rodolfo (*beve, ma osservando Mimì, la vede così intenta ai discorsi del viscontino che, preso d'ira, allontana da sè il bicchiere disgustato*)
Ah, va, Tokay ... Ancor sai di latino!
Perdrigeaux (*ritorna coi facchini*)
Permesso!
(*Marcello e Musetta fanno come prima*)
Musetta
Una mattina
volea spezzarsi il cuore ...
chi passava? ... un pittore.

them to take the furniture and group it at the far end of the courtyard. The morning light grows more intense.)

COLLINE (*blissfully sipping from a glass and pointing to the labels of the bottles*)
The Councillor
had a polyglot cellar.
(*drinks*)
This is pure Sanskrit.
SCHAUNARD (*dipping a biscuit in a glass full of champagne*)
See how
the French idiom is soaked up in this glass!
COLLINE (*forcing Rodolfo to drink*)
Drink!
RODOLFO (*tragically*)
Would it were poison!
SCHAUNARD (*pouring him some Burgundy*)
The local dialect
wonderfully strengthens the flavour of this wine! ...
(*all laugh and touch glasses with Schaunard*)
MARCELLO (*sitting apart on a couch with Musetta, both indifferent to what is happening around them*)
... at a *tilbury* – at a *coupé*
my heart would leap ...
MUSETTA
... if I saw a plush
hat ... there is Marcello!
PERDRIGEAUX (*with the porters, comes to take the couch*)
Excuse me!
(*not paying any attention, the two get up and go to sit elsewhere, continuing their conversation*)
MARCELLO
... A little blond,
the swirl of a petticoat ...
There ... that's Musetta!
COLLINE (*uncorks several bottles, pours for everyone, then bringing his glass to his lips, tastes and exclaims enthusiastically*)
What a classic Provence!
RODOLFO (*drinks, but looking at Mimì, he sees her so absorbed in conversation with the young Viscount that, seized with rage, he pushes away the glass in disgust*)
Ah, away, Tokay ... It still smells of Latin!
PERDRIGEAUX (*returns with the porters*)
Excuse me!
(*Marcello and Musetta do as before*)
MUSETTA
One morning
I thought my heart would break ...
who was passing by? ... a painter.

PERDRIGEAUX
Permesso.
MARCELLO (*spazientito*)
    Eh! seccatore!
PERDRIGEAUX
Signor, dell'asta è l'ora!
MUSETTA E MARCELLO
E andate alla malora!
(*I mobili son quasi tutti radunati in fondo al cortile a sinistra. I rigattieri si avvicinano: un suono di tromba annuncia il principio dell'asta. I bohèmi cogli invitati sono a destra, presso un tavolo che è rimasto, e sul quale stanno ancora bottiglie.*)
SCHAUNARD   (*ai rigattieri*)
Nobili rigattieri, grazie a voi.
Ci annunciate l'aurora!
(*rivolto al cielo*)
Oh rosea signora
ben alzata, buon dì!
(*dà i bicchieri colmi*)
A voi, Musetta! A voi, Mimì!
(*Mimì pone le labbra sul bicchiere, poi lo posa. Rodolfo lo afferra e barcollante col bicchiere in mano si avvicina a Mimì. Tutti lo guardano sorpresi.*)
RODOLFO
Mimì, il mio labbro tocca
il tuo bicchiere ancor.
Qui posasti la bocca,
vi agonizza l'amor;
implacato becchino
è il tuo labbro divino.
(*vuota d'un sorso il bicchiere*)

RODOLFO	MIMÌ (*spaventata si rifugia fra Musetta e Marcello*)	I RIGATTIERI (*suono di tromba*)
Come sopra una croce d'un bianco camposanto, levo ancora là voce,		COMMISS. ESTIMATORE Divano turco per scudi quindici.
canto l'ultimo canto! Odi, canta il mio cor. (*con immenso slancio*) Esci solo! Coi raggi, sulla fronte, del sole, quando sembra la vita una plaga fiorita sparsa di rose e viole e di giunchiglie in fior!	TUTTI GLI ALTRI (*interpolatamente*) – E' ubriaco! – Andiam! – L'aurora sorge. Via. Rincasiamo. – Straziarla non dovete! – Mimì partite! – Andiam! – Conducetelo via!	RIGATTIERI – Diciamo sedici! – Diciotto a me! – Venti! – Vent'uno – E mezzo … Due! – Tre!

PERDRIGEAUX
Excuse me.
MARCELLO (*impatient*)
Hey! Pest!
PERDRIGEAUX
Sir, it's time for the auction!
MUSETTA AND MARCELLO
And go to Hell!
(*Almost all the furniture has been grouped at the back of the courtyard to the left. The dealers approach: the sound of a trumpet announces the beginning of the auction. The Bohemians and guests are to the right, next to a remaining table, on which there are still bottles.*)
SCHAUNARD (*to the dealers*)
Noble dealers, our thanks to you.
You announce to us the dawn!
(*looking to the heavens*)
Oh rosy-fingered lady
welcome, good day!
(*giving out full glasses*)
To you, Musetta! To you, Mimì!
(*Mimì puts her glass to her lips, then sets it down. Rodolfo grasps it and unsteadily approaches Mimì, glass in hand. Everyone looks at him with surprise.*)
RODOLFO
Mimì, my lips touch
your glass again.
Here you placed your mouth,
here love dies in agony;
your divine mouth
is an unrelenting undertaker.
(*empties the glass with one draught*)

RODOLFO	MIMÌ (*frightened, hides between Musetta and Marcello*)	THE DEALERS (*trumpet call*)
As over the cross of a white gravestone, I raise again my voice, I sing my final song! Listen, my heart sings. (*with great passion*) You leave alone! With the rays of the sun on your face,	ALL THE OTHERS (*interrupting*) – He's drunk! – Let's go! – Dawn rises. Come. Home.	AUCTIONEER Turkish divan for fifteen scudi. DEALERS – I bid sixteen! – Eighteen here! – Twenty!
a flowery field strewn with roses and violets and with jonquils in bloom!	– He shouldn't torture her! – Leave, Mimì! Let's go! – Take him away!	– Twenty-one! – And a half ... – Two! – Three!

(*con tristezza*)
Ma il verno ... nei
   misteri,
fra il tepor della seta,
vivi! ... Tu sei un fiore
di serra! ... Fa terrore
la tosse all'ex poeta
cesareo del tuo cuor!
(*scoppia in un lungo
singhiozzo; Schaunard
e Colline lo trascinano
via*)

– E' ubriaco!
– Usciam di qui.
– Via, Rodolfo,
   t'accheta.
– Andiam, dunque.
– E' un poeta!
– Mimì, andate!
      Pietà
desta –
   Davver che fa
compassione ...
   Mimì
andate via di qui.
–V'allontanate!
      – Taci!
– Rodolfo, è giorno
   già!
– Strappatelo via!
–   Sì!
– Rodolfo!
– Andiam Mimì.

– Venticinque!
COMMISS.
ESTIMATORE
Uno! due! tre!
(*suono di tromba*)
Stipetto mogano.
RIGATTIERI
– Trenta.
   – Quaranta.
– Mezzo ...
   – Cinquanta.
– Cinquantatrè!
– Settanta!
   – Ottanta!
– Novanta!
   – Cento!
COMMISS.
ESTIMATORE
Il cero è spento!
(*suono di tromba*)
Un canapè.
Trenta.
RIGATTIERI
– Trent'uno.
– Mezzo.
   – Quaranta!
– A me cinquanta.
– Sessanta.
      – E sette!
– Settanta e tre!

(*Musetta e Marcello conducono via Mimì. Gli inquilini parte salgono, parte
si fermano a vedere l'asta.*)
(*Suono di tromba – L'asta continua.*)
   Cala il sipario

(*with sadness*)
But in winter ... in
mystery,
in the warmth of silk,

you live! ... You are a
hothouse
flower! ... Your cough
terrifies this ex-poet-
king
of your heart!
(*bursts into prolonged*

sobbing; Schaunard
and Colline lead him
away)

– He's drunk!
– Let's leave here!

– Come, Rodolfo,
calm down.
– Let's go, then.

– He's a poet!
– Mimì, go!
It's
pitiable –
it's really

tragic ...

Mimì
go away from here.
– Go away!
– Be quiet!
– Rodolfo, it's day
already!
– Take him away!
– Yes!
– Rodolfo!
– Let's go, Mimì.

– Twenty-five!
AUCTIONEER

Going! going! gone!

(*trumpet call*)

Mahogany chest.
DEALERS

– Thirty.
– Forty.
– Forty-five.
– Fifty.

– Fifty-three!
– Seventy!
– Eighty!
– Ninety!
– One hundred!

AUCTIONEER
Sold for one hundred!
(*trumpet call*)
A sofa.
Thirty.
DEALERS
– Thirty-one.
– And a half.
– Forty!
– Fifty here.
– Sixty.
– And seven more!
– Seventy-three!

(*Musetta and Marcello lead Mimì away. Some of the guests go upstairs, some*
stay to watch the auction.)
(*Trumpet call – The auction continues.*)
  The curtain falls

---

[1] The political scene published in section I above appeared in the memorial issue for
Giacosa of *La lettura*, 6 (October 1906), pp. 874f. The Cortile act, edited from a
collection of Illica's papers in the Biblioteca Passerini Landi in Piacenza by Mario
Morini, appeared in *La Scala* (December 1958), pp. 36–49. There is a previous
English translation by Rudolph Fellner, *Opera News* (4 February 1967), pp. 24–7.
[2] Edmond Texier, *Tableau de Paris* (Paris, 1852), p. 7.

Notes

1 The rise of Bohemia

1 Théodore Pelloquet, *Henry Murger* (Paris, 1861); *Histoire de Murger, pour servir à l'histoire de la vraie Bohème, par Trois Buveurs d'Eau* (by Adrien Lelioux, Léon Noel and Nadar [Felix Tournachon], [Paris, 1862]); Alfred Delvau, *Henry Murger et la Bohème* (Paris, 1866).

2 Jules Janin in *Le Journal des Débats*, 26 November 1849, and 31 December 1849, for the view of Murger as representing the French abandonment of revolutionary politics; Auguste Luchet in *La Réforme*, 3 December 1849, for the view of Bohemia as a reservoir of political passions and a demonstration of the contradictions within existing life.

3 Henri Murger, *Scènes de la vie de Bohème*, ed. Françoise Geisenberger (Paris, 1961), p. 31.

4 Ibid., pp. 31–2.

5 See the obituary of Privat in *Le Figaro*, 9 August 1859. On Privat, see Jean-Leo, 'Paris-Bohème. Alexandre Privat d'Anglemont', offprint from *Synthèses* (Brussels, 1949); Pierre Citron, 'Quatre lettres d'Alexandre Privat d'Anglemont à Eugène Sue', *Revue des Sciences Humaines*, n.s. 103 (1961), pp. 393–416. For Privat's writings, see the collections *Paris anecdote* (reprinted in 1885) and *Paris inconnu* (reprinted 1875).

6 On Vallès see Gaston Gilles, *Jules Vallès, 1832–1885* (Paris, 1941), and especially Roger Bellet, *Jules Vallès, Journaliste du Second Empire, de la Commune de Paris et de la IIIe République* (Paris, 1977). For a comparison with Murger, see for instance Helmut Kreuzer, *Die Boheme, Beiträge zu ihrer Beschreibung* (Stuttgart, 1968), and the much earlier but still interesting account by Jean Richepin. *Les Étapes d'un réfractaire* (Paris, 1872). Vallès's works have often been reprinted.

7 See for instance 'Culte de l'antiquité et culte jacobin', *Le Progrès de Lyon*, September 1864, and 'Les francs-parleurs', *Le Courrier Français*, August 1866, both reprinted in Vallès, *Littérature et Révolution*, ed. Roger Bellet (Paris, 1969).

8 Vallès, 'Les morts', reprinted in *Les Réfractaires. Oeuvres complètes de Jules Vallès*, ed. Lucien Scheler (Paris, 1955), p. 117.

9 See Baudelaire's preface to Léon Cladel, *Les Martyres ridicules*, in *L'Art romantique*, ed. L. J. Austin (Paris, 1968), p. 362.

10 Pierre Quillard, 'L'anarchie par la littérature', *Entretiens*, April 1892,

quoted in Eugenia Herbert, *The Artist and Social Reform, France and Belgium, 1885–1898* (New Haven, 1961), p. 129.

2 Synopsis

1 The *Capriccio sinfonico* has recently been published, in an edition revised and edited by Pietro Spada, by Elkan-Vogel (Bryn Mawr, Pennsylvania, c. 1978).

2 The musical element of the parody begins with a sequence of heavily accented, syncopated half-diminished chords. They mark, to these authors at least, an unmistakable reference to Verdi's *Otello*. The subject matter is, after all, not dissimilar.

3 In early nineteenth-century Italian opera, the *concertato finale* was usually in four parts of alternating 'kinetic' and 'static' function. First a 'kinetic' *scena*, almost always including the chorus; then a 'static' *largo*; then a 'kinetic' *tempo di mezzo*; and finally a closing, 'static' movement, in fast tempo, called the *stretta*. As was commonly the case in later nineteenth-century examples of the form, the *concertato* in *La bohème* omits the *stretta* in favour of a closing *coup de théâtre*.

4 According to one of Puccini's biographers, the music of this tattoo is the only occasion in *La bohème* on which the composer borrowed music from an existing French source (see Arnaldo Fraccaroli, *Giacomo Puccini: Si confida e racconta* [Milan, 1957], p. 99).

5 Compare with Iago's 'Temete, signor, la gelosia!' from *Otello* Act II. The connection was probably inescapable; in Ch. 15 of Murger's novel, for example, Marcello is discussed in the following terms: ' "Poor fellow," said Mimi, "and so jealous as he is." "Quite true," said Rodolphe. "He and I are pupils of Othello." '

6 For an account of the relationship between this theme and the opening motif of Debussy's *Pelléas et Mélisande*, and of Puccini's supposed reaction, see Alfredo Bonaccorsi, 'Note e commenti', *Rassegna musicale*, 33 (1958), p. 37.

3 The genesis of the opera

1 See Guido Marotti and Ferruccio Pagni, *Giacomo Puccini intimo* (Florence, 1926), pp. 47f.

2 See the summary of the protracted legal proceedings in the *Rivista musicale italiana*, 6 (1899), 833–7.

3 Arnaldo Fraccaroli, *Giacomo Puccini: Si confida e racconta* (Milan, 1957), pp. 87f.; Giuseppe Adami, *Il romanzo della vita di Giacomo Puccini*, 3rd ed. (Milan, 1944), pp. 129f.

4 Rodolfo – not Schaunard – is the leading baritone role in Leoncavallo's completed opera. William Ashbrook, *The Operas of Puccini* (1968; rpt. Ithaca, 1985), suggests that Leoncavallo had not yet proceeded very far with his project when he discussed it with Maurel (p. 49 n. 2). The letter is quoted from Howard Greenfield, *Puccini* (New York, 1980), p. 77.

5 Fraccaroli, p. 83, quotes Puccini's reminiscences, adding a 'confirming' discussion with two acquaintances on 9 February 1893 (p. 87). But see the critical view of these reminiscences in Claudio Casini, *Giacomo Puccini* (Turin, 1978), pp. 184f.

6 See M 143, CP 86, M 158. The fear of 'leaks' also seems to have restricted the number of working copies of the libretto (CP 133, 136).

7 See Mosco Carner, *Puccini: A Critical Biography*, 2nd ed. (London, 1974), pp. 57, 99ff., and 118 for Puccini's interest in subjects promised to other composers. One can sympathise with Leoncavallo's later outrage over rumours of Puccini's work on *Cyrano de Bergerac*, rights to which both he and Massenet had attempted to obtain. See *Musical Quarterly*, 37 (1951), p. 350f.

8 See Carner, p. 340; Marotti and Pagni, pp. 46f.

9 See Wolfgang Schivelbusch, *The Railway Journey: Trains and Travel in the Nineteenth Century*, tr. Anselm Hollo (Oxford, 1980), pp. 41–50 ('Railroad Space and Railroad Time'). The following account of Puccini's travels is derived from a variety of sources. In addition to the letters published in the *Carteggi pucciniani* (CP) and in Marek's biography (M), we have derived information from the collections in Arnaldo Marchetti, *Puccini com'era* (Milan, 1974), and Giuseppe Pintorno, *Puccini: 276 lettere inedite* (Milan, 1974), cited here as (P). Information in the *Gazzetta musicale di Milano* usually appears in the issue one week after the event described.

10 Cited from Piero Nardi, *Vita e tempo di Giuseppe Giacosa* (Milan, 1949), p. 756.

11 See the description of the still unpublished drafts in *Critica pucciniana* (Lucca, 1976), pp. 116ff.

12 See Carner, pp. 274–9.

13 See Ashbrook, p. 65, n. 19.

14 Marek, pp. 135f., provides a delightful description of the trial.

15 See the accounts in the *Gazzetta musicale di Milano* for 24 February, 10 March, and 5 May; and Marchetti, no. 187.

16 See the photograph reproduced in Marchetti, p. 225.

17 Nardi, pp. 759f.

18 See Fraccaroli, p. 99; Adami, pp. 141f.; Marotti and Pagni, pp. 70–2.

4 The libretto

1 The musical numbers for the play were composed by Pierre-Julien Nargeot, conductor of the Théâtre des Variétés orchestra.

2 The second and following editions bear the lumbering title *La bohème: Scene della Scapigliatura parigina di Enrico Murger, precedute dai* Paradossi del Pessimista, *dai cenni biografici e dagli studi critici raccolti dal medismo su Enrico Murger e sulla* Bohème (*La bohème*: Scenes of Parisian Bohemianism by Henry Murger, Preceded by *Paradoxes of the Pessimist*, Biographical Notes and Critical Notes Collected by the Same on Henry Murger and *Bohème*).

3 In defusing the political issue, Illica and Giacosa can scarcely have been concerned that the winter of 1830 was one of the most severe of the cen-

tury. Any Rodolfo gazing out of the garret window would have seen smoke pouring from chimneys and factories into the 'cieli bigi' of Paris – but also mountains of snow.

4 Puccini's letters to Clausetti (CP 127, 129, 132) also use the latter's newspaper connections to create pre-performance publicity for the opera and its conflation of Francine and Mimi.

5 Although Cherubini had already used the setting of a barrière in his *Les Deux Journées* (1800), this locale did not become frequent until later. See Pierre Citron, *La Poésie de Paris dans la littérature française de Rousseau à Baudelaire* (Paris, 1961), I, 365 and II, 321f., and Louis Chevalier, *Laboring Classes and Dangerous Classes in Paris During the First Half of the Nineteenth Century*, trans. Frank Jellinek (New York, 1973), pp. 101–7.

6 A more precise association is suggested by the fact that the Barrière d'Enfer is the nearest tollgate to the Latin Quarter and that Murger himself lived near it early in his career. See Champfleury [Jules Fleury], *Souvenirs et portraits de jeunesse* (Paris, 1872), pp. 83–5 and 93f.

7 Producers of the opera sometimes emphasise this motif visually by having Mimì wear fingerless gloves, which would allow her to work while providing a modicum of warmth.

8 Citing Murger's introduction, the librettists remind us in their preface that 'Bohemia has its special dialect, a jargon … Its vocabulary is the hell of rhetoric and the heaven of neologism …' ('la *Bohème* ha un parlare suo speciale, un gergo … Il suo vocabolario è l'inferno della retorica e il paradiso del neologismo …')

9 This verbal outrage provided the stimulus for a re-enactment of the episode by Puccini's friends when he finished *La bohème*. See Pagni and Marotti, *Giacomo Puccini intimo*, pp. 72f.

10 On the following, see Ariane Thomalla, *Die 'femme fragile': Ein literarischer Frauentypus der Jahrhundertwende*, Literatur in der Gesellschaft 15 (Düsseldorf, 1972).

11 See Rene and Jean Dubos, *The White Plague: Tuberculosis, Man and Society* (Boston, 1952), esp. pp. 44–66.

12 According to a letter of 20 June 1895 by Ricordi (M 151), Act III originally concluded with 'Vogliami bene' ('Love me'), inviting comparison with Violetta's 'Amami Alfredo' ('Love me, Alfredo').

13 Letter of 20 December 1910. Cited from Gabriele Baldini, *The Story of Giuseppe Verdi*, translated and edited by Roger Parker (Cambridge, 1980), p. 187.

14 See Dubos, *White Plague*, pp. 59–62.

15 See the brothers' discussion of the novel, including its medical source, in their Journal entry for 5 February 1869.

16 See William Ashbrook, *The Operas of Puccini* (1968; rpt. Ithaca, 1985), p. xiv.

5 The musical language of *La bohème*

1 See Walter Maisch, *Puccinis musikalische Formgebung, untersucht an der Oper 'La bohème'* (Neustadt a.d. Aisch, 1934), in particular p. 7.

2 For a recent assessment of Puccini's status here, see Roger Parker, 'Analysis: Act I in Perspective', in Mosco Carner, ed., *Tosca* (Cambridge, 1985), pp. 117–42.
3 Donald Jay Grout, *A Short History of Opera* (New York, 1965), vol. 2, p. 445.
4 Joseph Kerman, *Opera as Drama* (New York, 1956), pp. 17–21; see also pp. 252–8.
5 Mosco Carner, *Puccini: A Critical Biography*, 2nd ed. (London, 1974), p. 285.
6 Robert Donington, *Wagner's 'Ring' and Its Symbols: The Music and the Myth* (London, 1963).
7 See, however, the remarks made on this passage in connection with the autograph score, pp. 105–6 (eds.).
8 William Ashbrook, *The Operas of Puccini* (1968; rpt. Ithaca, 1985), p. 57, n. 12.
9 Maisch, p. 57.
10 Ashbrook, p. 56.
11 Carner, p. 345.
12 Maisch, p. 59; see also Carner, p. 345.
13 Carner, p. 289.

6 Puccini at work

1 This sketch, written on the same printed manuscript paper we find in much of the autograph, appears in a special issue of the now-defunct Italian journal, *L'approdo musicale*, 2/6 (1959). Then part of the Gallini collection, it is now in the Pierpont Morgan Library of New York, to which we owe thanks for permission to print the present reproduction.
2 The *libroni* are housed in Ricordi's archive in Milan, though microfilm copies are available for consultation at the American Institute for Verdi Studies, in the Bobst Library of New York University.
3 *Gazzetta musicale di Milano*, 13 February 1896, pp. 111–14.
4 See, for example, the extensive proof corrections discussed by Adelmo Damerini in his '*Suor Angelica* in una rara bozza di stampa', in *Giacomo Puccini nel centenario della nascità*. Comitato nazionale per le onoranze a Giacomo Puccini (Lucca, 1958), pp. 84–8.
5 William Ashbrook, *The Operas of Puccini* (1968; rpt. Ithaca, 1985), p. 65.
6 See *Carteggi pucciniani*, ed. Eugenio Gara (Milan, 1958), letters 111 and 126.
7 Giuseppe Adami, *Il romanzo della vita di Giacomo Puccini* (Milan and Rome, 1944), pp. 136–7. And to give Beckmesser what is owed to Beckmesser, we might point out that this anecdote was repeated by one of the present authors, in an earlier contribution to this series of Opera Handbooks (see Roger Parker, 'Analysis: Act I in Perspective', in Mosco Carner, ed., *Tosca* [Cambridge, 1985], p. 120).
8 This is confirmed by Carner and others, who tell us that 'Quando me'n vo'' was originally conceived on one of Puccini's hunting trips (see

Mosco Carner, *Puccini. A Critical Biography*, 2nd ed. [London, 1974], p. 340).

7 A brief stage history

1 The other principals were Camilla Pasini as Musetta, Evan Gorga as Rodolfo, and Tieste Wilmant as Marcello.
2 *Fanfulla*, 3 February 1896.
3 Quoted in the *Carteggi pucciniani*, p. 141.
4 Arnaldo Fraccaroli, *Giacomo Puccini: Si confida e racconta* (Milan, 1957), pp. 105f.
5 *Il Teatro Regio di Torino* (Turin, 1970), p. 135.
6 The poster is reproduced in *Il Teatro Regio*, facing p. 94.
7 *Gazzetta musicale di Milano* (1896), p. 175.
8 The 'bonnet' scene comprises the 87 bars between rehearsal nos. 15 and 16 of Act II. As Cecil Hopkinson points out, it is first seen in a French version of the vocal score published in May 1898. See his *A Bibliography of the Works of Giacomo Puccini* (New York, 1968), p. 17.
9 That the premiere was not given at Covent Garden was due to a certain resentment that lingered after Ricordi had made the rights to perform Verdi's *Falstaff* dependent upon an agreement to produce Puccini's *Manon Lescaut*. The latter opera had fared poorly, and Augustus Harris, the manager of Covent Garden, felt little temptation to take another flyer with Puccini three years later.
10 See Nellie Melba, *Melodies and Memories* (1926; rpt. Freeport, N.Y., 1970), p. 119.
11 On the following, see Harold Rosenthal, *Two Centuries of Opera at Covent Garden* (London, 1958), p. 297; John Hetherington, *Melba* (London, 1967), pp. 99–101; and Howard Greenfield, *Caruso* (New York, 1983), pp. 99–103.
12 See the table of performances in Pierre V. R. Key, *Enrico Caruso: A Biography* (Boston, 1922), pp. 398ff.
13 John F. Cone, *Oscar Hammerstein's Manhattan Opera Company* (Norman, Oklahoma, 1966), pp. 86–8.
14 Irving Kolodin, *The Metropolitan Opera 1883–1966* (New York, 1966), p. 184.

8 Aspects of the *La bohème* reception

1 *Fanfulla*, 4 February 1896. Reprinted in *Gazzetta musicale di Milano*, 6 February 1896, p. 82.
2 Beginning with the issue of the *Gazzetta musicale di Milano* cited in note 1, Ricordi made a point of quoting at length any favourable reviews of *La bohème* revivals. Sometimes these anthologies took up as much as a third of the entire issue.
3 For comparative statistics on Puccini's operas at the world's major opera houses, see Cecil Hopkinson, *A Bibliography of the Works of Giacomo Puccini* (New York, 1968), p. 68.
4 Igor Stravinsky and Robert Craft, *Dialogues and a Diary* (London,

1968), p. 58; George Marek, *Richard Strauss* (New York, 1967), pp. 320–2; François Lesure, ed., *Debussy on Music*, trans. Richard Langham Smith (New York, 1977), pp. 119–20; Hans and Rosaleen Moldenhauer, *Anton von Webern* (New York, 1979), p. 680.

5 Ludwig Karpath, *Begegnungen mit dem Genius* (Vienna, 1934), pp. 337f.; Alma Mahler, *Gustav Mahler: Memories and Letters*, 2nd ed. (London, 1968), p. 37.

6 'Born Again Italian Opera', in *Shaw's Music*, ed. Dan H. Laurence, vol. III (New York, 1981), pp. 214–21.

7 Published in Turin, 1912.

8 Donald Jay Grout, *A Short History of Opera*, 2nd ed. (New York and London, 1965), vol. II, p. 445.

9 'Die Bohème (1897)', in *Musikkritiker* (Leipzig, 1972), pp. 165–74; also: *Die moderne Oper*, vol. VIII (Berlin, 1899), pp. 75–85.

10 For a general account of Hanslick's attitude to Verdi, see Massimo Mila, 'Verdi e Hanslick', in *L'arte di Verdi* (Turin, 1980), pp. 316–30. For an English translation of Hanslick's review of *Otello*, see Eduard Hanslick, *Music Criticisms 1846–99*, trans. and ed. Henry Pleasants, rev. ed. (London, 1963), pp. 275–87.

11 *Revue des deux mondes*, vol. 148 (Paris, 1898), pp. 469–74.

12 Quoted in James A. Hepokoski, *Giuseppe Verdi: Falstaff* (Cambridge, 1983), pp. 33–4.

13 *The Magic Mountain*, trans. H. T. Lowe-Porter (New York, 1944; rpt. 1963), p. 641.

14 See the discography by Raffaele Végeto in the *Carteggi pucciniani*, ed. Eugenio Gara (Milan, 1958), p. 618.

15 *Ein Zeitalter wird besichtigt* (Berlin, 1947), pp. 273–81.

Bibliography

I. Books and articles about Puccini

Adami, Giuseppe. *Puccini*, 2nd edition (Milan, 1938).

Il romanzo della vita di Giacomo Puccini. 3rd edition, Milan and Rome, 1944.

L'approdo musicale, 2/6 (1959). The entire issue is devoted to Puccini.

Ashbrook, William. *The Operas of Puccini*. New York, 1968. Reprint, Ithaca, 1985.

Carner, Mosco. *Puccini. A Critical Biography*, 2nd edition, London, 1974.

Casini, Claudio. *Giacomo Puccini*. Turin, 1978.

Christen, Norbert. *Giacomo Puccini. Analytische Untersuchungen der Melodik, Harmonik und Instrumentation.* (Schriftenreihe zur Musik, vol. 13) Hamburg, 1978.

Critica pucciniana. Comitato Nazionale per le Onoranze a Giacomo Puccini nel Cinquantenario della Morte. Lucca, 1976.

Dukas, Paul. *Les Écrits de Paul Dukas sur la musique*. Paris, 1948.

Fellerer, Karl Gustav. 'Von Puccinis Arbeitsweise', *Die Musik*, 29/4 (1937), 692–5.

Fraccaroli, Arnaldo. *Giacomo Puccini: Si confida e racconta*. Milan, 1957.

La vita di Giacomo Puccini. Milan, 1925.

Giacomo Puccini nel centenario della nascita. Comitato nazionale per le onoranze a Giacomo Puccini. Lucca, 1958.

Hopkinson, Cecil. *A Bibliography of the Works of Giacomo Puccini*. New York, 1968.

Kerman, Joseph. *Opera as Drama*. New York, 1956.

Mann, Heinrich. *Ein Zeitalter wird besichtigt*. Berlin, 1947.

Marchetti, Leopoldo. *Puccini nelle immagini*. Milan, 1968.

Marek, George. *Puccini. A Biography*. New York, 1951.

Marotti, Guido, and Pagni, Ferruccio. *Giacomo Puccini intimo*. Florence, 1926.

Nardi, Piero. *Vita e tempo di Giuseppe Giacosa*. Milan, 1949.

Parker, Roger. 'Analysis: Act I in Perspective', *Tosca*. Ed. Mosco Carner. Cambridge, 1985, pp. 117–42.

Pizzetti, Ildebrando. *Musicisti contemporanei*. Milan, 1941.

Puccini, Giacomo. *Epistolario*. Ed. Giuseppe Adami. Milan, 1928. English edition, trans. Ena Makin. London, 1931.

Carteggi pucciniani. Ed. Eugenio Gara. Milan, 1958.

Puccini com'era. Ed. Arnaldo Marchetti. Milan, 1973.

Puccini: 276 lettere inedite – Il fondo dell'Accademia d'Arte a Montecatini Terme. Ed. Giuseppe Pintorno. Milan, 1974.

Lettere a Riccardo Schnabl. Ed. Simonetta Puccini. Milan, 1981.

Ricci, Luigi. *Puccini interprete di se stesso.* Milan, 1954.

Sartori, Claudio (ed.). *Puccini.* Milan, 1958.

Shaw, Bernard. 'Born-Again Italian Opera', *Shaw's Music.* Ed. Dan H. Lawrence. New York, 1981, III, 214–17.

Specht, Richard. *Giacomo Puccini. Das Leben – Der Mensch – Das Werk.* Berlin, 1931. English edition, trans. C. A. Phillips. London, 1933.

Tedeschi, Rubens. *Addio, fiorito asil.* Milan, 1978.

Titone, Antonio. *Vissi d'arte. Puccini e il disfacimento del melodramma.* Milan, 1972.

Torrefranca, Fausto. *Giacomo Puccini e l'opera internazionale.* Turin, 1912.

Valente, Richard. *The Verismo of Giacomo Puccini.* Diss. University of Freibourg, 1971.

II. Books and articles about bohemianism and *La bohème*

Baldick, Robert. *The First Bohemian: The Life of Henry Murger.* London, 1961.

Balestieri, Giuliano. 'Musetta è nata in barca'. *La Scala*, 15 (1951).

Bellaigue, Camille. *'La bohème'. Revue des deux mondes*, 148 (1898), 469–74.

Csampai, Attila, and Holland, Dietmar. *La Bohème. Texte, Materialien, Kommentare.* (rororo Opernbücher). Reinbeck b. Hamburg, 1981.

Delvau, Alfred. *Henri Murger et la Bohème.* Paris, 1866.

Hanslick, Eduard. 'Die Boheme (1897)'. *Musikkritiker.* Leipzig, 1972, pp. 165–74. Also: *Die moderne Oper*, VIII (Berlin, 1899), 75–85.

John, Nicholas (ed.). *La bohème.* English National Opera Guide 14. London, 1982.

Karpath, Ludwig. *Begegnung mit dem Genius.* Vienna, 1934.

Kreuzer, Helmut. *Die Boheme: Beiträge zu ihrer Beschreibung.* Stuttgart, 1968.

Lelioux, Adrien, Noel, Léon, and Nadar (Felix Tournachon). *Histoire de Murger, pour servir à l'histoire de la vraie Bohème, par trois Buveurs d'Eau.* Paris, 1862.

Maisch, Walter. *Puccinis musikalische Formgebung, untersucht an der Oper 'La Bohème'.* Neustadt a.d. Aisch, 1934.

Mila, Massimo. 'La novità di Bohème'. *Puccini.* Ed. Claudio Sartori. Milan, 1958.

Morini, Mario. 'Il cortile della casa di via La bruyère 8', *La Scala*, 109 (1959), 35–49. Translated by Rudolph Fellner, *Opera News* (4 February 1967), 24–7.

Murger, Henri. *Scènes de la vie de Bohème.* Ed. Françoises Geisenberger. Paris, 1961.

Pelloquet, Théodore. *Henry Murger.* Paris, 1861.

Puccini. La bohème. L'Avant-Scène, 20 (1979).

Santi, Piero. *'Nei cieli bigi ...'*, *Nuova rivista musicale italiana*, 1 (1967), 350–8.

Thomalla, Ariane. *Die 'femme fragile': Ein literarischer Frauentypus der Jahrhundertwende*. Düsseldorf, 1972.

Discography

BY MALCOLM WALKER

All recordings are in stereo unless otherwise stated
*   denotes 78rpm
(m)   mono recording
(e)   electronically reprocessed stereo
(4)   cassette version
(CD) Compact Disc version

For a full list of acoustic recordings from 1899 to 1928, see Raffaele Végeto, 'Discografia pucciniana', in Eugenio Gara (ed.), *Carteggi pucciniani* (Milan, 1958), pp. 615–22.

M	Mimì	*S*	Schaunard
Mus	Musetta	*C*	Colline
R	Rodolfo	*B*	Benoît
Mar	Marcello	*A*	Alcindoro

Complete Recordings

1918   Bosini *M*; Giana *Mus*; Andreini & Bolis *R*; Badini & Zani *Mar*; Baracchi *S*; Bettoni & Rubini *C*; Ceccarelli *B*; *A* / La Scala Chorus and Orch / Sabajno   HMV S5056/78*

1928   Torri *M*; Vitulli *Mus*; Giorgini *R*; Badini *Mar*; Baracchi *S*; Manfrini *C*; Baccaloni *B*; *A* / La Scala Chorus and Orch / Sabajno   HMV C1513/25*

1930   Pampanini *M*; Mirella *Mus*; Marini *R*; Vanelli *Mar*; Baracchi *S*; Pasero *C*; Baccaloni *B*; *A* / La Scala Chorus and Orch / Molajoli   Columbia 9846/58*

1938   Albanese *M*; Menotti *Mus*; Gigli *R*; Poli *Mar*; Baracchi *S*; Baronti *C*; Scattola *B*; *A* / La Scala Chorus and Orch / Berrettoni   MFP (m) MFP2076/77
    Seraphim (m) IB6038

1946   (broadcast performance) Albanese *M*; McKnight *Mus*; Peerce *R*; Valentino *Mar*; Cehanovsky *S*; Moscona *C*; Baccaloni *B*; *A* / NBC Chorus and Orch / Toscanini
    RCA (UK) (m) AT203
    (US) (e) VICS6019

1947   Sayão *M*; Benzell *Mus*; Tucker *R*; Valentino *Mar*; Cehanovsky *S*; Moscona *C*; Baccaloni *B*; *A* / Metropolitan Opera Chorus and Orch

/ Antonicelli   CBS (UK) (m) 78243
                      (US) (m) Y2 32364
1950   Tebaldi *M*; Gueden *Mus*; Prandelli *R*; Inghilleri *Mar*; Corena *S*;
       Arié *C*; Luise *B*; *A* / Santa Cecilia Academy Chorus and Orch /
       Erede   Decca (m) ACL121/122
                     Richmond (m) RS62001
1951   Ilitsch *M*; Boesch *Mus*; Delorco *R*; Baylé *Mar*; Oeggl *S*; Rus *C*;
       Siegert *B*; *A* / Vienna State Opera Chorus, Austrian SO / Loibner
                     Remington (m) 199-80
1951   Carteri *M*; Ramella *Mus*; Tagliavini *R*; Taddei *Mar*; Latinucci *S*;
       Siepi *C*; Zorgniotti *B*; *A* / Turin Radio Chorus and Orch / Santini
                     Cetra (e) LPS3237 (4) MC96/97
1951   Schimenti *M*; Micheluzzi *Mus*; Lauri-Volpi *R*; Ciavola *Mar*;
       Titta *S*; Tatozzi *C*; Passarotti *B*; *A* / Rome Opera Chorus and Orch /
       Paoletti   Remington (m) 199-99
c. 1952   (in Russian) Maslennikova *M*; Sakharova *Mus*; Lemeshev *R*;
       Lisitian *Mar*; Zakharov *S*; Dobrin *C*; Demyamov *B*; Belanov *A* /
       Moscow Radio Chorus and Orch / Samosud
                     Melodiya (m) D 07779/82
1955   Tyler *M*; Bijster *Mus*; Garen *R*; Gorin *Mar*; Holthaus *S*;
       Wolovsky *C*; Augenent *B*; *A* / Netherlands Opera Chorus and Orch
       / Bamberger   Musical Masterpieces Society (m) MMS141
1955   (in French) Angelici *M*; Castelli *Mus*; Gardes *R*; Roux *Mar*;
       Vieuille *S*; Depraz *C*; Hivert *B*; Herent *A* / Paris Opéra-Comique
       Chorus and Orch / Tzipine
                     EMI (m) 2C 053 10902/3M
1955   (in Russian) Shumskaya *M*; Yakovento *Mus*; Kozlovsky *R*;
       Burlak *Mar*; Tikhonov *S*; Korolev *C*; Demyanov *B*; Troitsky *A* /
       Chorus, Moscow PO / Samosud
                     Melodiya (m) D 09451/4
1956   De los Angeles *M*; Amara *Mus*; Björling *R*; Merrill *Mar*;
       Reardon *S*; Tozzi *C*; Corena*B*; *A* / Columbus Boychor, RCA Victor
       Chorus and Orch / Beecham
                     EMI (e) SLS896 (4) TC-SLS896
                     Seraphim (e) SIB6099
1956   Callas *M*; Moffo *Mus*; Di Stefano *R*; Panerai *Mar*; Spatafora *S*;
       Zaccaria *C*; Badioli *B*; *A* / La Scala Chorus and Orch / Votto
                     EMI (e) SLS5059 (4) TC-SLS5059
                     Angel (m) 3560BL
1957   Stella *M*; Rizzoli *Mus*; Poggi *R*; Capecchi *Mar*; Mazzini *S*;
       Modesti *C*; Luise *B*; Onesti *A* / Naples San Carlo Opera Chorus and
       Orch / Molinari-Pradelli
                     Philips (e) 6720 008
1958   Tebaldi *M*; D'Angelo *Mus*; Bergonzi *R*; Bastianini *Mar*; Cesari *S*;
       Siepi *C*; Corena *B*; *A* / Santa Cecilia Academy Chorus and Orch /
       Serafin   Decca 411 868-1DO2 (4) 411 868-4DO2
                     London 42002
                     Decca/London (CD) awaiting issue

1958   Beltrami *M*; Valtriani *Mus*; Antonioli *R*; Testi *Mar*; Oppicelli *S*; Ferrein *C*; Peruzzi *B*; *A* / Bologna State Theatre Chorus, Berlin Radio SO / Rigacci
               Eterna 820 168/9

1960   (in German) Lorengar *M*; Streich *Mus*; Kónya *R*; Fischer-Dieskau *Mar*; Günter *S*; Bertram *C*; Ollendorff *B*; F. Hoppe *A* / Berlin State Opera Chorus, Berlin Staatskapelle / Erede
               DG 2726 059

1961   Scotto *M*; Meneguzzer *Mus*; Poggi *R*; Gobbi *Mar*; Giorgetti *S*; Modesti *C*; Carbonari *B*; *A* / Maggio Musicale Fiorentino Chorus and Orch / Votto   DG 2705 038

1961   Moffo *M*; Costa *Mus*; Tucker *R*; Merrill *Mar*; Maero *S*; Tozzi *C*; Corena *B*; Onesti *A* / Rome Opera Chorus and Orch / Leinsdorf
               RCA (UK) VLSO3969 (4) VKO3969
               (US) AGL2-3969 (4) AGK2-3969

1962   Freni *M*; Adani *Mus*; Gedda *R*; Sereni *Mar*; Basiola Jr *S*;
/3   Mazzeoli *C*; Badioli *B*; Montarsolo *A* / Rome Opera Chorus and Orch / Schippers   EMI SLS907 (4) TCC2-POR 1545999
               Angel SBL3643
               EMI (CD) awaiting issue

1973   Freni *M*; Harwood *Mus*; Pavarotti *R*; Panerai *Mar*; Maffeo *S*; Ghiaurov *C*; Sénéchal *B*; *A* / German Opera Chorus (Berlin), Berlin PO / Karajan
               Decca SET565 (4) K2B5
               London OSA 1299 (4) OSA5-1299

1974   Caballé *M*; Blegen *Mus*; Domingo *R*; Milnes *Mar*; Sardinero *S*; Raimondi *C*; Mangin *B*; Castel *A* / Alldis Choir, LPO / Solti
               RCA (UK & US) ARL2-0371 (4) ARK2-0371

1979   Ricciarelli *M*; Putnam *Mus*; Carreras *R*; Wixell *Mar*; Hagegård *S*; Lloyd *C*; Van Allan *B*; *A* / Royal Opera Chorus, Royal Opera House Orch., Covent Garden / C. Davis
               Philips 6769 031 (4) 7699 116

1979   Scotto *M*; Neblett *Mus*; Kraus *R*; Milnes *Mar*; Manuguerra *S*; Plishka *C*; Tajo *B*; Capecchi *A* / Trinity Boys' Choir, Ambrosian Opera Chorus, National PO / Levine
               EMI SLS5192 (4) TC-SLS5192
               Angel SZBX3900 (4) 4Z2X3900

1979   Kincesová *M*; Dvorský *Mus*; Poka *Mar*; Banačk *C*; Bratislava Opera Chorus, Bratislava Radio Orch / Lenard
               Opus 9112 0931/32

Excerpts
1936   (Act 4) Perli *M*; Andreva *Mus*; Nash *R*; Brownlee *Mar*; R. Alva *S*; R. Easton *C* / LPO / Beecham
               EMI (m) HQM1234

1936   (in French) Corney *M*; Sibille *Mus*; Claudel *R*; Gaudin *Mar*; Payen *S*; Beckmans *C* / Paris Opéra-Comique Chorus and Orch / Wolff   Polydor 566077/81*

1936 (in German) Hüni-Mihacsek *M*; Jungkurth *Mus*; Rosvaenge *R*;
      Weltner *Mar*; Heyer *S*; Kasenow *C*; Hattemer *B*; Wenke *A* / Berlin
      Staatsoper Chorus and Orch / Weigert
                           Polydor 95362/66*
1940 Steber *M*; Dickey *Mus*; Tokatyan *R*; Cehanovsky *Mar*; Kent *S*;
      Alvary *C* / Chorus; Publishers Service SO / Pelletier
                           RCA (m) CAL222
1944 (in German – broadcast performance) Eipperle *M*; Gueden *Mus*;
      Anders *R*; Domgraf-Fassbaender *Mar*; Fuchs *S*; Windisch *C* / Berlin
      Radio Chorus and SO / Steinkopf
                           Acanta (m) BB21496
1951 Albanese *M*; Munsel *Mus*; Di Stefano *R*; Warren *Mar*;
      Cehanovsky *S*; Moscona *C* / RCA Victor Orch / Cellini and Trucco
                           RCA (US) (m) LM1709
1952 Meneguzzer *M*; Hopkins *Mus*; Gero *R*; Giorgetti *Mar* / Maggio
      Musicale Fiorentino Chorus and Orch / Ghiglia
                           Saga (m) XID5261
1954 (in German) Berger *M*; Köth *Mus*; Schock *R*; Fischer-Dieskau *Mar*;
      Prey *S*; Frick *C*; Hauck *A* / German Opera Chorus, Berlin SO /
      Schuchter   EMI (m) 1C 047 28572
1957 Amara *M*; Krall *Mus*; Barioni *R*; Valentino *Mar*; Harvout *S*;
      Moscona *C*; De Paolis *A* / Metropolitan Opera Orch / Cleva
                           Metropolitan Opera Guild (m) MO610
1960 (in French) Doria *M*; Cumia *Mus*; Vanzo *R*; Massard *Mar*;
      Giovanetti *S*; Legros *C* / SO / Ghiglia
                           Vogue LDM30132 (4) B.VOC413
1960 (in German) Eipperle *M*; Pütz *Mus*; Wunderlich *R*; Brauer *Mar*;
      Kofmane *S*; Roth-Ehrang *C*; Clam *A* / German Opera Chorus and
      Orch / R. Kraus   Eurodisc 7587 1R
1961 (in French) Jaumillot *M*; Poncet *R* / orch / Etcheverry
                           Philips 432 614
1963 (in German) Rothenberger *M*; Pütz *Mus*; Wunderlich *R*;
      Cordes *Mar*; Völker *S*; Frick *C*; Clam *A* / Berlin Komische Oper
      Chorus, Berlin SO / Klobucar
                           EMI 1C 063 28529
1966 (in German) Scheyrer *M*; Holm *Mus*; Kmentt *R*; Wachter *Mar*;
      Welter *C* / Vienna Volksoper Chorus and Orch / Bauer-Theussl
                           Eurodisc 80005ZR
1960s (in Hungarian) Házy *M*; László *Mus*; Olosfalvy *R*; Melis *Mar*;
      Bende *S*; Várhelyi *C*; Nádas *A* / Budapest PO / Erdélyi
                           Hungaroton SLPX 11503

Index